THE
BIBLE
AND
BEYOND

A Connection to Related Media

JUDITH MARIE JUDY

WESTBOW
PRESS®
A DIVISION OF THOMAS NELSON
& ZONDERVAN

This book is a work of non-fiction. Unless otherwise noted, the author
and the publisher make no explicit guarantees as to the accuracy of
the information contained in this book and in some cases, names of
people and places have been altered to protect their privacy.

WestBow Press books may be ordered through booksellers or by contacting:

WestBow Press
A Division of Thomas Nelson & Zondervan
1663 Liberty Drive
Bloomington, IN 47403
www.westbowpress.com
844-714-3454

Interior Image Credit: Judith Marie Judy

Scripture quotations are from New Revised Standard Version Bible,
copyright © 1989 National Council of the Churches of Christ in the United
States of America. Used by permission. All rights reserved worldwide.

ISBN: 978-1-6642-0187-3 (sc)
ISBN: 978-1-6642-0188-0 (hc)
ISBN: 978-1-6642-0186-6 (e)

Library of Congress Control Number: 2020914934

Print information available on the last page.

WestBow Press rev. date: 04/25/2022

Also by Judith Marie Judy under J. Marie Judy
Life on Torrez Road A Northern New Mexico Family History

This book is dedicated to all who seek.

CONTENTS

PART 1   THE BIBLE

SECTION 1   HEBREWS—ISRAELITES

Reflections Faraway Places
Ancient Civilizations
> Mesopotamia, Sumer, Akkad, Babylonia, Assyria, Elam,
> Media, Levant, Canaan, Hittites, Philistines, Phoenicia,
> Arameans, Amorites, Egypt, Jordan

Language Development

Source—Hebrew Bible
> Torah (Law), Yahwist, Elohist, Deuteronomic, Priestly,
> Redactor, Nevi'im (Prophets), Kethuvim (Writings)

PART 2   BEYOND THE BIBLE

SECTION 4   MOVING ONWARD

PREFACE

An author, writing before I was born, began his book with a proclamation indicating that there exists, from the beginning of time, a universal instinct leading toward a consciousness of a Divine Source. Every race or tribe, in some way, has worshiped and honored this Source—God—as named by some. The author went on to suggest that if there were no God, there would be no searching for God. That was the first time I saw in print that believing and searching for God gave evidence that God *IS*. Then, early in the twenty-first century from a book by Bruce Feiler, I saw the following quote, "There is a common psyche in the world in which humans lunge for the Divine. That is God's imprint left on us, which all religious people feel." In part, the revelation of holding that same undeniable belief, as presented by the two authors, spurred me on to write this book.

For a decade, I enjoyed readings of a biblical nature but still lacked a concise reference for connecting times and events of those long-ago years. Plus, questions arose regarding vocabulary and terms. Once again, I found myself putting down a book because the wording left me wondering and the ancient time frame, with changes in territorial names, puzzled me. I realized a compilation of my notes into one *easy to use resource* was long overdue. What an undertaking!

Covering the long years of biblical times, some repetition

seems necessary as details often overlap into other chapters. A *Glossary* covers the entire book plus related terms. *Timelines* present dates in a precise format and *Maps* provide a look at the physical placement of a few countries represented. Also, an *Index* helps in locating specific subjects. As a self-taught biblical student, I found these kinds of additions helpful.

My intent to withhold personal beliefs and opinions from the major text of this book has not been a total success. It seems basic life principles become a part of any endeavor. I include some personal thoughts in the form of *Reflections* at the beginning of each chapter and elsewhere in the book; they are in *italicized print*. Too, I think by inserting my memories, others will be inclined to recall their feelings regarding the various topics. Becoming personally involved deepens the meaning of everything we do.

More and more, it seems, I'm asked about the difference between religious and spiritual. I reply: *Spiritual* is the awareness of God within. It is a personal relationship with God. A knowingness that through every aspect of life, guidance and comfort are God's gift to humankind forever and forever. Some define God as *Divine Source* or *Light* or *Force* or *Spirit*. It is the thought that matters. *Religious* is the intellectual knowledge and following the exact teachings of a specific church, often called doctrine. Religious people can also be spiritual just as spiritual people can be religious.

This book is not an academic text nor is it an attempt to prove or persuade others of any religious or spiritual matters. It is a gift from my heart to those curious readers wanting a connection from biblical times to related media through the twenty-first century. My hope is that others will find this resource useful in unraveling the somewhat bewildering and overwhelming information of the Bible and ongoing interests.

INTRODUCTION

The Hebrew Bible covers God's relationship to humankind before the birth of Jesus. The New Testament tells of Jesus and the ensuing Christian religion. Christians combined their Scriptures with the Hebrew Bible into one book called the *Bible,* giving the name *Old Testament* to the Hebrew Bible and *New Testament* to their own Scriptures. In the process, Christians changed the placement of some books as shown in the Hebrew Bible. At times, the term Christian Bible is used to cover the combined Christian Old and New Testament. The Bible covers thousands and thousands of years. The following information is included to assist readers in approaching this book: *The Bible and Beyond.* . ..

The inspirational offering of the Bible and the desire for a history of humankinds' connection with God continue to be compelling forces for millions around the world. Biblical material dating back to Antiquity is daunting to many wanting to relate those older times with today's expanse of knowledge. Measurement of time, complexity of words, and the source of data, need to be considered in reading biblical material. Examples of these perplexing issues follow.

Measurement of time, a hurdle in unraveling biblical events, has changed from then to now. Most individuals in the World today focus on the exactness of time, unlike times of Antiquity. In looking at the counting of years, a number of variations have been observed over the years. In this book, dates from the Christian calendar are used followed by the designation of BCE (before current era), and CE (current era), nonreligious terms recognized in the twentieth century. The Jewish calendar, established in approximately 359 CE, is used for religious purposes by Jews all over the World and is Israel's official calendar. That calendar counts years since the creation, shown as 3760 BCE. The Christian calendar, a version of the Julian calendar, is used in the United States and most countries in the World. The Julian calendar originated in pre-Christian Rome.

Other ways of noting segments of time, as shown below, are helpful.

Bronze Age 3600-1200 BCE
Iron Age 1200-586 BCE
Babylonian Period 586-539 BCE
Persian Period 539-333 BCE
Hellenistic Period 333-63 BCE
Roman Period 63 BCE-330 CE

Time Based on the Christian Calendar (current era)
Antiquity or Ancient Times before the Middle Ages
Middle Ages (Medieval Period) 500-1500
Renaissance (revival of Classical art, literature, learning) 14th into the 17th century
Modern Period (recent times) 17th century-present

Marking of Centuries

BCE	CE	
499-400 5th century	0-99 1st century	10 years: decade
399-300 4rd century	100-199 2nd century	100 years: century
299-200 3nd century	200-299 3rd century	1000 years: millennium
199-100 2nd century	300-399 4th century	
99-0 1st century	400-499 5th century	

Abbreviations: century: c   approximately: circa or ca

The Hebrew Bible begins with their creation story which Bishop Ussher (1581-1656 CE) calculated at 4004 BCE. This date, different from the Jewish calendar, is questioned by some. Ussher's date is based on the generally accepted date of 1280 BCE for the Hebrews' Exodus from Egypt. Moving backward and incorporating additional biblical information, other dates were determined. Even now, dates given to Ancient Times are uncertain.

Complexity of words is another source of confusion found in books about the Bible. Often, *Bible* is referred to as *Scripture*. Words that have been determined to be *the very word of God* are considered Scripture. Scriptures are Sacred and Divine; they come from God. At times, Scriptures are mentioned as a *covenant*, a binding agreement with God. *Testament* is used much the same way as *covenant*.

The term *canon*, translated from the Greek word *reed*, meaning a straight stick used for measuring, indicates writings meeting the standard required for inclusion in the Bible. *Canon*, in a biblical sense, first used in 367 CE, applied to the Christian writings which became the New Testament. Even though the Hebrew Bible was in place prior to the New Testament, *canon* was extended to the three parts of the Hebrew Bible: Torah, Nevi'im, and Ketuvim. Another word used for the Hebrew Bible is *Tanakh*, an acronym from the first letter of each part, separated by the vowel *a*, and ending with the final letter of *Torah*,

In the multitude of biblical books, words referring to land territories and the Jewish people can be confusing. Presently, many books and maps refer to ancient Holy Land as Palestine. That land before given the name *Holy*, was Levant, then Canaan, followed by Israel, Israel/Judah, Judah, and then Judea. Romans, bringing an end to the final Jewish uprising in 135 CE, renamed the country *Syria Palestina*. After more changes and World War

I, the land became Palestine. Now it is Israel with Palestinian territories embedded within. In much the same manner, the name of the wandering tribe first known as Hebrews changed to Israelites after their Exodus from Egypt (1280 BCE) and then became Jews after the Babylonian exile (539 BCE).

Not only has there been a change in names of people and lands, titles of Bibles differ. A Jewish Bible translated in 1917 CE bears the name *The Holy Scriptures*; today, Jews prefer the name *Bible*. These are but a few of the differences in word usage found in literature of a biblical nature. Traditional historical names of territories and people are shown in this book.

Source of data is yet another question frequently asked regarding the Bible. In that long-ago time, history was recorded in a number of ways, still valid today. The compilation of the Bible reflects the importance of orally passing knowledge down through generations. Often times this form of record keeping is called *folklore*, which some believe to be unreliable. However, a story validating the importance of folklore was seen after the devastation of the Sri Lanka Tsunami of 2004 CE. From one of the outlying islands came the news of everyone fleeing to higher ground. They survived! Then, the often-repeated chant, learned through the years, surfaced: *sea goes out, run high*. No one remembered when it started, but, the old saying passed from generation to generation saved the island's population. While buildings were swept away—all humans escaped the tidal wave. Folklore, found in Scripture, is a dynamic form of history.

History is also seen in stones and altars as mentioned in Genesis, Exodus, and other books of the Hebrew Bible. Archeologists found altars dating back to about 2000 BCE. Altars were used to honor God in offering sacrifices plus marking other sacred and spiritual places. Altars ranged from piles of stones to finely built structures. With progression of humankind, written accounts evolved.

According to archeological findings, the earliest forms of writing, in Egypt and Mesopotamia, surfaced before 3300 BCE. Later, starting with small symbols baked into clay tablets came pictures connected as sentences that progressed into alphabets. Eventually, written accounts produced the Bible.

Apart from the Bible, scientists say the universe is at least fifteen billion years old. Through the years, news articles report various places and times where human life began. Archeology, starting in the mid-nineteenth century CE, is a crucial element in studying Jewish history. Some findings date early villages and city-states in the lands of present-day Israel and its surroundings to about 10,000 BCE. The earliest Canaan settlements date back to 9000 BCE. By 3000 BCE, Phoenicians settled along the Syrian coast; five hundred years later, Hebrew tribes moved into Canaan. By 1550 BCE, Philistines appeared along the same area; their territory was known as *Philistia*. Those *Sea People* were in conflict with the Israelites and Judeans.

Moving into Modern Times, discoveries have uncovered related biblical works hidden more than a thousand years ago; others have appeared from the black market. Writings not accepted as Scripture, along with views of historians from that early period, present a different tone of those times. Likewise, reviewing philosophical thought from the ages enlarges the scope of history by offering insight and meaning to Ancient Times. Writings from the past, as with other cultural practices, continue to affect the present.

In most aspects of life, changes continue. Modern Times bring additional ways of clarifying the past. Some find the new refreshing; others find it disturbing. Regardless, the Bible continues as a strong influence in life. Daily, biblical references occur in media of the 21st century CE. Building a connection from the old to the new widens the perspective. *The Bible and Beyond. . .* is a pathway to that goal.

PART ONE

THE BIBLE

SECTION ONE

HEBREWS—ISRAELITES

CHAPTER 1

Background (Hebrews— Israelites)

Reflections Faraway Places
Ancient Civilizations
    Mesopotamia, Sumer, Akkad, Babylonia, Assyria, Elam,
    Media, Levant, Canaan, Hittites, Philistines, Phoenicia,
    Arameans, Amorites, Egypt, Jordan
Language Development
Source—Hebrew Bible
    Torah (Law), Yahwist, Elohist, Deuteronomic, Priestly,
    Redactor, Nevi'im (Prophets), Kethuvim (Writings)

Judith Marie Judy

Reflections   Faraway Places

I wonder how many, like me, never gave places like Mesopotamia any thought at all. In fifth grade or so, our teacher pointed out the Mediterranean Sea and Egypt. That roll down map connected to the blackboard held vast places that intrigued me even at that age. In a seventh-grade social studies class, given a book about faraway lands, I was thrilled to be able to learn about other people and where they lived. Always an avid reader, my knowledge gleamed from books was an adventurous journey—my world became larger.

So, in looking at biblical accounts, I wanted to know about those lands and unravel the string of names that seemed to be ever changing. For me, it is FUN! The progression of people and lands led to an interest in their languages and how spoken words found themselves on leaves in a book. In learning, one thing leads to another.

From the Tower of Babel, sprang many wonders and conflicts. Even now, in the twenty-first century, words of turmoil blow across the world faster than one can compartmentalize them into a frame of understanding. Will people ever come together in harmony?

Ancient Civilizations

Reviewing some of the ancient people and places mentioned in the Bible helps connect them with each other and the approximate dates given to their importance. Dates in this section strictly adhere to the resources as cited, which are in close proximity with those shown elsewhere in this book.

Many people and places of the Bible began in the Fertile Crescent, a large semicircle of inhabited and cultivated land. This small area bordering the eastern coast of the Mediterranean Sea, reached from the Nile Valley through present day Israel and Lebanon, then across the border of Syria and Turkey. The crescent continued down through the land between the Tigris and Euphrates Rivers before they joined and emptied into the Persian Gulf. Archaeologists and historians use the term *Ancient Near East*, often abbreviated as *Near East*, for the ancient nations, people, and languages of the Fertile Crescent.

Key names associated with the Fertile Crescent are: Levant and Mesopotamia. The Greek word *Mesopotamia* means *land between the two rivers*. *Levant* is defined as *a strong easterly Mediterranean wind*. As history moved on, new names replaced old ones. Knowledge of those times has greatly increased with information collected through major excavations of the early twentieth century, CE. Inscriptions of wedge-shaped forms on clay tablets reveal records of advanced civilizations and provide insight into the beginning of written languages. History overlaps time and space; a brief account of some key names provides a means for integration.

Mesopotamia

The land of Mesopotamia curved across present day Syria and southern Turkey, then continued between the Tigris and Euphrates Rivers. The country of Iraq now covers a large portion of ancient Mesopotamia, while Iran shares the eastern border. Names associated with Mesopotamia are: Sumer (Ur), Akkad, Babylonia, Assyria, Elam, and Media.

Sumer

Biblical Shinar, Sumer, in the southern division of Babylonia, is now the southern part of Iraq. Evidence points to the Tower of Babel being built in *Shinar*. Archaeologists believe the people

3

of Sumer were the first advanced civilization (3300-2600 BCE). Sumerians developed the earliest from of writing using cuneiform script. Sumer fell to the Akkadians before 2334 BCE. Sumer experienced a revival, at Ur, about 2050 BCE, but fell as Elamites grew in power. The Babylonian ruler, around 1720 BCE, expanded his empire to include Sumer in the south and Akkad in the north.

Ur, thought the home of Abraham, on the Euphrates River north of the Persian Gulf, was the capital of Sumer for 200 years until captured by the Elamites. Excavated findings tell of Ur's advance culture, dating back to 2900-2500 BCE. Around 1900 BCE, foreigners from surrounding hills attacked and destroyed the city of Ur.

Akkad

Akkad, to the north of Sumer, invaded major city-states of Sumer, including Ur. Records from the clay tablets show that from 2334-2279 BCE, the Akkadians joined the city-states into one politic unit. The Akkadian Empire (2280-2150 BCE) covered today's southern Turkey, Lebanon, and east to the Persian Gulf. Through this period, authority was delegated to the regions of past city-states enabling them to gain power. By the twenty-first century BCE, much of Sumer had regained its original status. However, before long, other invaders, the Amorites, brought an end to the Akkadian Empire.

Babylonia

Babylonia (identified with the Tower of Babel) in southern Mesopotamia with Assyria to the north, was earlier inhabited by Sumerians. Sargon I united Babylonia under his rule about

2300 BCE. Babylonian power rose and fell between 2000 and 500 BCE. Much of their history covers struggles with Assyria. Babylon, capital of the Babylonia, is considered the oldest city of the ancient world. According to tradition, Babylon was built by the Sumer god Marduk. In its early history, the city became a small independent kingdom, conquering a large part of Mesopotamia (1792-1750 BCE). Around five hundred years later, Assyria overpowered (Old) Babylonia and then dominated the ancient world for seven hundred years. (New) Babylonia regained independence in 626 BCE and again rose to power, reaching its greatest strength. In 587 BCE, Babylonia destroyed Jerusalem and took most of Judah's habitants into bondage to Babylon, then, fell from power in 539 BCE with the Persian conquest led by Cyrus.

Assyria

Assyria, in the northwestern region of Mesopotamia, was populated by ancient tribesmen, probably migrating from Babylonia. Starting as a client state in the Old Babylonian Empire, Assyria became an independent kingdom by 1499 BCE. With continued expansion, Assyria conquered Babylonia around 1300 BCE. For close to 700 years, Assyria was a leading power in the ancient world. After a long siege, in 721 BCE, the Northern Kingdom of Israel fell to Assyria. Forty-one years later, as Assyrian armies set out to capture Jerusalem, they were victims of a plague. Over 150,000 Assyrian soldiers died; Jerusalem was saved. Following this incident, Assyrian power weakened while Babylonia became stronger.

Elam

Elamites, descendants of Elam, were ancient people dwelling east of the Tigris and Euphrates rivers. Their history is filled with struggles involving Babylonians, Assyrians, and Persians for control of the Mesopotamia region. Starting in 2000 BCE, Elamites expanded their kingdom, destroying Ur about fifty years later. By 1750 BCE, the Elamite Kingdom became a province* of Babylonia, lasting until 1200 BCE when Elamites regained control. Less than a hundred years later, Babylonia again dominated Elam. After years of struggle, Elamites fell to the Assyrians in 645 BCE and then came under Persia with the demise of the Assyrian Empire, leading to the end of the independence of Elam.

*province: a country or region brought under the control of a conquering country

Media

An ancient country of Asia, Media, is now included in parts of Iran, Iraq and Turkey. Its history is interwoven in the rise and fall of a number of nations. When Media joined forces with Babylonia, they brought the final destruction to the Assyrian Empire. Media reached its greatest power between 605-552 BCE, dominating Persia until defeated by Cyrus, of Persia. Media remained the most important province of Persia resulting in the joined name *Medes and Persians*. They were an Indo-European people known as Aryans with Zoroastrianism as their religion. The name became *Medo-Persia*, a great empire that ruled Asia until conquered by Alexander the Great in 333 BCE. The empire then became part of Syria and later was included in a new Persian Empire.

Levant

Levant (Latin *rising*), the land on the eastern coast of the Mediterranean Sea, became present day Israel, Palestinian Territories, Lebanon, and part of Syria. Names associated with the Levant are: Canaanites, Hittites, Philistines, and Phoenicians.

Canaan

Located between the Mediterranean Sea and the Jordan River with Egypt to the south and Phoenicia (Lebanon) to the north, the land of Canaan was settled by ancient tribes of Amorites and Canaanites long before 2000 BCE. The Canaanites became the dominant civilization with city-states, and from the north, cuneiform script containing a wedge-shaped alphabet surfaced. In this area, religious texts and other documents on clay tablets were uncovered early in the twentieth century CE. The script used by the Canaanites differed from that used by Babylonians and Assyrians.

Canaan was the land God promised Abraham and his people with the belief of one God, known then as Hebrews. During a time of famine, the Hebrews left Canaan and dwelled in Egypt where they became slaves (1700-1300 BCE). On their return to Canaan, as Israelites, they conquered the Canaanites who then fell from history.

Hittites

Hittites, from the name *Hatti*, another name for Anatolia (present day Turkey) flourished between 1900-1200 BCE. Later the people spread into northern Syria and on into Canaan while the Israelites were in Egypt. Israelites conquered the Hittites in reclaiming their Promised Land.

Philistines

Sea People, or Philistines as described by the Egyptians, are noted as being aggressive. Generally identified with the island of Crete, the Philistines migrated at two different times into Canaan. There were differences within the culture of the two groups. Early arrivals in Canaan appeared about the time of Abraham and offered friendship to the Hebrews. The later Philistines (1200-600 BCE) were enemies of the Israelites. Not only did Philistines conflict with Israelites over the division of Canaan, they struggled with the Assyrians. Under King David's reign over the United Kingdom of Israel (1005-965 BCE), the Philistines' power declined. Remaining Philistines were deported with the Israelites when they were exiled to Babylonia (587 BCE). Assyrians referred to the Philistines as *Pilisti* or *Palastu*; the Hebrew word was *Pelishti*, the bases of the name *Palestine*.

Phoenicia

Phoenicia (Phenicia) was given its name, the land of purple, by the Greeks. Its location, north of Canaan along the shore of the Mediterranean Sea, provided purple dyes made from shell-fish. Today, it is the country of Lebanon and coastal Syria. In biblical times, cedars from Lebanon were sent to Egypt and eastern Mesopotamia. Phoenicians had many contacts with Israelites. Arameans and Amorites reached across both Mesopotamia and the Levant; while Egypt and Jordan were separated, both played a part in the total history.

Arameans

People of Syria, Arameans, were a major nation northeast of Canaan. They were of the Aramaic language group; the word *Aram* is used in the Old Testament for Syria. The Arameans, part of the massive migration from about 3000 to 2100 BCE, eventually settled in several parts of the ancient world, including northern Mesopotamia. The Assyrian war with Syria (745-727 BCE), resulted in the defeat of Syria which then became part of the Assyrian Empire.

Amorites

Amorites, characterized as uncivilized, lived in the wilderness regions that are presently western Saudi Arabia, through a portion of Jordan, Iraq and southern Syria. About 2000 BCE, Amorites began their migration. Though a number of Amorites remained in Syria, Phoenicia and the southern desert regions, far greater numbers traveled eastward to Babylonia where they captured major cities and regions of Mesopotamia. Other Amorites settled in Canaan, being called *people of Canaan.*

The Bible speaks of Amorites being ancestors to the Canaanites. God promised the land of Canaan to Abraham, where he and his descendants, the Hebrews, lived until famine took them to Egypt (1700-1300 BCE). On their return to Canaan, the Israelites, as they became known, conquered the Amorites in reclaiming the Promised Land. The process was lengthy; it took until the time of King David (1005-965 BCE) before all the Amorites were defeated.

Egypt

Around 3000 BCE, all of Egypt fell under one king at the capital of Memphis. Irrigation systems increased Egypt's agricultural production leading into the Old Kingdom period of Egypt's history, the time when pyramids and pharaohs appeared. With the growth of government, by 2200 BCE, Egypt was decentralized leading to a period of weakness, known as the First Intermediate Period. The Middle Kingdom period (2000-1800 BCE) followed with new kings, again centralizing Egypt with an agricultural expansion. Enemies from other countries created instability once more and a Second Intermediate Period of weakness followed (1750-1570 BCE). Hyksos entered Egypt at that time, taking control of the nation until Egyptians were able to drive them out and the New Kingdom period (1570-1100 BEC) began.

Egypt was at the height of its power in 1280 BCE when Moses led the Hebrews, foreigners who had been in the country 430 years, out of Egypt. The Late Period of Egyptian history (1100-330 BCE) saw Israel as a greater power than Egypt, changing as Israel changed. Judah, for a short period, fell under Egypt. Romans took control of Egypt around 30 BCE.

Jordan

On a map of today, Jordan includes large areas east and south of the Jordan River, an important feature of biblical history. Starting above the Sea of Galilee, the river ends in the Dead (Salt) Sea. Hebrews crossed the Jordan River to enter the Promised Land. Pot shards from archaeological sites reveal early Hebrew settlements in the Jordan River Valley and rivers to the east.

Ancient Israel occupied territory on both sides of the river. John the Baptist baptized Jesus in the Jordan River.

Moving Forward

Persia defeated Babylonia in 539 BCE.
Alexander the Great defeated Persia, (333 BCE) ushering in the Hellenistic Period.
The final century before current era, Rome entered the scene.

Language Development

Genesis 11:1-9 tells of God stopping construction of the Tower of Babel and dispersing people over the earth with different languages. In time, oral languages became written words. Many inhabitants of the biblical land fell under the classification of *Semite*, used to identify people of ancient southwestern Asia including the Akkadians, Phoenicians, Hebrews, and Arabs. The term also covers modern people speaking a Semitic language. Scholars have categorized the Semitic languages groups as:

Northeastern groups—Akkadian and dialects of Babylonia and Assyria
Southern groups—Old South Arabian with various dialect
Northwest groups—Aramaic, Phoenician, Hebrew, (and others).
Within the Northwest group is the *Canaanite* branch of languages which includes Hebrew and Phoenician.

The development of written languages began at different times for the various civilizations in and around biblical lands. Some similarities are seen in the progression as shown in the brief accounts listed here. Times shown represents a general time period.

3300 BCE

Earliest forms of writing appear in Egypt and Mesopotamia.

The civilization of Sumer (3300-2600 BCE), in southern Mesopotamia, recorded their trading on clay tablets. Small symbols showing the type and amount of goods led to a script of pictures called pictograms. Eventually, symbols were used for thoughts or abstractions. Pictograms were then grouped together, known as **cuneiform script** because of the symbols' wedge-like shape. Most other groups in greater Mesopotamia adopted this advanced form of writing. Cuneiform script was used for 3,000 years; thousands of excavated baked clay tablets provide valuable information on the history of Mesopotamia. During that time, symbols were the bases of the Egyptian **hieroglyphic writing.**

2400 BCE

Sumer fell to the Akkadians (2334 BCE), whose language is classified as Semitic, though differed from the Sumerians. Amorites, after 2000 BCE, appeared in southern Mesopotamia; they adapted and translated old Sumerian texts into their Semitic language that evolved into Aramaic, Phoenician, and Hebrew. The written languages of all these groups were of cuneiform script, yet, they varied in style. Some examples of writings found on clay tablets follow.

The Epic of Gilgamesh, written. about 2100 BCE, describe the walls of Uruk (Iraq), a city-state of Sumer. (*I have been told;* The

Epic of Gilgamesh *contains the first version of the flood story. Also, I have heard music re-created from that clay tablet.*)

By 2000 BCE, Canaanites in the north had developed cuneiform script with a wedge-shaped alphabet, different from the Babylonians and Assyrians.

Information about Sumer is interpreted to suggest a possible time of Abraham's journey (2000-1800 BCE); proof of Abraham is not shown.

Tablets from Babylonia (1900-1200 BCE) tell of growing trade throughout Mesopotamia.

Cuneiform script was narrowed to nearly 600 characters.

Abraham arrived in the Promised Land, the home of Canaanites.

Aramaic, the language of the Arameans (Syria) was identified, eventually replacing many languages of the ancient world. The Semitic Aramaic language differed from the Canaanite branch.

1800 BCE

Tablets dating between 1799-1700 BCE, found on Syria's Mediterranean coast, indicate a change in symbols used for the cuneiform script. The new symbols are similar to an alphabet that could have evolved into the Hebrew alphabet. They provide some knowledge of Canaan and the surrounding region from Abraham, through the patriarchs and to the Israelites return from Egypt.

1500 BCE

Hieroglyphic inscriptions from Egyptian records (1600-1500 BCE) contain the words *eres-kena'an* (land of Canaan). Nomadic tribes living there were described as *Abiru* or *Habiru*, translated as *sand-dwellers* or *migrants*, possibly the root of the word *Hebrew*. Canaanites began using an alphabetic script. Crete replaced its hieroglyphic script with an alphabetic script.

1200 BCE

A pictographic form of writing arranged in alphabetic order, known as Proto (early) Canaanite, emerged in Canaan by 1150 BCE. At that time, Israelite communities were common in Canaan. About fifty years later, evidence of a spoken language, tentatively identified as ancient Hebrew, was noted. It was similar to the northwestern Semitic language spoken in Phoenicia. Some scholars think the language of the Hebrews began earlier, perhaps in Egypt or during the forty years in the desert.

A royal monument, constructed around 1050 BCE, documents a Phoenician alphabet. Shortly after, a Hebrew alphabet began to develop.

1000 BCE

The oldest example of Hebrew writing, discovered on a limestone tablet in Gezer (southern portion of middle Israel), dates the written language at 925 BCE. The writing is similar to the Phoenicians; however, sounds for consonant letters are different.

800 BCE

Greeks adopted the Phoenician alphabet but added separate symbols for vowels (*a e i o u*), still used today. Unlike the Greek language, the ancient Hebrew alphabet evolved as a separate branch of the Phoenician alphabet.

Between 799-700 BCE there is some evidence of literacy in Israel and Judah.

By 699 BCE, the Hebrew written language was clearly a distinct script with twenty-two letters. Much later, small points were added to indicate vowels. The language was written right to left. A few passages (Ezra 4:8, 6:18 7:12-26 and Daniel 2:46, 7:28) of the Hebrew Bible were written in Aramaic; others were written in Hebrew.

Between 650 and 400 BCE, Egyptians developed a cursive script based on their hieroglyphs. When Israelites returned to Judah from the Babylonian exile (after 539 BCE), the Aramaic language began replacing Hebrew. After the conquest of Alexander the Great, (333 BCE), Greek became the common language.

Around 250 BCE, the Jewish community in Egypt had translated the Torah into Greek. The translation is known as the Septuagint, or LXX. Over the next century or more, the other portions of the Hebrew Bible were also translated.

99 C

Jesus and his followers generally spoke Aramaic, though, the New Testament was written in the Greek language.

Jerome translated the entire Bible into Latin, the language of Rome.

1945 CE

Fragmented codices, volumes of pages bound into books, were found in Nag Hammadi (Northern Egypt). They had been translated from the Greek into a Coptic language of ancient Egypt. Thought to have been written around the time of the New Testament, the find is known as the **Gnostic Gospels**.

1949 CE

Writings on papyrus, pieced together and rolled into scrolls, were found in Qumran (east of Jerusalem). The hundreds of documents, known as the **Dead Sea Scrolls**, written mostly in Hebrew with a few in Aramaic, date nearly a thousand years older than any previous copies of the Hebrew Bible. Except for the book of Esther, partial copies of the rest of the Hebrew Bible were among the findings. Other scrolls told of the people living in the area, perhaps around 150 BCE.

Source—Hebrew Bible

Torah (Law)

Pre-modern Jews and Christians, without question, accepted Moses as author of the Torah, the first five books of the Hebrew Bible. The Greek name for *Torah* is *Pentateuch*, generally found in academic accounts whereas *Torah* (The Law or Teachings of Moses) designates a more religious nature. Into the twentieth century CE, there is disagreement over the authorship of the Torah. Some feel God gave all the words to Moses who then recorded them; others look at the final form of the Torah taking place later than the time of Moses.

The Renaissance (fourteenth into the seventeenth century CE), brought an interest in ancient texts resulting in a renewed study of the Hebrew Bible. Scholars, through the seventeenth and eighteenth centuries, identified distinct writing patterns in the Torah. Following is a brief description of the findings.

Yahwist Source 900s BCE (J) from the name YHWH for God

German scholars were the first to write of the various sources of the Hebrew Bible; in the German language YHWH begins with J. The writings attributed to this author, from the Southern Kingdom of Judah, tell of the development of humankind and of people with the belief of one personal God. It is thought that the Yahwist wrote during the time of King Solomon (968-928 BCE), though it could have been more than a century later.

Elohist Source 800s-700s BCE (E) from the Hebrew word Elohim

Elohim is a general term for God, sometimes shown as El. The Elohist author, a priest, was from the Northern Kingdom of Israel. The Elohist writings are only found within the Yahwist writings. The priest left the north after that kingdom fell to Assyria (721 BCE) and settled in the Southern Kingdom. He took his writings with him and they were then incorporated into the Yahwist narratives noted as JE.

Deuteronomic Source 600s BCE (D) from the final book of the Torah

The source of the book of Deuteronomy is not combined with other writings, though there are repetitions of earlier narratives. Deuteronomy is different from the first four books of the Torah in that no other source is identified within the writing. Deuteronomy includes Moses' last days and his advice to the

Hebrews for entering the Promised Land. Apparently, Levites who left the Northern Kingdom for the Southern Kingdom preserved the material and compiled it into a book. Scholars generally agree that the book found in the Temple in 622 BCE (2 Kings 22) is the central part of Deuteronomy.

Priestly Source 500-400s BCE **(P)** from the writings of priests

During the Babylonian exile (587-539 BCE) and extending through the return of the Israelites to Judah, priests recorded religious traditions and practices so they would not be lost. In the absence of a Temple, the efforts of the priests maintained and reinforced the Israelites faith during their bondage in Babylonia.

Redactor **R**

Some scholars assume an editor or a group of editors, called redactors, combined the various sources mentioned into the Torah. The lengthy process was completed in stages, most likely during the Babylonian exile (586-538 BCE). Other scholars feel there was little editing to the final Torah and use the word *compiler* for the process instead of *redactor*.

Marc ZVI Brettler, in his introduction to The Jewish Study Bible, presents the view that reading the Bible as it was written before concern regarding authorship, brings a clarity to the meaning of the messages that prevailed for thousands of years. Brettler also suggested that, perhaps, concentrating on individual sources leads to a lack of appreciation for the very reason the Bible came to be. As with all things, thoughts differ.

Canonization, the designation of biblical material as Inspired (Scripture), covered many years. At the time Hebrew writings were noted as central to the Jewish faith, the term *canon* had not come into use regarding the Bible. Many scholars feel it was after the Israelites return from Babylonia and Ezra's help in restoring the faith (458 BCE), when the Torah (Law) was looked on as Scripture.

Nevi'im

The section of the Hebrew Bible, Nevi'im (Prophets), deals with the final days of Moses then moves on through reclaiming the Promised Land of Canaan. That was a time when prophets and kings were influential. Prophets extended into the Babylonian exile and beyond; their spoken proclamations eventually became written words. The long-complicated history was recorded by more than one author and reflected various stages and interests. Once written, the complex compositions were edited and expanded. The Nevi'im was considered Scripture before 300 BCE.

Kethuvim

A variety of material from diverse time periods is found in the Kethuvim (Writings), the last section of the Hebrew Bible. There is no central theme or idea portrayed in these writings covering Israel's past, prayers, wisdom literature, and apocalyptic prophecy. The Kethuvim is significant for understanding the Hebrew Bible as a whole while providing insight into the development of Jewish thought after the rebuilding of Jerusalem and into the beginning of Roman persecution (515-63 BCE). These writings came together and were considered Scripture by 70 CE.

CHAPTER 2

The Hebrew Bible

Reflections Bible
Hebrew Bible—A Review
    Torah (Law), Nevi'im (Prophets), Kethuvim (Writings)
Books of the Hebrew Bible and Old Testament
Early Hebrew Lineage

Reflections *Bibles*

The Hebrew Bible covers thousands of years, from oral tradition, continuing through the time of messages left on stone pillars, before advancing to written words. Of course, growing up I never knew of a Hebrew Bible. The Old Testament came before the New Testament. It made sense to me.

There was more for me to remember about the Old Testament than the New Testament. At Sunday school, we memorized the Twenty-Third Psalm. And how I loved those stories! Noah's flood, a baby left in a basket among reeds, and David killing a giant, were among my favorites. In my childhood, the order of events never mattered; they all just seemed special. It was hard for me to figure out Solomon and keep track of Jacob's family, though Joseph with his colorful coat and dreams never left my mind. Bedtime stories for my children came from a book of Old Testament Stories, still on a bookcase shelf. About ten years ago, I wanted to know more about those writings.

As I progressed in my biblical self-study, a Jewish friend mentioned she had several copies of Hebrew Bibles and offered me one. Of course, I accepted. She gave me an old one that had belonged to her father; his notes still intact. The faded words of his personal affirmation of God are an inspiration to me. This torn and tattered Bible is a treasure unto its own. It is a first translation into the English language by a group of English-speaking Jewish scholars, with a 1917 copyright and titled The Holy Scriptures.

Hebrew Bibles, like others with a more current copyright, come in a variety of titles. My friend's generation refers to the ancient writings as Scriptures. *I'm told younger ones prefer the word* Bible; *they say it is more precise. Regardless, they are all dear to my heart.*

Hebrew Bible—A Review

Torah (Law)

Torah, meaning *teachings* or *instructions*, contains historical accounts of early Hebrew times and revelations given from God to Moses. Torah, with a small *t*, first referred to the oral tradition of passing on God's creation story and the Hebrews' relationship with God. Close to four thousand years later, when the remembered words were written, they became Torah—with a capital T. At times called the *Five Books of Moses*, the Divine revelations from God set the foundation of the Hebrews' spiritual and communal life. Those early times led to Abraham, advancing to Moses with the deliverance of Hebrews from Egypt, commencing with God's direction for living and worship. There is no final agreement among scholars as to the dating and authorship of the Torah. Nevertheless, materials compiled and edited, seemingly around 458 BCE, were officially recognized as Scripture. Into present time, biblical scholars, Jewish and non-Jewish, continue their in-depth study of the Torah.

In comparing the Torah with the first five books of the Christian Old Testament, there is no change in the order of the books: **Genesis, Exodus, Leviticus, Numbers,** and **Deuteronomy**. Biblical references are taken from *The Jewish Study Bible*.

Genesis tells of God creating the World. Included are two different origins of humankind and the first people, Adam and Eve in the Garden of Eden. Some biblical scholars date that time at 4004 BCE. Adam and Eve were sent from the Garden because of their disobedience to God. Births of Cain, Able (killed by Cain), and Seth followed; lineage from Seth led to Noah. At that time, Hebrews, with a growing belief in one God, still moved from place to place. Genesis continues with Hebrew history.

Once more, because of their evil ways, people felt the wrath of God. He first directed Noah to build an ark to save his family and pairs of the animal kingdom; then, the rains came. It rained for forty days and nights. Noah and his family did not perish. A questionable date of 2348 BCE is noted for that period. After departing the ark, Noah's sons and their sons, spread over the earth. Noah's sons are: Ham, Japheth, and Shem. Canaan, a son of Ham, settled land along the Mediterranean Sea, which carried his name. Descendants of Japheth spread to the north, both east and west. Eber, from Shem and ancestor of Terah, father of Abram, located through the area of the Euphrates and Tigris Rivers [Mesopotamia].

A Hebrew like Noah, Abram answered God's call and set out for a land He promised would bring forth a great nation. Abram's entire household and that of his nephew, Lot, journeyed to the land of Canaan. After some time of travel, the combined herds and flocks required larger pasture lands with adequate water. They crossed into Egypt where Abram introduced his wife, Sarai, as his sister. Complications followed when young men sought out Sarai. Yet, Abram and Sarai, with all the households and goods, left Egypt without trouble.

Back in Canaan, the need for suitable grazing required Abram and Lot to settle in different areas. Lot chose a section in the lower Jordan Valley, at that time, a den of wickedness. At one point, one of the feuding kings took Lot and his household as prisoners; they were freed by Abram's intervention. Lot then pitched his tents near the city of Sodom which was destroyed along with Gomorrah because of their sinful ways. Lot, his wife and two daughters fled, as directed; however, the wife became a pillar of salt when she looked back upon the wreckage.

Abram resumed his searching for the Promised Land. It was there, in Canaan, when God gave that land to Abram and his descendants—the Promised Ones. Before long, Abram fathered

Ishmael with Hagar, handmaiden of his wife Sarai. Then God changed Abram's name to Abraham and Sarai to Sarah. In time, Sarah gave birth to Isaac, a second son of Abraham. God tells Abraham that through both Ishmael and Isaac great nations will raise.

From Ishmael, the Islamic faith grew. Islam, a religion based on the teaching of Muhammad, centers on the belief of one God, Allah. Muhammad, born in Mecca of Arabia, became a prophet in 610 CE. Early biographers of Muhammad traced his tribe's lineage back to Ishmael. Previously, Jewish interpreters connected Ishmael with the Arabs. The Quran (Koran), the Islamic Holy Book, tells of Muhammad's life and his messages from God. People of the Islamic faith are called Muslims. The religious center for Muslims is Mecca.

Returning to Genesis, the Hebrew faith continued with Isaac. The time set as a possibility for Abraham, and with him—the Age of Patriarchs—is 2000-1700 BCE. Much later, 30 CE, Christianity, based on the life of Jesus, surfaced from that very heritage—carrying forward the worship of one God.

God tested Abraham by asking for the sacrifice of his son, Isaac. Abraham made all the arrangements and set about to take Isaac's life when God sent an angel to halt the action. Then, God knew Abraham to be obedient and rewarded him with abundance and numerous descendants. Later, God directed Isaac to the land of Abraham's youth where he [Isaac] found Rebecca, who became his wife. They had twin boys, Esau and Jacob. Jacob tricked his father by taking on the appearance of Esau, the first born. Isaac then gave his son Jacob the blessing to carry on the faith and lineage first given to Abraham.

Jacob, with his wife Leah, and her handmaiden, birthed eight sons and one daughter. With his wife Rachel, and her handmaiden, Jacob fathered four additional sons. The Twelve Tribes of Israel sprung from the twelve sons of Jacob, whose name God changed to Israel.

Joseph, the favorite son of Jacob, sold by his brothers into slavery, found favor with the Egyptian Pharaoh and grew in power. A dream Joseph interpreted predicted seven years of plenty followed by seven years of drought. With this insight, Egypt stored enough wheat to last through the lean years. As the famine reached Canaan, Joseph brought Jacob and all the families to Egypt.

Exodus begins with more years in Egypt and a progression of Pharaohs; Hebrews had become slaves in the land of Egypt. Fearing the strength of their growing numbers, the Pharaoh order all male Hebrew babies killed. Then, a Hebrew boy was born and saved by the Pharaoh's daughter. She named him Moses and raised him as her own child. Moses grew to manhood and when learning of his birth people, he rose up against the Pharaoh and led the Hebrews out of Egypt. The year of the Exodus is another question; however, a number of scholars have set it at 1280 BCE. Hebrews, as decreed by God, spent forty years in the wilderness of Sinai because many had reverted to the worship of idols.

The book of **Leviticus** covers The Law as given to Moses while in the wilderness. It instructs Hebrews on ways to relate to God. The priesthood is formed through the lineage of Aaron, high priest and older brother to Moses. General laws with conditions for five annual feast days are established.

In **Numbers**, spies seeking the means of a conquest enter Canaan. The Hebrews rebel against God and question Moses' leadership. God denies Moses and Aaron entry into the Promised Land of Canaan because they did not trust Him to provide for His people. Aaron died a short time later. Even at that point, God revealed land allocations for the Twelve Tribes of Israel [descendants of sons of Jacob/Israel]. The division was to take place on their arrival in Canaan.

The Ten Commandments and the greatest commandment to love God above all else are given to Moses in **Deuteronomy**. God gave instructions for building an ark to hold the Ten Commandments and other details for entry into Canaan. Moses died and Joshua, from the tribe of Ephraim, led the people into the Promised Land.

Torah ends with Deuteronomy. After the completion of the Torah, additional Jewish writings received the status of Scripture. The Hebrew Bible groups these inclusions into Nevi'im (Prophets) and Kethuvim (Writings).

Nevi'im (Prophets)

Nevi'im tells of prophecy, seen throughout a thousand years of Israel's history. Prophets—messengers of God—fulfilled many duties. They were considered *holy*, intermediaries between God and the people, for the keeping of God's commandments. Proclamations of the prophets are often called *oracles*. Prophets also carried messages from the people to God. When God punished the people, prophets told them that it was God's will; with proper moral behavior there would be no punishment. Prophets could be either men or women. They informed people of God's warnings or revelations and spoke of His comforting words. Kings conferred with prophets when seeking knowledge regarding state affairs. Prophets addressed universal human mysteries of Divine intervention.

Prophecy altered as the nation changed. Early prophets were often asked about private matters such as family sickness or lost objects. With the onset of kings, prophecies included God's choice for kings. Later, prophets had a voice in international affairs and spoke on the issues of social justice. Then, in Babylonia, Ezekiel told of God's justification for destroying Jerusalem and a possible future with the rebuilding of the Temple.

While a few books of Nevi'im are not titled with the name of a prophet, prophecy played an important part throughout that history. **Joshua** is thought of as the prophetic successor to Moses. In **Judges**, oracles are often consulted. Elijah, Elisha, and other prophets provided a substantial role in the selection of kings; it is stated that all kings or dynasties depended on sanctioning by a prophet.

It appears that all of the prophetic books were compiled and edited over a period of time, some covered centuries. The books focus on the individual prophet's words; repeated through the years until the Hebrews developed a written language, then they were recorded by written words. Scholars have been able to determine where most prophets lived and where they prophesied; yet, uncertainty surrounds those editing the writings. Before 300 BCE, the prophecies were compiled into Nevi'im and grouped with Torah, in the category of Scripture. There are references to *the law and the prophets* in the New Testament.

Nevi'im consists of eight books: **Joshua, Judges, Samuel, Kings, Isaiah, Jeremiah, Ezekiel**, and **The Twelve**. In the Medieval Period, the books were divided according to the subject, with the term *Former Prophets* given to the first four books dealing with historical accounts. *Latter Prophets* follow; they center more on prophecy. The designation of *former* and *latter* indicates their placement in the Bible, not a chronology order.

Christian Bibles contain the same books as Nevi'im; the ordering differs. Some are placed with Historical Books while others are listed with Prophetic Books. A major difference is the Prophetic books coming at the end of the Christian Old Testament, perhaps as a way of pointing into the future and the fulfillment of a messiah, as prophesied. In some Bibles, the Latter Prophets are further categorized as Major (Isaiah, Jeremiah, Ezekiel, Daniel), and Minor for the remainder. [Daniel, in the Hebrew Bible is placed in Kethuvim.]

Returning to the Hebrew Bible, Nevi'im tells of the Hebrews' entrance into Canaan where they became Israelites. The distribution of lands, struggles of independent tribes under judges, unification under kings, division of the kingdom and their demise, are covered.

The first book in Nevi'im is **Joshua**. He led the Hebrews into the Promised Land (1240 BCE), where they became known as Israelites, and officiated over the allocation of lands to the Tribes of Israel.

A portion of land went to each tribe descending from sons of Jacob Israel: Joseph, Benjamin, Reuben, Simeon, Levi, Judah, Issachar, Zebulun, Dan, Naphtali, Gad, and Asher. Joseph's portion was divided between descendants of his two sons: Manasseh and Ephraim.

Lands east of the Jordan River were given to Reuben, Gad, and a half to Manasseh. Lands west of the Jordan River were given to Judah, Ephraim, Benjamin, Simeon, Zebulun, Issachar, Asher, Naphtali, Dan, and a half to Manasseh.

The tribe of Levi did not receive a specific territory as they were devoted to religious duties; therefore, they were assigned forty-eight cities with surrounding pastureland. Six of the cities offered a place of refuge for individuals awaiting judgment regarding questionable killings.

Joshua, descendant of Ephraim, received a city for his guidance (Joshua 19:49-50).

Scholars have long questioned the exactness of the tribal borders; the division of land covered centuries. The final disbursements seem to have occurred through the times of King David and King Solomon (1005-965/968-928 BCE).

The book of **Judges** follows Joshua. It tells of Israel's struggles as they conquer Canaan. For more than two hundred years after entering Canaan, no form of political authority within the Tribes of Israel existed. That time period (roughly 1200-1000 BCE) is referred to as the Period of Judges, as Israelites relied on judges to act as tribal leaders. Judges judged Israelites' enemies, not fellow Israelites. It took several generations before Israelites successfully conquered the Canaanites. Conflicts, between Israelites and invasions from outside, kept Israel in a state of war. Israelites faced other difficulties as well, for they remained wanderers; moving about in an effort to maintain herds of sheep and goats. Israelites, an independent people with men and tribes all going their own way, lacked cohesiveness. Also, during that period, prophets, were called on for counsel and political direction.

Generally, Samuel is regarded as the first prophet because of his importance; yet, there were prophets before him. Samuel is also recognized as the last judge. All of Israel knew Samuel. When he became an old man, people realized they needed a centralized government with a strong leader for their survival. They asked Samuel to appoint such a person. In 1025 BCE Samuel anointed Saul, from the tribe of Benjamin, as the first King of Israel. Saul proved to be a poor choice for king; therefore, a short time later, Samuel anointed David as king.

The books **First and Second Samuel** contain history related to Samuel, Saul, and David. Saul, the first king, ruled twenty years. King David, son of Jesse from Bethlehem of Judah, replaced Saul. David, known for killing the giant Goliath, is often noted as Israel's greatest king, even though problems plagued his reign.

David had an affair with Bathsheba, whom he married after having her husband killed. Discord among his sons pitted one against the other over the throne. Although, before his death, David recognized his son, Solomon, as king. David reigned forty years (1005-965 BCE).

The story of King Solomon, son of David and Bathsheba, is found in **First Kings**. One of Solomon's most noted accomplishments is building the Temple in Jerusalem, completed around 950 BCE, after seven years of construction. Solomon's extensive architectural achievements led to political unrest because of the required heavy taxes and forced labor. Another disturbing element of Solomon's reign was his numerous wives, many of whom were foreigners and worshiped multiple gods. In many ways, Solomon was considered wise, despite his actions which left the country in a devastating situation.

Not long after Solomon's death (928 BCE), the Ten Tribes in the north revolted against the heavy taxation of Solomon's reign. Furthermore, they no longer wanted to be under rulers of the line of David. The tribes in the south sought to retain Solomon's legacy, including the lineage of David. The dispute resulted in a permanent division between the Israelites. The tribes in the north retained the name Israel as the Northern Kingdom of Israel with Samaria as the capital; the tribes in the south had united as Judah and became the Southern Kingdom of Judah with Jerusalem as the capital.

In Solomon's time, worship centered around the Temple he built in Jerusalem; the practice continued for the Kingdom of Judah. The Kingdom of Israel established its own places for worship. However, lacking close ties to the Temple, many Israelites there turned to idol worship.

Second Kings covers both Judah and Israel as they encounter internal and external turmoil. Assyria and Babylonia were threats to both kingdoms. Meanwhile, prophets condemned the Northern Kingdom for the elite benefiting from a growing economy while the lower class faced loss of land and poverty. Similarly, the Kingdom of Judah received the prophets forecast of doom because of the weakening state of God's covenant.

After a three-year siege of Samaria, in 721 BCE, the Northern Kingdom of Israel fell to Assyria. Most of the Israelites were resettled in lands farther north. Some historical accounts refer to the Ten Northern Tribes of Israel as the *Lost Tribes;* they never again completely emerged in world history. Assyrians resettled the land of Israel with other conquered people, most of whom worshiped idols. The new population became known as *Samaritans*—heathens in the eyes of the Southern Kingdom of Judah.

Assyrians longstanding threat to the Kingdom of Israel also affected the Kingdom of Judah, who earlier had become a vassal* of Assyria. Judah revolted against Assyria in 701 BCE, bringing about Assyrian's invasion of Judah and their capturing of a number of towns. However, an angel of God saved Jerusalem and destroyed the Assyrian army. By 640 BCE Judah was released from Assyrian dependency.

*vassal: had use of land but had to pay tribute to the oppressor for protection

Babylonia (called Chaldeans at that time) then rose in power and by 612 BCE, brought an end to the Assyrians. Shortly after, Judah became a vassal of Babylonia. Judah revolted in 598 BCE refusing to pay the required tribute. Nebuchadnezzar, King of Babylonia, retaliated by seizing Jerusalem and taking most nobles and officials to Babylonia. Little more than ten years later, 587 BCE, Judah again exerted independence. Nebuchadnezzar re-entered Jerusalem which fell after an eighteen-month siege. Solomon's Temple and all of Jerusalem were destroyed. Most inhabitants of Judah and Jerusalem were either killed or taken to Babylonia where they lived in exile until 539 BCE.

In exile, the Israelites received a considerable amount of personal liberty. Many became involved in business. Israelites were allowed to practice their faith and scribes began writing down their Sacred writings. Before long, scribes became more important than prophets and the first rabbis and synagogues appeared. Old tribal divisions among the exiles diminished, replaced by unity.

Continuing through *The Jewish Study Bible,* the book of **Isaiah** with prophetic sayings and poetry is next. In addition, close to two hundred years of Judah's history, the Assyrian period; the Babylonian exile; and the restoration of Judah, are found in Isaiah. One of the best-known prophets, Isaiah lived in Jerusalem toward the end of 700 BCE. Two more names listed among the Former Prophets are **Jeremiah** and **Ezekiel**, each covered in separate books.

In the years of turmoil within the Kingdom of Judah, before conquered by Babylonia, people ignored warnings of doom from the prophet **Jeremiah**. While Judah was experiencing a time of freedom and prosperity, Jeremiah began his prophecies, which lasted until the fall of Jerusalem (587 BCE). His messages were unpopular to most, especially the Temple priests. Jeremiah believed that it was not enough to just attended services in the Temple. Faith in God, shown by moral living and complete loyalty, indicated righteous living. Jeremiah condemned fellow Israelites, the king and the people, for their idolatry and injustice. Many Judeans believed God lived in the Temple; therefore, a disaster would not fall on Jerusalem or Judah. Yet, by 587 BCE, Babylonia completely destroyed Jerusalem and the Temple. Jeremiah was excepted from the mass exile of Judeans because of his earlier encouragement for the king of Judah to surrender.

Ezekiel was a priest in Jerusalem and part of the deportation of 598 BCE. In a vision, Ezekiel saw winged spirits transporting an *appearance similar to the glory of YHWH,* which Ezekiel interpreted as God giving the voice of prophecy to him [Ezekiel]. Through that vision, the Israelites realized that God was with them, in exile. God did not live in the Temple in Jerusalem.

Ezekiel prophesied for his people in Babylonia over the next twenty-seven years. Like Jeremiah in Judah, Ezekiel gave messages that God was punishing the Israelites because they had fallen away from His covenant. Ezekiel prophesied the destruction of Jerusalem followed by the restoration of the Temple. The dedication of Jeremiah in Judah and Ezekiel in Babylonia kept the long-held faith of one God alive for enough people—the belief did not die.

Other prophets of the Hebrew Bible, listed as *The Twelve*, are: Hosea, Joel, Amos, Obadiah, Jonah, Micah, Nahum, Habakkuk, Zephaniah, Haggai, Zechariah, and Malachi. The Hebrew Bible concludes with Kethuvim.

Ketuvim (Writings)

Ketuvim contains historical accounts and treasured stories handed down through generations. This collection includes times of the wandering Hebrews to the beginning of Judaism. Age old songs and prayers, literature of heroes and heroines, with events of downfall and survival, are all vital to the enduring faith. Long thought of as Israelites, their faith in one God saw a dramatic change. In the years before the destruction of Jerusalem, Israel and Judah were considered a region of land. With the Babylonian exile and no land to call their own, they became *the people of one God*. When allowed to return to their homeland, the name *Israelite* became *Jew*.

The term *Jew,* from the Hebrew word *yehudi,* meaning *Judean,* applied first to people from the tribe of Judah, as they were the majority of exiles. Later, *Jew* and *Jewish* identified Hebrew descendants, those devoted to YHWH. At the time of exile, some Israelites had settled throughout the ancient Middle East. When Judah, once again, became a place for worship, many of those in their new countries chose to stay. The movement away from the once *Promised Land,* called *Diaspora,* or Dispersion of the Jews, is still evident today. With Jews living in various places around the world, those living in the present state of Israel are in the minority.

As mentioned, Israelites from the Babylonian exile, on returning to Jerusalem, ushered in a new way of defining themselves. No longer tied to a specific land era, as Jews and the Jewish faith, the people were identified by their ethnicity along with their religious and social practices. Events before the exile are considered the history of Israel; after the return to the homeland, it is the history of Judaism. Judaism evolved as Jews living across many lands, and those in Judah, adapted to the diverse culture and political environment of their surroundings. With Judah remaining a client state (dependent) to ongoing empires, adjusting to the situation was critical. Learning to live as minorities resulted in different ways of being a Jew.

The books of Ketuvim, in their final form, date to the post exile period. Jews of Judah, after their struggles in Babylonia, felt a need to connect with their past as they moved into their future. They collected vast and varied material from their early history and incorporated their return from Babylonia, into the collection *Ketuvim.* Categories of the writings and placement in the Hebrew Bible follow.

Songs and prayers to God are found in **Psalms. Proverbs** and **Job** are labeled as wisdom literature. **Song of Songs**, **Ruth**, **Lamentations**, **Ecclesiastes**, and **Esther**, are grouped as the Five Scrolls, each one read at the appropriate celebration. **Daniel** is classified as apocalyptic literature. **Ezra**, **Nehemiah**, and the **Chronicles** are historical literature. The Christian Old Testament separates the books, inserting them in a more chronological order. It took until roughly 70 CE, before Ketuvim was included with Torah and Nevi'im as Scripture.

The above descriptions, along with titles, generally provide insight into the contents of the books; a few exceptions follow. **First and Second Chronicles**, like First and Second Samuel, cover the Kings: Saul, David, and Solomon. **Lamentations** is a sequel to the prophet Jeremiah. **Ezra** and **Nehemiah** are both key biblical figures to the post exile period.

The book of **Ezra** begins with Cyrus, king of Persia allowing Israelites to return to their homeland and rebuild their Temple. Objections from local inhabitants plus financial hardships halted the rebuilding. People of Samaria, brought-in to populate that area when the Northern Kingdom of Israel fell to the Assyrians, asked to help with the rebuilding because in their new home, they worshiped the Israelite's God. Their offer was refused, creating lasting ill will from the Samarians (Ezra 4-6). Dedication of the rebuilt Temple did occur in 515 BCE. The years from 515 BCE to 70 CE (Roman destruction of the new Temple) is referred to as the Second Temple Period.

In 458 BCE, (a questionable date) Ezra, born in Babylonia, journeyed to Judah. Ezra, descended from the line of Aaron through Zadok, was a scribe and a royal administrator. The Persian government permitted Ezra to assist the people of Judah, many who had intermarried with non-Israelites, to restore their faith of YHWH and the Law of Moses. Ezra called together all Jewish adults in Jerusalem and read them the torah—words that were not yet *Scripture*. Writings had to be translated from Hebrew into Aramaic, the new language of Jews. Ezra's role in reading and reinterpreting the Law of Moses integrated the old Law into new circumstances. Ezra's work provided the foundation for a new form of worship—Judaism—and influenced the Torah being recognized as Scripture.

Nehemiah was an official in the Persian Empire assigned as governor of the province of Judah. After his arrival in Jerusalem, 445 BCE, he rebuilt the walls surrounding the city. Even with resistance from Samaritans and others, the task was completed in fifty-two days. During his twelve years in Jerusalem, before returning to Babylonia, Nehemiah further restored the Jewish faith by enlisting support for the Levites, restricting trade on the Sabbath, and prohibiting mixed marriages.

Historical writings taking place between Kethuvim and the New Testament, not considered Hebrew Scripture but included in some Christian Bibles, are considered the Apocrypha. Some books are supplemental to Kethuvim; others cover additional history and literature. Chapter 3 contains Information on the Apocrypha books.

Books of the Hebrew Bible and Old Testament

A short version of previously stated material is given here as a concise reference to the books of the Hebrew Bible and Christian Old Testament.

Dating and authorship of the sections in the Hebrew Bible are not certain. Although, scholars have been able to give an approximate time they were compiled and noted as being of central importance to the Jewish people.

Torah (Law of Moses) contains the creation story, genealogy records with family histories, the life of Moses and instructions given to him by God. Scholars date canonization (recognition as Scripture) during the Persian Period (539-333 BCE).

Nevi'im (Prophets) covers more than a thousand years of the Israelites' history: judges, kings, prophets, and the fall of a divided kingdom. Apparently, this section was canonized during the late Persian (539-333 BCE) or early Greek period (333-63 BCE).

Kethuvim (Writings) includes literature and history starting with the Hebrew times and ending after the Babylonian exile with changes resulting in a renewed faith. This was the last group of books to be canonized, very well, around 70 CE.

Christians gave the name *Old Testament* to the Hebrew Bible at the time they compiled and canonized their writings with the name *New Testament,* in 367 CE. Following the Torah, placement of books in the Old Testament differs from those in the Hebrew Bible. The Old Testament follows a more chronological order.

Contents from: The Jewish Study Bible Second Edition

Torah (Teaching, Instructing)

Genesis, Exodus, Leviticus, Numbers, Deuteronomy

Nevi'im (Prophets)

Joshua, Judges, I Samuel, II Samuel, I Kings, II Kings, Isaiah, Jeremiah, Ezekiel, The Twelve: Hosea, Joel, Amos, Obadiah, Jonah, Micah, Nahum, Habakkuk, Zephaniah, Haggai, Zechariah, Malachi

Kethuvim (Writings)

Psalms, Proverbs, Job, The Five Megillot (Scrolls): Song of Songs, Ruth, Lamentations, Ecclesiastes, Esther
Daniel, Ezra, Nehemiah, I Chronicles, II Chronicles

Contents from: The New Oxford Annotated Bible

New Revised Standard Version With The Apocrypha

The Hebrew Bible

The Pentateuch: Genesis, Exodus, Leviticus, Numbers, Deuteronomy

The Historical Books: Joshua, Judges, Ruth, 1 Samuel, 2 Samuel, 1 Kings, 2 Kings, 1 Chronicles, 2 Chronicles, Ezra, Nehemiah, Esther

The Poetical and Wisdom Books: Job, Psalms, Proverbs, Ecclesiastes, Song of Solomon

The Prophetic Books: Isaiah, Jeremiah, Lamentations, Ezekiel, Daniel, Hosea, Joel, Amos, Obadiah, Jonah, Micah, Nahum, Habakkuk, Zephaniah, Haggai, Zechariah, Malachi

Early Hebrew Lineage

Bishop James Ussher (1581-1656 CE), by looking at the genealogies noted in the Hebrew Bible, proposed the date of 4004 BCE for the Creation of the World and the story of Adam and Eve.

Genesis lists descendants from Adam through the children of Jacob. There are ten generations from Adam to Noah.

Sons of Adam and Eve: Cain, Abel, **Seth**
(Cain killed Abel)
From **Seth** came Enosh
From Enosh came Kenan
From Kenan came Mahalalel
From Mahalalel came Jared

From Jared came Enoch
From Enoch came Methuselaj
From Methuselaj came Lamech
From Lamech came **Noah**

Using Ussher's dates, Noah's Flood is recorded as 2348 BCE. There are ten generations from Noah to Abram.

Sons of Noah: Ham, Japheth, **Shem**
From **Shem** came Arphaxad
From Arphaxad came Shelah
From Shelah came Eber
From Eber came Peleg
From Peleg came Reu
From Reu came Serug
From Serug came Nahor
From Nahor came Terah
From Terah came **Abram**
(God changed Abram's name to Abraham [Father of a host of Nations].)

Genesis continues with descendants through Jacob.

Sons of Terah: Nahor, Haran, Abram

Nahor's children with wife Milcah
    (Haran's daughter): Milcah, Iscah

Haran's son: Lot

Sons of Abram: with Hagar, handmaiden of Saria: **Ishmael**
    (Islamic faith followed)

with wife, Sarah: **Isaac**
(God changed Saria's name to Sarah [Princess].)

Sons of Isaac: with wife, Rebecca,
(Nahor's granddaughter): **Esau, Jacob** (twins)

Esau: wives: Judith and Basemat from the Hittite Nation,
(Esau's descendants also listed in Genesis)

Sons of Jacob: with wife Leah: **Reuben, Simeon, Levi,
Judah, Issachar, Zebulun,** and **daughter, Dinah** with
Zilpah, handmaiden of Leah: **Gad, Asher** with wife
Rachel: **Joseph, Benjamin** with Bilhah, handmaiden of
Rachel: **Dan, Naphtali** (God changed Jacob's name to
Israel.)

The birth of Abram (Abraham) to the death of Jacob (Israel)
is noted as the Age of Patriarchs, from 2000 to 1700 BCE.

A questionable date 1921 BCE is assigned to the time Abram
followed God's call and journeyed to the land of Canaan. Genesis
13:14-17 speaks of God giving Abram and his offspring all the
land he [Abram] could see. This land is generally known as *The
Promised Land.*

The birth of Ishmael (God Hears), by Sarah's handmaiden
Hagar, and God's promise of making Hagar's descendants too
many to be counted, are found in Genesis 16:10-11. Later (Genesis
17:20-22) Abraham through Sarah fathered Isaac (He Laughed)
and God told Abraham that His covenant would be fulfilled with
that son.

Genesis 24-25 tells of Isaac's marriage to Rebecca. Abraham
wanted Isaac to take a wife from his family in the north, not
from the land of Canaan. A servant was sent to select such a wife;
Rebecca was granddaughter to Abraham's brother, Nahor. Twins,

Esau and Jacob, were born to Isaac and Rebecca. Esau (Covered with Hair), first born, sold his birthright to Jacob (He caught by the Heel), the second born.

In Genesis 29, Jacob's journey to find a wife is recorded. His search took him to the land of Abraham's father, similar to the story of Isaac and Rebecca. On his arrival Jacob met Rachel, daughter of Laban, his mother's brother. Jacob agreed to seven years of work in return for the gift of Rachel as his wife. Laban tricked Jacob and he was married to Leah, Rachel's sister. Jacob worked another seven years for Rachel. In time, Jacob and his families returned to the land of Canaan. Jacob struggled with a man [angel] for God's blessing in Chapter 32. In victory, Jacob's name was changed to Israel (God Strove) because he had fought with God and prevailed.

The story of Jacob and his descendants' sojourn in Egypt is told in Genesis 47-50. After a number of years of prosperity, Canaan experienced an extended time of famine. Joseph, sold by his brothers as a slave and taken to Egypt, predicted a time of plenty would be followed by a time of drought. When the drought came, it reached into Canaan. Sometime around 1700 BCE, Joseph brought Jacob and the families into Egypt where provisions had been stored for the lean years. More years passed and the Hebrews became slaves to the Egyptian Pharaoh.

Another look at generations from Abraham through Jacob:
Sons of Abraham: Ishmael, **Isaac**
Sons of Isaac: Esau, **Jacob**
Children of Jacob: Daughter—Dinah
Sons—**The Twelve Tribes of Israel: Joseph, Benjamin, Reuben, Simeon, Levi, Judah, Issachar, Zebulun, Dan, Naphtali, Gad, Asher.**

SECTION TWO

SPANNING OLD AND NEW

CHAPTER 3

Background (Spanning Old and New)

Reflections Four Hundred Years
Condensed Timeline
Lands and People
    Samaritans, Galilee, Persia, Zoroastrianism, Parthians,
    Greece, Hellenistic Culture, Hellenistic Philosophers,
    Rome, Jews in Diaspora
Related Writings
    Apocryphal/Deuterocanonical Books, Flavius Josephus
    (37-100 CE)—Jewish Historian, Mishnah and Talmud,
    Kabbalah—Ancient Jewish Mysticism

Reflections   Four Hundred Years

Roughly, a period of four hundred years separates the Hebrew Bible and the New Testament. In my childhood and through most of my adult years, I never gave any thought to the passing of time between the Old and New Testaments contained in my Bible. I knew the New Testament came after the death of Jesus, sometime around 30 CE, but never questioned beyond that. Names in the New Testament: Sadducees, Pharisees, scribes, are but a few that left me bewildered. Then, too, I couldn't keep track of all the Herods and I wondered how Pompey, Julius Caesar, Marc Antony, and others fit into the times.

When my interest in the Bible deepened, I realized those four hundred years cover a critical time for the Jews, which impacted Christianity. The social and political climate of Jewish life changed dramatically. Even before Rome, conflicts and influence from other countries caused tensions while factions within the Jewish population of Judah grew. Yet, the Jews retained their devotion to God and survived.

Condensed Timeline

Before Current Era (BCE)

928   Death of King Solomon, division of United Israelite Nation

721   Kingdom of Israel fell to Assyrians—they resettled Israelites farther north

587   Kingdom of Judah fell to Babylonians—they took most remaining Israelites to Babylonia

539   Babylonia fell to Persia—Israelites allowed to return to Judah

458 Ezra, born in Babylonia, arrived in Jerusalem, restored Jewish faith with the help of Nehemiah, arriving in 445 Torah considered Scripture

333 Judah submitted to Alexander the Great—became Greek *Judea*

301 Judea fell under Egyptian Rule
ca 300 Hebrew *Nevi'im* (Prophets) considered Scripture

198 Judea fell under Seleucid Kingdom of Syria

164 Maccabean Revolt led to Judean independence
Jewish Hasmonean Dynasty governed Judea

63 Pompey of Rome conquered Judea

37 BCE-4 CE Reign of Herod the Great—appointed by Rome

4 BCE-30 CE Life of Jesus

Current Era (CE)

50s Apostle Paul wrote letters to early Christian Churches

70s Gospel of Mark appeared

70 Roman commander Titus Vespasian destroyed Jerusalem and the Second Temple—Jews killed or taken to Rome as slaves
Hebrew *Kethuvim* (Writings) considered Scripture

80s Gospel of Matthew appeared

90s Gospel of John appeared

110s Gospel of Luke appeared

132 Jews revolted against Rome—self-government in Jerusalem

135 Rome recaptured all of Judea—Jews dispersed

Lands and People

With the passage of time, civilizations rise and fall. Accompanying the changes are adjustments to the way of life for those affected. Different factions appear, promoting additional shifts—some disappear over the years—others are long lasting. Samaria and Galilee, countries with history going back to the days of early Israelites, then continuing into early Christianity, are still seen on twenty-first century maps. In my early years, both places tugged at my heart. Among the stories connected to Samaria, I was especially drawn to the woman at the well (John 4:7-10). Of course, Galilee, home of Jesus, has always been dear to me. I have even envisioned myself, walking from Galilee to Jerusalem, hurrying through Samaria. Lands and people connected to ongoing biblical times are given a closer look on the next pages.

Samaritans—People of the Land

With the division of lands when Hebrews returned from Egypt to the Promised Land, the region of Samaria in the uplands of central Canaan was allocated to the tribe of Ephraim and a portion of the tribe of Manasseh. The area, noted for its fertile soil, became a center of trade; nations with foreign religions influenced the Israelites. After the tribes in the north became the Northern Kingdom of Israel, the city of Samaria (constructed around 853 BCE), became their capital.

The Assyrian conquest of 721 BCE led to the deportation of most of the Ten Tribes in the Northern Kingdom. Assyria resettled the area (Samaria) with foreigners from farther north, people who worshiped idols. Prophets spoke against the idolatry and immorality of Samaria (Hosea 7:1, 8:5-7). However, a number of the settlers married with the remaining Israelites and adopted the worship of one God.

The people of the land, inhabitants of what once was the Northern Kingdom, thought of themselves as Jewish descendants. Israelites from the Southern Kingdom, on their return to Judah after the Babylonian exile (539 BCE), saw *the people* as descendants of foreigners. Conflicts arose between the two groups in building the new Temple. *The people* were not allowed to be a part of the restoration as noted in Ezra 4:1-5: *Adversaries of Judah and Benjamin heard of rebuilding the Temple [and said] let us build with you. We have worshiped your God since we were brought here. The offer was refused and the people of the land undermined the building.* The strife never healed. Eventually more Assyrians arrived in Samaria and the inhabitants took the name Samaritans.

Beginning with Ezra and Nehemiah, intermarriage between Jews and Samaritans was forbidden. To be recognized as Jews, men had to divorce their foreign wives. The Jewish restrictions caused Samaritans who continued worshiping the God of Israel, to build their own temple; they refused to accept the one in Jerusalem as sacred. In addition, they only accepted the Torah as Scripture. Samaritans do not follow the Jewish calendar.

Galilee Early History

Galilee, situated in the northern part of present-day Israel, continues to have the highest rain-fall and the most fertile lands of the region. The historian, Josephus, wrote of Galilee as having rich and fruitful soil where all regions were cultivated.

Canaanites dominated Galilee for many years during the time Israelites were claiming their Promised Land. On the return from Egypt, Ten Tribes of Israel received land in the northern region. After King Solomon's death (928 BCE), conflicts during his reign caused the Tribes in the north to break away from the United Kingdom of Israel. They formed the Northern Kingdom of Israel.

In 721 BCE, Assyria conquered the Northern Kingdom (Samaria/Galilee) and resettled most of the population farther north. The Ten Tribes of Israel were lost to history. Assyria then moved a mixture of races into the area. In time, both Jews and heathens settled in the region of Galilee. Under the Hasmonean dynasty (164-63 BCE), Jews reclaimed Galilee.

At the time of Jesus' birth, Nazareth was a Jewish town surrounded by Hellenized communities. Their culture influenced the Jews; even their language had a notable change. Jews of Judea thought little of the Jews in Galilee. The distance between the Temple in Judea and Galilee further set the two groups apart.

Galilee, as noted in the first three Gospels of the Christian Writings (New Testament), was home of Jesus (4 BCE-30 CE). Nazareth and Capernaum of Galilee are mentioned in accounts of Jesus' public ministry.

Persia

As early as 2000 BCE, a migration from the hills of present-day Russia settled along the coast of the Black Sea, becoming Persia (Iran). After conquering other nations, Cyrus II, in 559 BCE established the Persian Empire. Twenty years later, Persia defeated Babylonia and Cyrus allowed exiled Israelites to return to Judah. Cyrus gave Judah, as a vassal state, a great deal of freedom and treated the Jews, as Israelites became known, with kindness.

The Persia Empire continued its expansion. After the death of Cyrus, his son conquered Egypt. Persia's next ruler, Darius I, not a direct descendant of Cyrus II, defeated even more nations until twenty-three provinces fell under Persia's domain. Darius I, like the rulers before him, respected Jews and assisted their efforts in Judah. Not only did Darius I order the completion of rebuilding the Temple in Jerusalem, he provided ample funds for the project. Sixteen years previously, the work had stopped.

In 333 BCE, Alexander the Great of Greece claimed the Persian lands. At Alexander's death (323 BCE), generals divided his empire and the Greek general, Seleucid I obtained Persia. Seleucid and his sons built their own dynasty. Around 250 BCE, Parthia, a district in Persia, revolted against the Seleucids, gaining control over all of Persia.

Episodes of history relating to the Persian Period and Cyrus are found in the Hebrew Bible and Old Testament books of Ezra, Daniel, II Chronicles, and Isaiah plus the Apocrypha Book of Esther. In connection with Persia, the religion Zoroastrianism is noteworthy.

Zoroastrianism

A prophet, Zoroaster (Greek pronunciation), is tied to the religion known as *Zoroastrianism,* surfacing around the sixth century BCE in ancient Medes*. The date of Zoroaster's birth and his writings are uncertain. Like Judaism, the belief of one God shaped Zoroastrianism. In a slightly different manner, Zoroaster's view of life reflected dualism: forces of *good* and *evil* with *good* ultimately overcoming *evil*. One of Zoroaster's collections of hymns, the Gathas, names Ahura Mazda as the Wise Lord and Angra Mainyu as the evil spirit. From the time of creation until the final judgment, the two will struggle. In other writings, the Avesta, Zoroaster claimed Ahura Mazda helped him in achieving his mission of enlightening. A decline in Zoroastrianism occurred with the rise of the Islamic faith; yet, the religion is ongoing to a lesser extent in western India and Iran.

*Medes: part of Media, involved in the rise and fall of several nations   In 549 BCE, Cyrus II (Persia) defeated Media. Cyrus allowed the continuation of Zoroastrianism.

Parthians

The Parthians began as a tribal group southeast of the Caspian Sea in ancient Persia (Iran). In 586 BCE, the Babylonians settled some of the Israelites in Parthia, after their exile from Judah. The historian Josephus wrote of Israelites given the right to practice their own faith in their new land.

Parthia, one of Persian administrative districts established by Darius I, fell with Persia, to Alexander the Great (333 BCE) then the Seleucids (323 BCE). Parthians revolted against the Seleucids, close to seventy-five years later, and became the ruling power throughout all of Persia. Parthians entered Judea in 40 BCE, capturing Jerusalem. Nevertheless, in 37 BCE, Rome proclaimed Herod the Great, King of Judea.

Greece

As with other regions that grew into civilizations, Greece had a long history of nomadic tribes evolving with the advancement of knowledge. Located in southeastern Europe, with the Aegean Sea on the east and the Mediterranean Sea on the west, Greece grew into a country of city-states. Differences among the populations led to internal conflicts. The region remained powerless with no central government until 338 BCE when Philip II of nearby Macedon conquered the southern peninsula of Greece. After Philip's death in 366 BCE, his son Alexander the Great extended the Greek Empire throughout Asia Minor (lower Turkey), to

Egypt, and the borders of India. Persia, with its vassal state Judah, was among those claimed by Greece. The name *Javan* is shown for *Greece* in Genesis 10:2, 4 and Isaiah 66:19.

At Alexander's death (323 BCE) Judea (Greek spelling of Judah) fell under the rule of Ptolemy, who claimed Egypt and Syria. Seleucus claimed most of Mesopotamia. More changes occurred; through it all, the Greek culture flourished. A number of Jews accepted the new ways while others felt adapting foreign influences weakened Judaism. Around 200 BCE, descendants of Seleucus defeated one of the surviving Ptolemy rulers and all of Judea fell under the Seleucus Kingdom. The new regime forced all Judeans to comply with Greek practices, resulting in the Maccabean Revolt (164 BCE) and an independent Jewish nation until the arrival in 63 BCE of the Romans.

Hellenistic Culture

People of ancient Greece are *Hellenes*. Greek expansion and culture altered lives around the Mediterranean Sea and beyond. Alexander the Great, of Greece, conquered Persia in 333 BCE. Hellenistic culture, shown in architecture, theater, literature, philosophy and political concepts, reached Judah.

Greeks saw life different than the civilizations they defeated. Among the new ideas challenging the people they conquered were: democratic government, recognition of moral choices, and acceptance of both the seen and unseen worlds. Jews, in Judea and elsewhere, were alarmed by aspects of Hellenism. The Greek public display of nudity and worship of many gods, reflected in Greek literature, theater, and art, appalled the Jews. The priestly right to rule, given to Jews by God, apposed a government of the people. Too, the common Greek belief of immortality divided the Jews. Some Jews accepted portions of Hellenism; they adopted Greek names and a number of Jewish thinkers welcomed Greek rationalization. However, scores of Jews felt their fundamental beliefs were at stake.

In time, the Greek language replaced Hebrew. Around 250 BCE, the Torah was translated into Greek and given the name Septuagint. Later, other portions of the Hebrew Bible were translated. Many Jews no longer spoke or read the Hebrew language.

Hellenistic Philosophers

Philosophers through time and across the world seek meaning and purpose in life. A few Greek and a Jewish Hellenistic philosopher are summarized here to illustrate the ongoing effect of Greek culture

Many philosophers were drawn to the Greek city of Athens where differing philosophical beliefs flourished. The ending of the old city-state system of Greece (338 BCE), weakened the nation and culture; **Hellenistic philosophies** answered the resulting crisis of values. Athens remained the philosophical center until 87 BCE when Romans plundered the city and drove many philosophers into exile. Most of their philosophical writings were lost at that time. Brief accounts of a few familiar philosophers offer a glance at their lasting influence.

Socrates (469-399 BCE) believed that a life studied is the only life worth living. Noted for his intellectual brilliance and personal integrity, he questioned his fellow citizens over their own moral attitudes. Socrates spent his days arguing his beliefs. His ideas and personality drew many followers, including young people. There were a number of reasons Athenians disliked Socrates. A vast number of elders thought he corrupted the youth. Too, Socrates refused to acknowledge the gods of the city; he introduced new ones. Likewise, his distain of others' lack of ethics, which he always asserted, created enemies. Also, Socrates voiced the opinion that only those who studied political matters should be allowed to make governmental decisions. Athens, a democracy, welcomed all voices in forming public policy. Charges were brought against Socrates for challenging the city's control over religious matters and his refusal to end philosophical questioning. The trial lasted only one day with Socrates being found guilty and sentenced to death by poison. Socrates left no writings; Plato's works about Socrates became a source of inspiration and ideas for future philosophers.

Plato (427-347 BCE), born into a powerful aristocratic family of Athens, became a follower of Socrates. Disenchanted with politics after Socrates trail and death, Plato studied in Italy. There, he returned to politics but failed in advancing his ideas to the existing government. Returning to Athens in 387 BCE, Plato established the Academy, a place centered on research and teaching.

Plato saw abstract objects as *Forms* (slightly different from *Ideas*). He defined Forms as eternal and changeless, having no material substance. Knowledge of Forms, conceived in thought, exist even in the absence of thought. Plato saw Forms as the source of moral and religious inspiration and when people become acutely aware of Forms, they experienced tremendous improvement in their lives. Plato's view of Forms led him to understand the observable world as an imperfect image of an unobservable and unchanging realm.

Through fifty years of writing his philosophical beliefs, Plato utilized the style of dialogue between speakers. Socrates was the subject of many of his works. Plato's school and his writings influenced future philosophers; Aristotle joined the Academy at the age of seventeen, staying until the death of Plato.

Aristotle (384-322 BCE), another outstanding Greek philosopher and a student of Plato, left Athens after Plato's death. His travels included a stay in Macedonia where he tutored Alexander the Great. Returning to Athens in 335 BCE, Aristotle began his own philosophical school.

Aristotle viewed choice and action as providing human good, unlike Plato's Form position. Practical wisdom, according to Aristotle, is necessary for living well. He further broke down wisdom as a result of intellectual and moral virtue. Intellectual virtue determines the best way to achieve goals. Obtaining the goals requires moral virtue. Aristotle simplifies his concept as: the ability to reason, a cognitive function, combined with theoretical (abstract) activity, both based on virtue, results in happiness.

Nearly all of Aristotle's writings, covering virtually all topics of philosophical importance, were lost. Only detailed lecture notes, working drafts, and accounts of his lectures written by others, survived. Years after his death, some organization of Aristotle's writings took place. However, it took until 1831 CE before critical editions of his work were published. The publications are still used by scholars today.

Philo (ca 20 BCE-40 CE), the son of a respected Egyptian Jewish family became the first to combine Hebrew Scripture with Classical Philosophy. Often mentioned as the Jewish Plato, some Orthodox Jews still question Philo's views. Also setting Philo apart from other philosophers are the number and diversity of his explanations of hidden spiritual meaning in the Hebrew Sacred texts. The majority of Philo's work consisted of interpretations presented in thoughtful and orderly verbal exchanges. He told how the Scriptures agree with Plato's thoughts of God and the soul's search for God. Additionally, Philo connected the general laws of nature (order and rational) to Moses' commandments.

Philo saw God as loving, just, and the eternal unknowable creator of the material world. He believed in the intrinsic truth of the Torah; the inner knowledge observed only by few. He spoke of a Divine mediator connecting the supernatural deity (God) with the lower world, unifying the law of the universe. Philo went on to say the world of ideas are God's thoughts and can only be known by intellect.

Although Philo left a vast amount of philosophical works, he was unknown to Medieval Jewish philosophers. Nevertheless, he had a lasting impact on early Christianity as Clement of Alexandria and Origen found value in Philo's words.

Rome

Capital of the ancient Roman Empire, Rome, located on a hill near the Tiber River before it enters the Mediterranean Sea, became the largest force of the ancient world. From its beginning as a small Italian village in the eighth century BCE, by 510 BCE it advanced to the Republic of Rome. As a republic, a ruling council called the Senate handled Rome's affairs based on the interests of the citizens. Less than two hundred and fifty years later, Rome dominated the Italian peninsula and began conquering other domains. With expansion, it became more difficult for the Senate to maintain control of the empire. By 88 BCE, conflicts between generals led to a civil war, resulting in power given to General Sulla, a dictator. Ten years later, on Sulla's death, Jules Caesar, finding favor with the people of Rome, formed a triumvirate (government by three people) with successful generals Crassus and Pompey. Despite disagreements among the three, the Roman Empire grew in power and territory.

In 66 BCE, Pompey forces took a former kingdom near the Caspian Sea. Then in 65 BCE, Anatolia (Turkey) fell to Pompey, followed by Syria in 64 BCE. The next year Pompey entered Judea and claimed Jerusalem in 62 BCE. At that point, Judea became a Roman vassal state. Pompey took thousands of Judean prisoners to Rome and annexed 30 Judean cities.

On Pompey's return to Rome, Caesar plotting against Pompey

and Crassus while claiming his own victories, created another civil war. In 53 BCE, Crassus was killed in battle with the Parthians. After a defeat by Caesar, in 48 BCE, Pompey fled to Egypt where he was assassinated. A year later, Caesar took control of Judea and set out to claim additional territories. He took sides with Queen Cleopatra in Egypt's civil war; a prolonged affair between the two followed.

When Caesar arrived back in Rome, the Senate named him *Dictator,* though the people wanted the title *king.* Caesar began planning for his great-nephew and adopted son, Gaius Julius Caesar Octavianus (Octavian) to inherit the dictatorship on his death. Although, certain members of the nobility questioned Caesar's power and did not want another authoritative dynasty.

Brutus, a close friend and ally to Caesar, was among those alarmed by the situation. He and his brother-in-law, Cassius, drew others into a plot that led to the assassination of Caesar in March of 44 BCE. Mark Antony, Caesar's most trusted friend, turned the people against Brutus and his followers who then escaped to Greece where they gained power and planned a return to Rome. Meanwhile, Antony and Octavian, with another Caesar loyalist, Lepidus, were raising their own army to resist Brutus and Cassius. The Senate named Antony, Octavian, and Lepidus, as the Second Triumvirate: the official rulers of Rome. This action assured Octavian the right to follow Caesar in power.

Two years after Caesar's assassination, the armies of Brutus and Antony battled in Greece. Both Cassius and Brutus committed suicide rather than be taken as prisoners with the Second Triumvirate victorious return to Rome. A year later, Lepidus was expelled from the Triumvirate and rivalry between Antony and Octavian accelerated. Antony, while in Egypt, became involved with Cleopatra, leading to a civil war between Antony and Octavian. By 30 BCE, following defeat, Antony and Cleopatra committed suicide. Three years later, Octavian received the name

Augustus (*splendid*), though he was not officially proclaimed Emperor. Augustus became the supreme authority of the Roman Empire, bringing an end to the Republic. Soon the people of Rome simply referred to Augustus as Emperor.

The Roman Empire, with emperors: some good, but numerous cruel, expanded their territory. During the reign of Diocletian (284-305 CE) the empire became too large for one person to manage. Diocletian divided the realm into East and West regions; plus, he assigned three other officials as emperors to share the administration of the Roman Empire. Rome became the capital of the Western Roman Empire while in the east, Emperor Constantine created a capital at Byzantium (ca. 330 CE) and renamed it Constantinople.

High taxation, political infighting and immorality brought a decline to the Western Empire of Rome. Ongoing attacks from barbaric invaders further weakened Rome, bringing an end to that empire in 476 CE. The surviving Eastern Byzantine Empire fell to Muslim Turks in 1453 CE.

Jews in Diaspora

Diaspora, the Greek word for *scattering*, refers to the movement or dispersion of the Jewish people from their homeland, sometimes noted as: The Promised Land, Israel, Judah, Judea, and Palestine.

The dispersion began in 721 BCE after the Kingdom of Israel fell to the Assyrians who then deported the Ten Tribes of Israel farther north. They are considered the *Lost Tribes* as they vanished from history. In 587 BCE, the Babylonian Empire conquered the Kingdom of Judah and took most of the Israelites to Babylonia as captives. When Babylonia fell to Cyrus of Persia (539 BCE), he allowed Israelites to return to their homeland; however, many stayed in Babylonia where they had continued to worship their one God, formed a community, and prospered.

After Judea fell under Ptolemaic rule (301 BCE), a large Jewish community was established in Alexandria, Egypt. Previously, small numbers of Jews settled in Egypt where they worshiped in their own temple and maintained contact with Jerusalem. Jewish communities in Egypt continued to grow.

Another major dispersal of Judean Jews occurred after the Roman destruction of the Second Temple in 70 CE and the Bar Kokhba Revolt of 135 CE. By that time, successful Jewish communities were found across Turkey, Greece, Rome, Egypt, Carthage, and Spain. Presently, *Diaspora* often identifies Jewish communities outside of Israel.

Related Writings

The recording of years between the Hebrew Bible and early Christianity relied on a number of sources. The Torah and Nevi'im are mentioned in the New Testament. Some writings eventually becoming the Kethuvim also influenced those that came later. The three parts of the Hebrew Bible were crucial in maintaining the wisdom and history needed for survival of the Jewish faith. Incorporating their long-held practices with adjustments needed for new situations, created ongoing directives, some still active in the twenty-first century.

Apart from biblical sources, historian Flavius Josephus (ca 37-100 CE) wrote for the general population. His works are quoted even today. Likewise, the influx of other lands and people brought new sources which were intermingled with the old. In continuing, a closer look is given to those works.

Apocryphal/Deuterocanonical Books

Some writings, originally in Hebrew, Aramaic, and Greek, were familiar and important to a number of Jews, especially those living outside of Judea. Not considered Scripture by the Jews, they are included in various Christian Bibles under the term Apocrypha (hidden books).

Scholars today question the title *Apocrypha* as in Antiquity *hidden books* were those available only to individuals with intellectual dept and insight. The translation of the Hebrew Bible into the Greek Septuagint contained the hidden books. Around 400 CE, Jerome translated the Septuagint and the Christian New Testament into Latin (Vulgate version). He gave the name *Apocrypha* to the Jewish non-scriptural writings included in the Septuagint. During the Protestant Reformation (sixteenth century CE), the Apocryphal Books were removed from the Christian Old Testament and were placed in the category of *Apocrypha*.

Inclusion of Apocrypha Books remains controversial. Some Christian Churches have some or all of them in their Bibles, other denominations exclude the books. They are not part of the Hebrew Bible. *Deuterocanonical* (canonized at a later date) is used by Catholics to indicate the Apocrypha Books they proclaimed as Scripture.

The Apocrypha contains books or parts of books written in pre-Christian centuries. Some of the books are additions to books in Kethuvim (Writings) of the Hebrew Bible. Others refer to history not previously covered. The different types of Apocrypha Books follow.

Category of Apocryphal Books

Devotional and Liturgical literature: Psalm 151, Prayer of Manasseh

Wisdom literature: Wisdom of Solomon, Sirach
(or Ecclesiasticus, or the Wisdom of Ben Sira)

Five Scrolls: The Song of Songs, Ruth, Lamentations, Ecclesiastes, Esther

Additions: Tobit, Judith, Additions of Esther, Baruch, Letter of Jeremiah

(The Five Scrolls are included in the Kethuvim [Writings] of the Hebrew Bible. The Additions provide a deeper look at those important times from the past.)

Apocalyptic literature: Additions to Daniel
(Prayer of Azariah, Susanna, Bel and the Dragon)

Historical literature: 1 Maccabees, 2 Maccabees, 1 Esdras*,
2 Esdras, 3 Maccabees, 4 Maccabees

*Esdras: Greek name for Ezra

Understanding the development of Jewish life and thought at the end of the era before current time is found in the Apocrypha.

Flavius Josephus (37-100 CE)—Jewish Historian

Generally, Flavius Josephus (Joseph), son of Matthias, a priest of Jerusalem, is considered the best-known historian of Jewish affairs. At the beginning of the Jewish War against Rome (66 CE) Josephus led Jewish troops in Galilee fighting against the Roman General Vespasian. After Rome's victory, Vespasian took Josephus as captive, followed shortly by Josephus' prediction that Vespasian would become Emperor of Rome. [The prediction was fulfilled in 69 CE.] As the war continued, Vespasian used Josephus as an interpreter and insisted that Josephus encourage Jews, remaining within the walls of Jerusalem, to surrender; the offer was declined. After the total destruction of Jerusalem in 70 CE, Josephus was taken to Rome and given his freedom. He remained there, accepting the Vespasian's family name (Flavius) and the role of Vespasian's historian.

Josephus spent most of his remaining years writing about Jewish history. Critics feel his six-volume work on the Jewish Wars was written from a Roman point of view. *An Antiquity of the Jews,* a twenty-volume history, covers the time of Adam and Eve and extends through Josephus' life. Scholars today cite Josephus' work—accounts of history written by a knowledgeable and capable individual who personally experienced a portion of those years.

Mishnah and Talmud

Jews continued to rely on Oral Law even with the written Torah. Oral Law included scribes' interpretation of The Law as given to Moses. For generations, prophets, elders, scribes, Pharisees and rabbis depended on Oral Law for instructing students. Many scholars, instrumental in passing on Oral Law, died during the two revolts against Rome (70 CE and 135 CE). To preserve the knowledge, it became necessary to write down the Oral Law. The writing, accomplished by scribes, is called the *Mishnah,* first edited about 200 CE.

As Judaism evolved, a need for explanations and adaptations of the Mishnah was necessary. A work of the Pharisees, the *Talmud* (learning), provided the additional information. The Talmud repeats the Mishnah, followed by commentaries. In time, two specific books of the Talmud became available: the Jerusalem or

Palestinian (fourth century CE) and the Babylonian (fifth century CE). Many Jews viewed the Talmud as the religious and civil constitution of their people, which could be carried into Diaspora. Others saw the Talmud as a summary of all traditional Jewish knowledge contained in one book.

Oral Law, Mishnah, and Talmud reflect the changes between the writing of the Torah and Christianity. Into the second millennium, current era, some Jews question the need to study details of Temple sacrifices and say the Talmud causes disagreement among their people.

Kabbalah—Ancient Jewish Mysticism

A learned friend speaks of the original Kabbalah being founded as early as 40 BCE. The Mystical school of thought, known as the modern form of Kabbalah, began between 1250-1300 CE. By the end of the twentieth century and into the twenty-first, mention of Kabbalah, in relationship to Jewish studies, has become almost common. I have read that modern teachings of Kabbalah, by some Jewish and non-Jewish individuals, have distorted the ancient teaching. After my limited reading on the subject, the modern classes I'm aware of, offered for a few weeks and without any prior knowledge, would be unable to explore the original Kabbalah. Like many topics related to history, meanings and interpretations are often altered to fit changing times. Sometimes I think the old *is better than the* new. *It is with hesitation, I include Kabbalah in my writing; as non-Jewish, my wish is to honor all aspects of their faith. I question writing about a subject that seems deeper and more hidden than mere history. Nevertheless, I submit the following taken from Lawrence Joffe:* The History of the Jews From the Ancients to the Middle Ages.

Kabbalah, like other forms of mysticism, seeks complete union with God, unbound by the material world. Differing from other forms of mysticism, Kabbalah centers on helping God repair a world in need and that it is only possible with intrinsic knowledge of the Hebrew Bible and the Talmud. Traditionally, this mysticism was conferred to those with advanced knowledge and had reached the age of forty.

Though Jewish mysticism diversified over centuries, the fundamental bases of Kabbalah came from the writing of prophets and the second century CE Mishnah. Two primary mystical thoughts of that time centered on creation [Genesis] and Ezekiel's vision of a chariot. Some scholars, looking at Kabbalah in a worldly manner, have found traces of Gnosticism and Zoroastrianism within the framework of Kabbalah. Likewise, Kabbalah has influenced Christians and Muslim Sufis.

Through the Middle Ages (500-1500 CE), a number of mystical teachings of Kabbalah were written. The *Zohar** contains secret ancient writings or compilations of those works. The mystical school of thought came to be known as Kabbalah, from the Hebrew meaning *to receive, to accept*. The dictionary defines *Kabbalah,* a variant of *cabala,* as a medieval and modern system of Jewish theosophy with a belief in creation through emanation (flowing out from God) and a cipher (coded message) method of interpreting Scripture. The definition includes Kabbalah as an esoteric, occult, or secret matter.

*Zohar: Hebrew meaning splendor or radiance   The Zohar is a group of books containing explanations on mystical aspects of the Torah, scriptural interpretations, and material on mysticism. The books first appeared in Spain in the thirteenth century CE, published by a Jewish writer. However, the concepts are attributed to Simeon bar Zakkai, a second century CE Palestinian.

CHAPTER 4

Judaism

Reflections Moving Forward
Need for Change
  Priests, Synagogues and Rabbis, Sabbath, Sanhedrin,
  Scribes, Pharisees and Sadducees, Essenes and Dead Sea
  Scrolls, Maccabees and Hasmoneans, Zealots

Reflections   Moving Forward

Older books that I started with, in learning more about the Bible, lacked explanations regarding the change of names from Israelites to Jews. It makes so much sense to me now. Of course, many of their people lived elsewhere, after the Babylonian exile and ties with the original Twelve Tribes of Israel were far removed. It seems to me, times when people must move forward, adopting new ways, or even a name, fills the void of what was lost. The newer books tell of the practical reasons for changes within the faith of those steadfast individuals with a belief of one God. I wonder how the people felt. Generally, personal names hold special feelings for folks. Wouldn't it be so for the name defining one's heritage?

Need for Change

When Israelites returned to Judah (539 BCE), they faced new challenges. No longer was there one geographic semi-sovereign state. Only a remnant of what was once the United Kingdom of Israel remained, with Jewish populations residing elsewhere. In Judah, no Temple existed. The returning Israelites rebuilt the Temple and restructured their religious practices. Regardless of their location, Israelites were united as *the people of God*.

The name *Israelites* no longer described their new situation. Those from the tribe of Judah were the ones returning from the Babylonian exile; therefore, they took the name *Jew*, from *Judean*, and proceeded under a faith called *Judaism*. The Law of Moses remained the foundation of Judaism. In compiling The Law into the written Torah, it became necessary for learned individuals to adapt and explain to others how God continued in changing times. Some pre-existing groups altered long-held practices while new ones surfaced in the midst of up-coming affiliations. The outcome: a splintered people. Peace, even though a time of Judean Independence, was short lived. This chapter summarizes some critical changes within that fluctuating period.

Priests

During the Babylonian exile, with the absence of a Temple, there were no sacrifices but priests still upheld other religious practices. On returning to Judah and rebuilding of the Temple, the priestly role as set forth in the Torah resumed. The high priests continued from the lineage of Aaron until the Hasmonean Dynasty (164-63 BCE), then the Hasmoneans made the appointment from within their family.

At that time, the role of priests changed in other ways. High priests still took care of Temple functions. However, scribes and Pharisees were interpreting the meaning of the Torah and became more powerful than most priests. In addition, synagogues and rabbis replaced the Temple for many Jews. After the destruction of the Second Temple (70 CE), priests and Levites melted into the general Jewish population.

Thousands of years earlier, starting with the Hebrews, priests were honored. In the days before Moses and Aaron, priests carried out a tradition of the head of a tribe (sons of Jacob), or the father of the family. They represented the family before God and offered rituals for cleansing them of sins. An example of this is found in Job 1:5. The person mediating between God and others is referred to as *priest*. In Exodus 2:16 the word *priest* denotes the head of a family.

While in the wilderness of Mount Sinai, God, through Moses, appointed Aaron and his sons as priests, officially establishing the priesthood (Exodus 40:13-15). Aaron, like Moses, was of the tribe of Levi. Future priests were to be descendants of Aaron;

other Levites, not Aaron's direct descendants, would be assistants to the priests. Priests offered sacrifices for atonement from sins; Levites took care of the Tabernacle (tent or temporary place of worship), then the Temple when it was built (Numbers 18:1,7). A high (chief) priest with specified duties officiated over other priests. Dedication of the Levites to God is shown in Exodus 32:25-29. The Hebrew word for priest is *Kohen*, perhaps taken from *Kohath*, son of Levi (Exodus 6:16). Moses and Aaron were *Kohathites.*

Returning to Canaan, Hebrews took the name Israelites, in the land that became Israel, as Joshua allocated lands to the Twelve Tribes of Jacob/Israel. Levites did not receive a specific section of land. Instead, they were given forty-eight cities, with pasture lands, throughout Canaan (Joshua 21). Priests, with the Levites, had the responsibility to maintain Gods' laws across the land and to settle disputes among the Israelites (Deuteronomy 17:8-13). The book of Leviticus deals with priests and the worship of God.

The passing of centuries saw greater numbers of priests and some changes. In the time of Samuel and the priest Eli, appointment of a high priest came from a collateral branch, not a direct descendant of Aaron (1 Samuel 2). King David divided the group into smaller units. King Solomon appointed Zadok as high priest, returning that position to a direct descendant of Aaron. As long as priests maintained their loyalty to God and His laws, they were highly respected and influenced the people. However, this too changed.

The prophet Ezekiel (22:23-31) states that priests had sunk to immorality, departed from God and worshiped idols, like many of the people. The first two chapters of Malachi, another prophet, points out neglect and corruption of priests. Starting with a lofty family position, the role of *priest* declined with events no one could control.

The Gospels of the New Testament contain numerous accounts of Jewish priests and their opposition toward Jesus. The term *priest* is seen elsewhere in the New Testament and in reference to the Christian religion.

As mentioned, in the Hebrew language, *kohen* translates to *priest*. In the Greek printings of the New Testament, *hiereus* indicated the Jewish priesthood. The English word *priest* or *elder* came from the Greek word *presbyteros*, all are found in the Christian religion.

Synagogues and Rabbis

While in Babylonia, Israelites continued their own religion. Scribes began writing down their ancient practices, then the rise of rabbis (*great teachers* in Hebrew) and synagogues (*houses of assembly* in Greek) appeared. Synagogues were a place of religious services where ten or more adult men gathered to study the Law of Moses. The service, officiated by a rabbi, was based on the scribes' writings. When Israelites returned to their homeland, the worship in synagogues with rabbis grew, in Judah and throughout lands with a Jewish population.

Before and after Alexander the Great conquered Judah (333 BCE), Hellenistic civilization penetrated the land. Following Alexander's death, when Judea (Greek spelling of Judah) fell under Egyptian rule, the Jewish people were exposed to even greater Hellenistic influence. By then, many Jews were living in Egypt, partaking in the economic opportunities brought on by a new era of prosperity and peace. In their desire to preserve the new faith of Judaism, Jewish settlements began building synagogues.

Egyptians recorded the construction of a synagogue in the

third century BCE; others might have been built earlier. Remains of a synagogue at Masada (Judea) date about 31 BCE. Functions of synagogues differed from the Temple. In synagogues, no sacrifices or expensive priestly rites took place. Jews gathered for readings and discussions of the Torah; plus, the Jewish community came together for other religious events. With the changes, the Aramaic language replaced Hebrew for many Jews, then Greek replaced Aramaic and the Torah became available in those languages. The Aramaic translation is the *Targum*; the Greek translation, from Hebrew, is the *Septuagint*.

During the Hasmonean Period (164-63 BCE) and an independent Judea, many Pharisees became rabbis, leading to a rabbinic tradition which further defined their role. With the destruction of the Second Temple (70 CE) and the final dispersion of Jews from Jerusalem after the failed Bar Kokhba Revolt (135 CE), synagogues became the official place for Jewish services and the role of rabbi continued. Rabbis transcribed the Talmud, a constitution for Jews wherever they lived. Into the twenty-first century, rabbis serve as legal and spiritual guides. Worship is held in synagogues that contain the Torah scroll.

Sabbath

The Hebrew word for Sabbath is *Shabbat*, meaning *rest*. Genesis 2:1-3 states that after God completed the creation of the heavens and earth, He blessed and hallowed the seventh day and rested that day. In giving the Ten Commandments to Moses, God stipulated that the Sabbath be remembered and kept holy. No one was to work. Once more, God blessed and consecrated the Sabbath (Exodus 20:8-11). Keeping the Sabbath *holy* required not only resting from labor, but honoring God with visits to places of worship and holding a joyous attitude.

The Sabbath took on a deeper meaning for the Babylonian exiles. In continuing their faith, they regarded honoring the Sabbath as one way of proclaiming their long-held belief and devotion to God. The Jewish Sabbath begins at sundown Friday and ends Saturday at sundown.

Nehemiah, in his effort to bring the Jews of Judah back to The Law, warned of the dangers in profaning the Sabbath. He further prohibited selling of merchandise on that day (Nehemiah 13:15-22). After that, Jewish religious leaders added even more restriction to the Sabbath, making the day burdensome.

The early Christian Church observed Sabbath on the first day of the week, Sunday, the day of Jesus' resurrection.

Sanhedrin

I came across the term Sanhedrin often in my biblical readings and thought of it as a Jewish group somewhat connected to Pharisees and Sadducees. Searching for more exact wording, I found my references gave differing definitions. In connecting the various information, defining the Sanhedrin as a high court of long standing for both religious and legislative aspects of Judaism, seems valid. Yet, the Sanhedrin is more than that. Sanhedrin is often mentioned in the New Testament, though its formation began as the written Torah took shape. To simplify my findings, I offer a variety of resources and structure.

The New Oxford Annotated Bible defines Sanhedrin as the religious court, whose membership was drawn from the Jewish ruling classes, holding authority over Palestine [Judea] under the Roman Empire. Among their duties, the court could decide cases on its own and send cases on to the Roman governors.

Bandstra defines *Sanhedrin* as a legislative and judicial

body from the period of early Judaism and into rabbinic times, traditionally composed of seventy-one members.

Early Judaism refers to the time when Ezra (458 BCE), from Babylonia, arrived in Judah and restructured the Hebrew faith into a living religion of Judaism. In so doing, he organized a *Great Assembly* which became Judah's legislature and high court, taking the place of a king. Rabbinic times denote the period when rabbis, who came from the group of Pharisees, transcribed the Talmud into a form that defined the Torah for Jews in and away from Judea.

Both Ezra's time and the New Testament are included in Youngblood, Bruce and Harrison's *Sanhedrin* definition. It states the Sanhedrin grew out of the council of advisors for high priests under Persian and Greek rule. The council, made up of seventy-one leading priests and aristocrats, later included scribes. Eventually Sadducees and Pharisees were accepted into the Sanhedrin. After 6 CE, the Sanhedrin only had authority in Judea. Leaving most of the governing of Jews to the Sanhedrin, Romans always had the right to intervene. The Sanhedrin could not issue a death sentence.

The Sanhedrin survived the first Jewish Revolt against Rome (70 CE). Before the final attack, a rabbi was helped in leaving Jerusalem. He made his way to the southern coast of Judea and later Roman authorities approved his reinstating the Sanhedrin.

After the Bar Kokhba Revolt (133 CE) surviving Jews were banned from Jerusalem and Judea was renamed Palestinae [Palestine]. A short time later, Jews slowly returned to portions of their original homeland and re-established the Sanhedrin assembly, continuing as a judicial court for Jews in Palestine until it was absorbed by the Byzantine Empire (ca 395 CE).

Scribes

Scribes served as teachers during the Babylonian exile. After the return to Judah and the Torah became a written source, it had to be copied, interpreted, and taught. The task fell to scribes. Before long, the revelations of prophets became written words, changing the emphasis to studying the interpretation of prophecies and away from prophets' oral declarations. In this way, scribes replaced prophets. The scribes' teaching of the Scriptures with their interpretations, became known as the Oral Law.

Additionally, scribes wrote official documents and took dictation for other matters. Thought of as lawyers, scribes were scholars with expertise on interpreting the meaning of the Torah and the words of the prophets. In the Hebrew Bible, Ezra is described as a priest of high standing and a scribe (Ezra 7:11).

Scribes worked to build a strong cohesive bond within the Jewish population: those who had remained in Judah, those returning from exile, and those in Diaspora. The scribes' interpretations of Hebrew Scripture were compiled and written as the Mishnah. Starting around 200 BCE and ending with the destruction of the Second Temple (70 CE), the Mishnah covered all areas of Jewish life. Pharisees expanded the Mishnah to show how God's words offered direction in changing times; that work is the Talmud.

Pharisees and Sadducees

Between 200-100 BCE, in Judea, two distinct groups, Pharisees and Sadducees emerged. Both groups had connections to the Hasmoneans and the Sanhedrin. Pharisees, a name taken from the Hebrew *perushim*, meaning *the separated ones,* began as a small group with knowledge of The Law. They formed from a group known as *Hasidim*, faithful Jews who supported the Maccabean Revolt. Sadducees, a name thought to have been taken from Zadok, high priest appointed by King Solomon, claimed direct lineage to Aaron. Sadducees were high priests, leaders of the priesthood, plus influential aristocrats. Following are some key issues of each group.

Pharisees
Stressed sincere worship and social justice over Temple rites
Believed God was everywhere, not just in the Temple
Balanced predestination with free will
Accepted immorality of souls and resurrection of the dead
Looked for the coming of a messiah
Preferred worship in a Synagogue over the Temple
Opposed Hellenistic ways, Sadducees, and Rome

Pharisees upheld the Law of Moses as set forth in the Torah and adapted it to meet the changing needs of Judaism. They added to the scribe's interpretation (Mishnah) of the Torah, making it suitable for survival in changing times. The result is the *Talmud*. The work of the scribes and Pharisees is known as the *Oral Law*. The term *Written Torah* designates the Hebrew Bible, without interpretations. The combination of the Oral and the Written Torah gave the directive for daily living and faith of Jewish communities. This new way of observing the Torah is often referred to as *Pharisaic Judaism*. Rabbis taught this form of Judaism. Eventually, Pharisaic Judaism led to Rabbinic Judaism.

Knowledge regarding Rabbinic Judaism comes from surviving Targums, translations of the Hebrew Bible into the Aramaic language. Targums, not literal but paraphrases, spoke of how Jews understood the Hebrew Bible.

There is little mention of Pharisees in the Hebrew Bible; they have a continued presence in the New Testament.

Sadducees
Supported priestly authority
Stressed Temple rituals, including sacrifices and tithes
Strictly enforced the literal Written Torah
Believed only in free will and no afterlife
Regarded their wealth a sign of blessedness
Held religious and non-religious power
Approved Roman appointment of high priests
Opposed Pharisees and Jesus

After the destruction of Jerusalem and the Second Temple (70 CE), Sadducees fled Judea. Without the Temple, their role ceased to exist. There is no mention of Sadducees in the Hebrew Bible, some in the New Testament.

Essenes and the Dead Sea Scrolls

Essenes, numbering about 4,000, appeared around 150 BCE. Alluded to in Hebrew and Aramaic sources, Essenes are not mentioned in the New Testament. Until the twentieth century, knowledge of that group came from ancient writers as illustrated by the following.

Collins references Josephus' *Jewish War* and *Antiquities*.

A portion states:

> Josephus describes the common life of the sect [Essenes] by emphasizing that they are not restricted to one town but "in every town several of them form a colony." They live a peaceful, simple life, and have the possessions in common. They do nothing unless ordered by the superiors. Before sunrise, they recite ancestral prayers to the sun, as if entreating it to rise. When they assemble

for meals, they bathe in cold water to purify themselves. Purity is required for entry into the refectory. A priest recites prayers before and after meals.

Philo of Alexandria (*Quosomnis probus liber sit*,5-91) is referenced by Collins with:

> Philo, who calls them Essaeans, says that they were exceptionally virtuous people who lived in villages. They refrained from animal sacrifices and avoided cities. They lived "without goods or property," but had all things in common. They had common meals, and whatever belonged to each belonged to all. They had no implements of war, and they rejected slavery. They had no time for philosophy, since it did not lead to the acquisition of virtue, but devoted themselves to the study of ethics, by studying the ancestral laws, especially on the seventh day, when they met in synagogues.

Collins also references Pliny the Elder (23-79 CE) a Roman writer, *in his [Pliny] Natural History* 5.17.4 (73).

> [Pliny] affirms that the Essenes are "people (*gens*) unique of its kind," without women and renouncing love entirely, without money, and having for company only the palm trees. He marvels that this celibate community had managed to renew itself "for thousands of centuries." Pliny seems to know only one Essene settlement, to the west of the Dead Sea, where they "have put the necessary distance between themselves and the insalubrious shore."

Scholars, in the nineteenth century CE, trying to come to some certainty regarding the Essenes, looked at them as part of

Christianity. Yet, in other ways they were connected to Judaism. Then in 1947, scrolls were discovered near the Dead Sea.

A Bedouin youth, Muhammed-ed-Dib, herding goats near the northwest shore of the Dead Sea threw a stone into a cave and from the sound, realized he had broken something. Entering the cave, he found a number of scrolls in an ancient jar. Muhammed sold his scrolls in Bethlehem. After the purchase, they were divided and resold in two lots. A professor of the Hebrew University obtained one portion; the other went to the Syrian Orthodox Metropolitan Monastery. Within a few weeks, more scrolls surfaced; like the first set, they changed hands a number of times. Eventually, the seven scrolls came together in Jerusalem and by 1965, for safe keeping, were placed in a special building: The Shrine of the Book. Within two years, excavation began in other caves.

Excavation around the Dead Sea, in a place given the name *Qumran*, continued from 1949 to 1956. The findings ranged from complete scrolls to scraps which took years to piece together. At the conclusion of the work, nine hundred documents were represented. Most were written in Hebrew, some in Aramaic, and a small number in Greek. Partial copies of every book of the Hebrew Bible, except for Esther, were found. Dating from 200 BCE to 100 CE, the copies are close to a thousand years older than any previously known manuscripts of the Hebrew Bible.

In addition to biblical material, other documents provided new information or affirmed what was only known through fragmented copies. For instance: The *Temple Scroll* relates to the temple structure, its practices and procedures concerning sacrifices, plus, Sabbath and feast regulations. Another scroll, *The Community Rule*, seems to cover the constitution of the community living near the Dead Sea. Those two documents are among the ones seen for the first time.

The scrolls left questions regarding the Qumran community. Scholars still debate whether they were Essenes. However, the *Community Rule* and other scrolls do offer an insight into the way of life for the community, which apparently surfaced during the early Maccabean period (164-63 BCE). Its members, Jews, objected to the practices of the Hasmoneans, primarily the appointment of a high priest not of the Zadok lineage. The scrolls indicate the Jews of Qumran stressed the laws of Moses and observed their own ritual purity. The community was led by a *Teacher of Righteousness* and the general belief was *dualism*, a force of good (sons of light) and a force of evil (sons of darkness) existed and *good* would eventually win over *darkness.*

Communities, other than the one at Qumran, lived around the Dead Sea area. Scholars think Jews from the nearby communities, and maybe some farther away, hid their writings in the caves at the beginning of the Jewish Revolt against Rome (66-70 CE). The Jews, thinking their Temple would be destroyed, wanted their writings to survive. Finding the scrolls, almost two thousand years later, has been described as the greatest discovery of the twentieth century. The documents have been studied intensively by an ever-growing number of Jewish and Christian scholars plus sociologists of religion and philosophers.

Controversy over whether Essenes were the ones living at Qumran when the scrolls were hidden, remains. Some scholars point out that a similarity of ideals and doctrines, of Essenes, are seen in the teachings of John the Baptist and Jesus. However, Essenes, unlike early Christians, lived apart from others; Christians lived and worked among many different people. The Essenes disappeared in the early Christian era.

The Dead Sea area, a Judean wilderness for ages, remains an interest to many. The following list conveys some it its long history.

1025 BCE	David sought safety in the caves of the Dead Sea while hiding from King Saul.
587 BCE	There is no question; a fort existed at Qumran in the pre-exile period.
100-50 BCE	Occupancy of Qumran is unsure. A religious group (Essenes) might have lived in the area. When the area was occupied, there was trade among the groups.
64-63 BCE	Under the Hasmonean Dynasty, there was a chain of fortresses around the Dead Sea, but it is questioned if one was at Qumran.
	Archeologists have suggested that Rome converted the fortresses for its own use, with smaller buildings surrounding a large square structure. A tower, used as a lookout, is questioned.
31 BCE	An earthquake and fire destroyed Qumran.
01-68 CE	Most scholars agree that a religious group lived at Qumran. Essenes are questionable.
66-73 CE	During the Jewish-Roman War (68 CE) the pre-exile fort was destroyed. The remains of a tower were among the ruins.
132-135 CE	Simon Bar Kokhba, leader of the final Jewish Revolt against Rome, retreated to a site southwest of Qumran (letters were found during excavation).

Maccabees and Hasmoneans

After a little more than two centuries of Persia control, Alexander the Great of Greece conquered all Persian lands. Ten years later, with the death of Alexander, Judea (Greek spelling of Judah) was divided among his generals. Before long, Judea fell under Ptolemy rule of Egypt and was able to continue with a high priest officiating over the Jews. During that time, Jews were encouraged to settle in Egypt; many took the opportunity of the acceptance and prosperity Egypt offered. A clash between Egypt and Syria resulted in Judea falling under the Seleucid Empire of Syria (198 BCE). At first, with this new domain, a high priest continued as before. Although, that changed as the Syrian monarchs imposed stronger Greek influence in Judea.

In 175 BCE a new Syrian ruler, Antiochus Epiphanes, enforced stricter rules over Jews. He gave the priesthood to the highest bidder, vandalized the Temple, made practicing the Jewish faith a capital offense, and required Jews to make sacrifices to Greek gods. Jews revolted in 164 BCE.

Mattathias, a priest from the Hasmonean family, killed a fellow priest who was preparing a sacrifice to a Greek idol. Mattathias and his five sons then fled to the hills of Judea and the revolt was in motion. Mattathias' oldest son, Judas (named *Maccabeus* for *Hammerer*) led the rebellion, known as the Maccabean Revolt against the Syrians. Three years later, the Maccabees regained Jerusalem. The first act of renewing Jewish worship was the cleansing of the Temple. Only enough oil was found to light the Temple lanterns for one day; yet, the flame lasted eight days.

Today, the reclaiming of the Temple and the right to worship as before is celebrated in December as Hannukah. Individual candles are lit for eight consecutive nights. With the restored freedom, Hasmoneans appointed a member of their own family to the position of high priest. No longer did a descendant of Zadok fill the office. For many Jews, the change was unforgivable.

Following the initial victory in Jerusalem, fighting continued in an attempt to extend the realm of Judea. Judas was killed and his brother Jonathan made peace in the land. On Jonathan's death, the last remaining brother, Simon, became high priest plus army commander. Syria gave Judea political independence (142 BCE), and Rome confirmed the action a few years later. After five hundred years, a free Jewish state existed, ruled by the Hasmonean Dynasty. Internal unrest, created in part by Hellenistic culture and the role of high priest, weakened the Jewish nation to the extent they were unable to overcome the power of Rome. The Hasmonean Dynasty (164-63 BCE), ended with the advancement of Pompey.

The Books of Maccabees, contained in the Apocrypha, recounts the time leading up to the revolt, the conflict, and Judea becoming an autonomous state.

Zealots

Zealots were similar to a group that formed around 50 CE, known as the Sicarri, the Latin word for dagger, which they used in assassinating Jewish officials who cooperated with the Romans. Zealots, with a strong resentment to Roman domination of Judea, surfaced a few years later. They felt God had given the land to their people and they alone had a right to that land. The historian, Josephus, uses the term *Fourth Philosophy* to describe the Sicarri and Zealots.

With headquarters in Galilee, Zealots left for Jerusalem at the beginning of the Jewish Revolt against Rome (67 CE). In Jerusalem, the Zealots violently brought down the priestly aristocrats. Then the Zealots urged fellow Jews to use force in overthrowing the Romans. Three years later, the Jewish uprising led to Rome's total destruction of Jerusalem. Surviving Zealots and their families fled to Masada, the last Jewish outpost, to resist the Romans. In 73 CE, Rome breached the walls of Masada and found all seeking refuge there had committed suicide.

CHAPTER 5

Roman Rule

Reflections   Long Lasting Influence

Rome!! The word alone brings so many images to my mind. As a teenager, Rome seemed a romantic paradise where dreams come true. The many Hollywood stars slipping in and out of the streets of Rome, with cathedrals and fountains in the background, easily carried me into a world of make believe. I hardly connected that far away land to biblical times. Of course, some movies centered on early Christians and the torture they faced at the hands of the Romans. Somehow, I thought the martyrdom of Christians was admiral—able people dying for their beliefs. In those years, I was hardly aware of Rome's impact on Jews. One thing I knew from Shakespeare was Julius Caesar. The adaptation we read in high school thrilled me. We even memorized certain passages.

The Rome I know now is nothing like those gilt-edged scenes of my past. Rome, in biblical times, brought so much destruction to so many. Probably, no more than other civilizations, but for some reason, I am overwhelmed with anguish of Rome's brutality in creating their empire. No longer can I carelessly envision: "All's fair in love and war."

Rome!! A word of many images, lingers.

Judea Under Rome

A power struggle between different factions of Judea created an opening for advancement of Roman General Pompey, conqueror of neighboring Syria. A year later, 63 BCE, Jerusalem fell to Pompey who placed Hyrcanus of the Hasmonean Dynasty in the position of high priest and subordinate ruler. Pompey's reorganization of Judea left Jews devastated. The Hasmonean domain was reduced to two small sections, Judea and Galilee, separated by Samaria.

By 60 BCE, the Roman world was controlled by the Roman Triumvirate: Jules Caesar, Gnaeus Pompeius (Pompey), and Marcus Crassus. Each of the three fought for complete power. After Crassus was killed in battle, struggles between Pompey and Caesar resulted in a Civil War. Battles continued; Caesar, in 48 BCE, defeated Pompey's forces. Making his way to Egypt for protection, Pompey was assassinated. Caesar made Judea a province of Rome in 47 BCE.

During the final years of Pompey and Caesar's conflict, secret Jewish resources provided Caesar with reinforcements. In return, Caesar allowed Jews a greater degree of religious freedom. Antipater, a Jewish convert and twice ruler of the neighboring territory, Idumea, south of Judea, formed an alliance with Caesar. He received Roman citizenship and was named procurator (governor) of Judea. Antipater appointed one son, Phasael, governor of Judea and Perea (Transjordan). Another son, Herod, became governor of Galilee.

In 44 BCE, Caesar was assassinated. Within a year, Antipater died of poisoning. Parthians invaded Judea in 40 BCE and successfully captured Jerusalem. Phasael committed suicide and Herod fled to Rome where the Senate named him king of Judea. However, Judea remained under the Parthians. Again, with the help of the Roman Senate, Herod, in 37 BCE, fought his way through Judea and captured Jerusalem. Herod's reign of Judea lasted until his death in 4 BCE.

Soon after his appointment as king, Herod, with the addition of Great to his name, had forty-seven members of the Sanhedrin killed and then restricted the Sanhedrin's duties to religious matters. Not Jewish by birth, Herod, in hopes of claiming Jewish support, married Mariamne, descendant of the Hasmonean Dynasty. Herod felt he was king of all Jews, in Judea and elsewhere. In compensating Jews, he appointed a descendant of Zadok as high priest and supported Jewish establishments in Antioch (Syria), Babylonia (Iraq), Alexandria (Egypt), and Rome. Herod generally favored Pharisees over Sadducees. However, he catered to the Hellenized Jews over those holding to traditional Jewish ways.

Herod is noted as a master builder and economic genius. He controlled the extraction of asphalt from the Dead Sea; he imported Egyptian grain into Judea during a period of drought. Herod revived the Olympic Games, refurbished and built new fortresses, and in Jerusalem, constructed an amphitheater. Seemingly, he rivaled King Solomon in his accomplishments of a material nature. Though, Herod is remembered as a cruel king.

In spite of his achievements, Herod saw treason all around him. During his reign, he had Hyrcanus II, a Hasmonean nearing eighty years old, executed. The same fate fell on Herod's wife Mariamne, her mother and her brother, plus additional members of Herod's own family.

As recorded in the New Testament Gospel of Matthew, Jesus' birth in Bethlehem of Judea came during the time of King Herod. Frightened by news of a child being born *king of the Jews*, Herod ordered the killing of all children two years of age and under, in and around Bethlehem. Herod the Great died in 4 BCE, leaving a legacy of continued terror.

Heirs to Herod's Kingdom

The lineage chart below offers a quick look at the division of Herod's kingdom.

Herod the Great: King of Judea and Surrounding Lands from 37 to 4 BCE

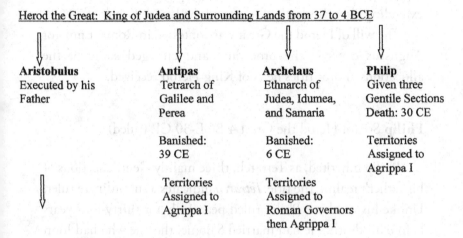

Aristobulus
Executed by his
Father

Antipas
Tetrarch of
Galilee and
Perea

Banished:
39 CE

Territories
Assigned to
Agrippa I

Archelaus
Ethnarch of
Judea, Idumea,
and Samaria

Banished:
6 CE

Territories
Assigned to
Roman Governors
then Agrippa I

Philip
Given three
Gentile Sections
Death: 30 CE

Territories
Assigned to
Agrippa I

Agrippa I
Assigned governing Posts:
part of Judea 37 CE
Galilee and Perea 39 CE
All of Judea, Idumea, and
Samaria 41 CE
Death: 44 CE

Territories
Assigned to
Roman Governors

Agrippa II
Assigned large portion of Agrippa I's
Territory: 48 CE
Loss of power: 66 CE
Jewish Revolt: 70 CE
Regained kingship: 73 CE
Death: 90 CE (?)

The following pages provide additional details.

A common practice for descendants of Herod the Great in adding *Herod* to their own names resulted in the name *Herod* appearing often in the New Testament. Sons, a grandson, and a great-grandson, continued the cruelty of the first Herod—extending after the death of Jesus and the Jewish Revolt of 70 CE.

The will of Herod the Great was contested in Rome. Emperor Augustus oversaw the procedure and changed some of the allocations and/or titles heirs of King Herod received.

Philip Son of Herod the Great 4 BCE-30 CE (ruled)

Philip inherited, as Tetrarch, three mainly Gentile sections of his father's realm. The title *Tetrarch* indicates a subordinate ruler. Unlike his brothers, Philip ruled peacefully for thirty-four years before his death. He had married Salome, the one who had John the Baptist killed. On Phillips's death, his territories were assigned to Agrippa I.

Archelaus Eldest Son of Herod the Great 4 BCE-6 CE (ruled)

Archelaus was named Ethnarch over Judea, Idumea (south of Judea), and Samaria. The title *Ethnarch* designates a subordinate ruler over a province or a people without the title of *king*. The title *king* would be given when Archelaus proved worthy. Shortly after Archelaus took over his allotted territories, there were Jewish revolts against Rome. Antipas and Philip sent complaints to Rome about Archelaus' oppressive reign and his inability to keep peace; Archelaus was banished to Rome two years later.

After Archelaus' banishment, Rome combined Judea, Samaria, and Idumea into a Roman province, causing a separation of Jews as the Jewish population of Galilee remained under Antipas.

Roman procurators ruled the Roman province until 41 CE when the territory was assigned to Agrippa I. Three years later, with the assassination of Agrippa I, Judea, Samaria, and Idumea again fell under direct Roman rule.

Antipas Son of Herod the Great 4 BCE-39 CE (ruled)

Antipas, named *Tetrarch* of Galilee and Perea, is often mentioned as Antipas the Tetrarch. In addition, Antipas added Herod to his name, resulting in the frequent appearance of *Herod Antipas* in the New Testament.

Herod Antipas married his half-brother's wife, Herodias, mother of Salome. John the Baptist spoke ill of Herod Antipas because of the marriage. Shortly thereafter, Herodias and Salome plotted the death of the Baptist. Herod Antipas ordered the deed to be carried out (Matthew 14:1-12). On the morning of Jesus' crucifixion, Pontius Pilate sent him [Jesus] to Herod Antipas (Luke 23:6-12).

Pilate, Roman governor of Judea appointed in 26 CE, immediately began tormenting Jews. His questionable treatment increased over the next ten years, leading to his removal from the position.

Even though problems arose for Antipas the Tetrarch, Galilee and Perea experienced a time of peace and prosperity. In assuring the linage of Herod the Great, Antipas assigned his nephew, Agrippa I, a governing post. When Rome banished Antipas to an obscure section of France (39 CE), Galilee and Perea were then given to Agrippa I.

Agrippa I Son of Aristobulus, Grandson of Herod the Great 41-44 CE (ruled)

Agrippa I, already in a government post, created some conflicts. However, in 37 CE, a new ruler, Emperor Caligula, appointed him vassal king of a large area in Judea. As noted, on Antipas' banishment, Agrippa I received Galilee and Perea. After the death of Emperor Caligula (41 CE), the rest of Judea plus Samaria and Idumea fell under the domain of Agrippa I. In 44 CE Agrippa I died suddenly; his territory fell under the direct rule of Rome as his heir (Agrippa II) was only seventeen years old.

Agrippa II Son of Agrippa I, Great-grandson of Herod the Great 48-90 CE (ruled)

In 48 CE, Agrippa II received his father's territory and two years later became a Roman vassal king. As noted in Acts 25:13-27 and 26:32, the apostle Paul appeared before Agrippa II. By then, the second Agrippa's constant companionship with his niece Bernice, oldest daughter of Agrippa I, created ill will among Jews. Nevertheless, Agrippa II maintained his position.

By 66 CE, Agrippa II could no longer control the continual fighting between opposing factions of Jews. Rome, alarmed by the violence, invaded Judea and relieved Agrippa II of his duties. Judea's political instability intensified, leading to Rome's destruction of Jerusalem in 70 CE. Three years later, Rome ended the revolt with the capture of Masada; Agrippa II regained kingship and served under Rome for another seventeen years.

Jewish Revolts Against Rome (Current Era)

After Agrippa I's death in 44, Roman governors, less receptive to the Jewish population, were appointed to rule Judea. In that atmosphere, four years later, Rome named Agrippa II as Judea's vassal king. In Judea, Greek settlers, wealthy Jews, along with Romans, benefitted financially with the situation. Impoverished Jewish farmers were burdened with heavy taxation and little protection from thieves. By 62, the death of the presiding Roman governor left a void leading to increased friction between Rome and various Jewish factions.

Jewish Zealots called their downtrodden fellow citizens to join with them in a revolt against Rome. As the fighting spread, Jews from outlining areas sought shelter in Jerusalem and by 66, Jerusalem was overflowing with Jewish refugees. Rome took action; their troops entered Jerusalem, killing Jews in their shops and streets. Jewish rebels retaliated and the stunned Roman troops retreated. Jews continued the uprising until Agrippa II was overthrown, then they formed an independent government in Jerusalem. Within months, a Jewish civil war weakened their position. Rome took advantage of the situation and set out to reclaim the region.

In 67, Roman troops led by General Vespasian defeated Galilean Zealots commanded by Josephus, the historian. Two years later, Vespasian became emperor as a civil war divided Rome. Titus, son of Vespasian, took his father's place in defeating the Zealots. For over a year, Jerusalem had fought off Rome's attempts of a siege; Titus' first action was to strengthen the siege. He built walls around the city, starved those inside and killed all Jews trying to escape. Soon the walls of Jerusalem gave way. Titus' troops methodically moved toward the Temple—headquarters of the Zealots. By the end of August, 70, the Temple lay in ruins. No mercy was given to survivors. It is estimated that over one hundred thousand Jews lost their lives in the siege and that many more were taken to Rome as slaves. Jews were banished from Jerusalem and prohibited from re-entry. Sadducees, having no purpose without the Temple, disappeared. Some Pharisees survived.

Titus returned to Rome a hero; however, a large group of surviving Zealots led a few remaining Jews to Masada, a mountain top fortress in the southern desert of Judea. There, Jews felt safe in their stronghold; but before long, renewed Roman troops marched to Masada. They built a ramp which gave them access to the top of the sheer cliffs. Those hiding there since the destruction of Jerusalem, prepared for the attack as troops came closer and closer. When Roman troops broke through the walls of Masada, they discovered all Jews inside had committed mass suicide. Three years after the fall of Jerusalem, Jewish statehood was completely lost. Agrippa II regained his throne, remaining for seventeen years. In time, Rome allowed Jews to return to Jerusalem.

The Temple ceased to be; Judaism survived. Diaspora Jewish communities continued in numerous locations in the vicinity of Judea. Across these new communities, Kohens, Levites, and surviving Pharisees, continued the Jewish faith with meetings in synagogues. Sadducees, Zealots, and Essenes became history; Pharisees became rabbis and controlled the re-established Sanhedrin, eventually centering in Galilee.

Hostilities between Romans and Jews surfaced once again, coming to an end as Hadrian became Emperor (117-138). Jews welcomed this Emperor until he prohibited circumcision and prepared to build a Roman city, Aelia Capitolina, on the ruins of Jerusalem. With that news, Simon Bar Kokhba (Aramaic: son of a star) mounted an attack against Rome: The Bar Kokhba Revolt of 132-135. Jewish forces in Diaspora and Judea were united, bringing victory to Jerusalem and all of Judea. Under the sovereign Jewish State, a coin was minted inscribed: *Year one of Israel's redemption*. Rome retaliated in a most vicious war. Roman casualties were enormous; Jews were decimated. It is estimated, close to six hundred thousand Jews were killed, fifty towns and close to a thousand villages were destroyed. Jewish survivors were taken as slaves or forced to flee in exile. Judea was a wasteland. In Galilee, some Jewish life continued.

Wanting an end to any future Jewish uprisings spurred Rome to drastic measures. Hadrian tried to end the Jewish religion by burning scrolls and executing rabbis. Furthermore, he banned the study of the Torah and all other observances of Judaism. The Temple grounds became a place for worshiping Hadrian and the Roman god Jupiter. A new name, *Aelia Capitolina*, was given to Jerusalem and Judea became *Syria Palestina*. Though badly beaten, Jews survived in rural settlements of their homeland and beyond.

Diaspora Jews maintained the Jewish religion and culture. The Talmud became a Jewish constitution, traveling wherever Jews located. Eventually, Babylon replaced Galilee as the Jewish center. A noticeable separation occurred between the Jewish and Christian faiths with the end of Jerusalem and Judea.

SECTION THREE

CHRISTIANS

CHAPTER 6

Background (Christians)

Reflections Cherished Years
Terms Linking Faiths
Roman World of Jesus
People of the New Faith
   Jesus, John the Baptist, Jesus' Disciples, The Marys, Paul
   (Saul)

Reflections   Cherished Years

As I write about Christianity, I recall my early years with awe. For some reason, from a little child, God was real to me and I found joy and comfort in the little Methodist Church I attended with my family. Certain phrases used in some of the sermons are still remembered. With all of those beloved memories and the heart-warming celebrations of Christmas and Easter, I knew little about how the Bible came to be written words. I guess it was the meanings *that reached into my soul—and so it must be—to sustain a life.*

In Sunday School and Vacation Bible School, we memorized John 3:16, colored pictures of Jesus and the disciples, and of course, at Christmas we put on the pageant of Jesus' birth. Cardboard wings with tinsel halos and shepherds in bathrobes transformed us all into that beautiful story.

I was ten when the church gave me a Bible. Like others in those years, it had the standard black cover with a zipper, embossed with gold words: Holy Bible Illustrated. *I cringe today when looking at the childish printing of my name on one of the first pages. Right after I put those letters on the line beneath* Presented to, *I felt sad because my printing wasn't pretty. I had marred* The Bible, *so special to me. After all these years, the zipper is unstitched in places but I still cherish my first Bible. It brings to mind my rural farm days. Of interest to me now is that it conforms to the King James Version edition of 1611. I don't read my first Bible often. The* New English Bible with the Apocrypha, *copyright of 1970, is easier to read. I purchased that Bible myself; I smile looking at the fine lines of my name on the inside cover.*

My daughter, about eleven, received a Bible when she was baptized into the Baptist Church that nurtured us for many, many years. It was the church of my children's great, great-grandparents. Their dedication help shaped all of our lives. A couple of years ago, while making a move, my daughter came across papers she had written describing her thoughts on the meaning of baptism. How precious that she still has those. I reminded her of the time, probably close to her baptism, when she was over-come with tears as we were driving at night and she saw a lighted cross on the mountain side. How dear—life memories shared between generations.

Returning to my own writing about the Bible, I appreciate all that I've learned about both the Hebrew Bible and the New Testament. It is a knowledge that enlarges my reverence to long held beliefs. I wish for others, a knowingness of a Greater Power that forever and ever, dwells within the realm of life.

Terms Linking Faiths

To some extent, the words of the New Testament reflect the Hebrew Bible. Nevertheless, some terms and sayings are used in a slightly different manner. To clarify, explanations on some key elements follow. Additional supporting information is covered later in this section.

Apostles (from the Greek word *sent*) continued the teachings of Jesus after his death. Disciples became apostles along with others who traveled to surrounding countries spreading the message of Jesus.

The title of **Christ** (Greek meaning *anointed one*) was not used in reference to Jesus during his lifetime. The Hebrew word meaning *anointed one* was used for kings and priests, which came to include *messiah.* The Greeks gave their word *Christos* for the *anointed one,* which then became the English *Christ.* The Christian Church is based on the life of Jesus, his death and resurrection. People believing Jesus died for the sins of mankind are called Christians. There is no mention of the word *Christianity* in the New Testament; the word *Christians* is mentioned twice.

Jesus selected twelve **disciples** to join him in telling people about God. Generally, twelve disciples are mentioned. A disciple is a follower; one who is taught.

Epistles (Greek *letters*), are formal letters sent with specific information related to an identified topic. The Apostle Paul wrote letters to Christian communities that had someone who could read them to others. The letters contained encouragement and instructions to fellow Christians. The New Testament contains Paul's letters in addition to others.

Gentiles, in the Roman World, were people neither Jewish nor Roman citizens. Pagans often were classified as gentiles. When used by historians, *gentile* and *pagan* are not considered negative titles.

A **good shepherd** characterized a leader who comforted [sheep/people]. Genesis 4:2 states that Abel is a *keeper of sheep*. King David, in the 23rd Psalm of the Hebrew Bible, refers to God as a shepherd. Jesus, in the New Testament Gospel of John (10:11), describes himself as a *good shepherd*.

The **Gospels** (Greek *good news*), tell of Jesus' life, death and resurrection. There is no accurate indication of the authors of the Gospels. They were written decades after Jesus' death and no doubt the messages had changed somewhat with the retellings of the events.

Hope is defined in the dictionary as: to expect with confidence, to trust; it is alluded to in many passages of the Hebrew Bible. Often the word *trust* is shown. All the prophetic books give hope for the future, a rebuilding of the relationship between God and the people of Israel. Isaiah, Chapters 40-53, addresses the expectations of those in the Babylonian exile. Isaiah 40:31 reads: ...*But they who trust in the Lord shall renew their strength...* Moving into the Psalms, Chapter 39:8 asks: *What, then, can I count on, O Lord? In You my hope lies.*

The Letters of the New Testament contain many references to *Hope*. Romans 5:2 states, ...*we boast in our hope of sharing the glory of God*. Chapter 1 verse 3 of the First Letter of Peter tells of Jesus giving a new birth into a living hope through his resurrection. In Hebrews 11:1, the words are: *Now faith is the assurance of things hoped for, the conviction of things not seen*.

Kingdom of God, mentioned often in the Gospels, pertains to God's grace in the world: happiness, peace, and joy. Jesus' ministry revealed the Kingdom of God. He taught of a world where everyone had what they needed and had no fear: it is the Kingdom of God. John the Baptist, baptizing Jesus, told those present that *the kingdom of heaven was near* (Matthew 3:2). In Matthew 19:23-24, *Kingdom of Heaven* denotes the same meaning as *Kingdom of God*.

Love is described in 1 Corinthians, Chapter 13, as being important for the Christian Community. The chapter concludes with: *And now faith, hope, and love abide, these three; and the greatest of these is love*. In writing about Christianity, Houston Smith speaks of the two most important facts about life: God's overwhelming love of humanity, and the need for people to accept that love and let it flow through them to others. A dictionary definition of *charity* is Christian love, taken from the Late Latin *caritat*.

The word **messiah**, from Hebrew *anointed one*, translates to Greek *Christos* then to English *Christ*. The word *messiah* as a future deliverer of Israel became part of the language only after 587 BCE when Judea fell to the Babylonians.

The Gospel of Matthew (1:1-17) begins with a genealogy from Abraham and concludes with an indication the messiah would extend the lineage. The birth of the messiah follows. In the telling of Jesus' birth, Matthew calls Jesus *Emmanuel*, meaning *God is with us*. Isaiah 7:14-16 speaks of a child to be born of a young woman and will be called Emmanuel, connecting Jesus with God. As the Gospel of Matthew continues, the term *messiah* is repeated. Yet, during Jesus' life, few thought of him as the messiah. Matthew ends with Jesus saying *I am with you always*, likely meaning: Jesus is Emmanuel, *God with us.*

Pagan *like gentile*, spoken in a historical setting contains no negative connotation. During the Roman period, paganism referred to the belief of many gods. Numerous religions of the ancient Mediterranean region were considered pagan.

Sin, as defined in the dictionary, is a lack of upholding God's Law. John the Baptist baptized for the forgiveness of sins. The New Testament is the first written account that a future messiah will suffer (Greek *passion)* and die for the sins of the people. The concept of people being sinful, before birth, is rarely mentioned in the Hebrew Bible. Christianity developed the notion of original sin.

The title **Son of God**, like *messiah*, was not given to Jesus until after his death. During the time of Jesus and before, Jews used the title *Son of God* for miracle-workers, which were common in the first century CE. A clearer definition as a Jewish title is one who mediated between God and humans; kings and others were given the title. Some Christians believe Jesus was the Son of God all his life, while others feel direct communication with God came after his baptism when the Spirit of God descended on him.

Son of Man, like Son of God, has conflicting meanings. In the Hebrew Bible, Daniel (7:13-14) sees *One like a human being. . .* defined as *son of man.* However, in the passage, the celestial being is *like* a human being. Bandstra defines Son of Man as a Divine authority figure with the appearance of a human being. Some Christians today, unlike Jesus and his followers, view Son of Man as a real human being.

The **Spirit of God**, ancient Israelites believed, were *revelations* from God. Those filled with the Spirit had the ability to accomplish miracles. The Gospel of Luke (4:14-21) relates the incident when Jesus spoke words of the Prophet Isaiah, beginning with: *The spirit of the Lord is upon me because he has anointed me.* Jesus then proclaimed: *Today. . . this text has come true.* The underlining meaning of this episode is that Jesus was filled with the *Spirit of God,* at times called the *Holy Spirit.*

The Hebrew word for **truth** conveys firmness and reliability. 1 Esdras 4:33-41 speaks of truth. Verse 36 says: *The whole earth calls upon truth, and heaven blesses it.* The speech ends with: *Blessed be the God of truth!* People's response: *Great is truth, and strongest of all.* In John 4:23-24, Jesus is speaking*: But the hour is coming, and is now here, when the true worshipers will worship the Father in spirit and truth, for the Father seeks such as these to worship him. God is spirit, and those who worship him must worship in spirit and truth.*

The United States Declaration of Independence, dated July 4, 1776, states: *We hold these Truths to be self-evident, that all Men are created equal, that they are endowed by their Creator with certain unalienable Rights, that among these are Life, Liberty, and the Pursuit of Happiness.*

Will of God, surprisingly, received little mention in my many references. The dictionary defines *will* as a desire or wish. In Matthew 6:9-13, Jesus tells his followers to pray to God and includes the words: *Your will be done, on earth as it is in heaven.* Again, Jesus calls on God before his crucifixion: *My Father, if it is possible, let this cup pass from me. . . if this cannot pass unless I drink it, your will be done* (Matthew 26:39-42).

In biblical circles, God's will is often heard. Many times, prayers conclude with: thy will be done. Years ago, my question was: What is God's will in my life? A pastor explained something to the effect that what I wished for—from the heart—and it was good, God wanted that for me. Otherwise, I would not have that longing. Another way of looking at it is: *that which would fulfill my life, is God's will. God bestows His desires upon the hearts of mankind. It is there if one searches.*

Word of God is used by Christians in reference to Jesus and the New Testament; sometimes simply *Word* is used.

Terms used in the Hebrew Bible and the New Testament, though recorded long ago, are spoken across the world today. In looking closer at the time of Jesus, new languages surfaced. For many, Aramaic replaced Hebrew followed closely with Greek. Writings of the new faith reflect the times at that point in history. Before long, Latin replaced the Greek language.

Roman World of Jesus

Christianity is based on the life and teachings of Jesus. His birth (4 BCE) and death (30 CE) are generally accepted as being close to the actual events. After Jesus' death, his disciples received a sign that they were to go forth and carry on his ministry. History, shown in the Hebrew Bible and the years that followed, provide the background on how Christianity surfaced and grew.

Jesus and his followers were Jews living in the time of oppressive small kingdoms and large empires using violence to control the less fortunate. Frequent wars threatened any hope of long-lasting peace. It was a time when the Roman Empire expansion covered vast areas. Like other Roman providences, Judea was forced to pay annual tribute to Rome. Additional hardships resulted when wealthy aristocrats took over small lands and created large estates to grow, sell, and export produce. Those forced from individual farms could no longer sustain even a meager existence. Yet, in those harsh times, there was the feeling among the poor that their status was God's will and kings ruled by Divine right.

As Rome's demands on Judea became more and more

burdensome, Jews wanting change resulted in the surfacing of differing factions. Pharisees focused on a strict practice of the Law of Moses. The wealthy Sadducees wanted peace with the Romans and leaned toward the Hellenistic culture. Essenes withdrew from mainstream Judaism, while Zealots sought the destruction of Rome through armed uprisings. Most Jews were not a part of these factions. Nevertheless, all Jews were influenced by the climate of that time and they sought change.

Though oppressed outwardly, the Jewish spirit could not be crushed. Hope remained. Followers of Jesus believed he was the long-awaited savior that would triumph over their enemies and restore moral stability to their people.

Jesus' life was centered mostly in Judea and Galilee, traveling between the two through Samaria. The Sea of Galilee and the River Jordan were vital connections to the time of Jesus. Those areas, and the ones surrounding them, were part of the Roman Empire at a time when there was no middle class. Few people belonged to the upper class; most were considered lower class with almost no hope of ever changing their status. In largely populated areas, one-third of the people were slaves with better lives than the poor. Most people were uneducated, ninety percent were illiterate. There were no cures for most diseases and many babies died. The dangers of travel prevented journeys far from home. The Roman World impacted Jesus' life, from birth to death.

People of the New Faith

The Gospels, from the Greek *Good News,* provide nearly all accounts of Jesus written within decades after his death. Later historians mentioned Jesus in their writings. Jewish Flavius Josephus (ca 37-100) acknowledged Jesus; there are a few others. Roman Suetonius (75-130) wrote of disturbances instigated by one named *Chrestus*. Another Roman, Tacitus (56-117), writing about Nero, uses the term *Christians* with a leader named *Christ (Christus)*. Jesus' birth and death, along with events of his ministry, are given in the Gospels. Unless noted otherwise, the following accounts of Jesus, John the Baptist, Jesus' disciples, and the Marys, are taken from the Gospels. The first part of Acts (of the Apostles) continues with Apostles spreading the *Good News*; Paul's life and ministry is given in the final portion of Acts.

Jesus 4 BCE-30 CE

Toward the end of Herod the Great's reign over Judea (37-4 BCE), a child was born. An angel appeared to Mary with news she would give birth to a savior, the longed-for messiah. Joseph took Mary for his wife and near the time of birth they left their home in Nazareth of Galilee and journeyed to Bethlehem of Judea, the House of David. Caesar Augustus had called a census requiring people to report to the city of their lineage. While there Mary gave birth to Jesus—the child many believed to be the messiah (Matthew 1:18-24) (Luke 2:1-6).

Around the time of Jesus' birth, a great light appeared in the sky, perhaps from a nova or planets coming together. Wise Men, seeing the bright light, came looking for an infant prophesied as the King of the Jews. On hearing the news, Herod ordered the killing of all male babies in and around Bethlehem. To escape the slaughter, Joseph took Mary and Jesus to Egypt. After Herod's death, the family returned to Nazareth (Matthew 2).

The House of David refers to lineage from David, anointed King of Israel by the prophet Samuel. Jerusalem, once known as Zion, became the *City of David*. The Hebrew Bible, Micah 5:1-2, indicates a child with a heritage from Ancient Times would come out of Bethlehem and rule Israel. Also, Isaiah 11:1-10 speaks of a descendant of Jesse [father of David], who would be given the spirit and knowledge of the Lord and bring peace. Jesus descended from the House of David. The Gospel of Matthew begins with the lineage from Joseph back to David's son Solomon. Luke 3:31 traces the blood line from Jesus' mother, Mary, through her father, Heli, to David's son Nathan (brother of Solomon).

Luke's Gospel tells of a time when twelve-year old Jesus and his family journeyed to Jerusalem for the Passover celebration. *Passover* is the time from Moses when Hebrews smeared lamb's blood over their doors so the Pharaohs' evil curse would *passover* their household. Returning from Passover, Mary and Joseph noticed Jesus was missing and went back to the Temple. Jesus had remained there, talking with the rabbis (Luke 2:41-47) (Exodus 12:21-27).

There is little information regarding Jesus during the years between the Passover when he was twelve and the beginning of his ministry. Some accounts place him studying in the East. Others indicate he was living a normal life as a young Jewish male. He would have been attending the synagogue while learning about God, as related in the Torah, and words of the prophets. During that period, Jesus, probably worked in the fields and helped with family chores. In conversations, I've heard questions regarding the need for Jesus to seek knowledge elsewhere, as God imparted all wisdom to Jesus. From within, Jesus was prepared for his life. Today, as in the past, questioning has value.

Following the account of young Jesus in the Temple, all the Gospels carry the story of his baptism by John the Baptist. Some scholars place John at the Jordan River in 26 CE, preaching and baptizing. Leaving the shores of the Jordan, Jesus spent time in the wilderness being *tempted by the devil.*

After forty days and nights in the wilderness, Jesus returned to Galilee and began preaching and healing. [Wilderness is not mentioned in John.] Jesus then selected disciples to work with him in teaching of a loving God and in healing the sick. Large crowds followed them as they extended their ministry beyond Galilee (Matthew 3, 4) (Mark 1) (Luke 3, 4) (John 1).

In his teaching, Jesus used *parables,* short simple stories containing profound meaning. When the disciples questioned Jesus about the parables, he replied: *To you has been given the secret of the kingdom of God, but for those outside, everything comes in parables in order that they may indeed look, but not perceive. . . .* In Matthew, Jesus continues by referring to a prophecy of Isaiah being fulfilled: . . . *[they] will turn and I would heal them.* Jesus had given the disciples the ability to see and understand his teachings at a deeper level, which other followers lacked. However, in questioning and turning inward to know God, all could be healed (Matthew 13) (Mark 4) (Luke 8).

The four Gospels, with some differences, tell of Jesus and his disciples preparing for a trip to the Temple in Jerusalem for Passover. Regardless of the danger, the disciples agree to make the trip. On their arrival, Jesus made a triumphant entrance into Jerusalem. For a few days, Jesus visited the Temple, creating hostility and anger over questions and answers regarding his authority and purpose. Later that week, Jesus and his twelve close disciples secluded themselves for a traditional meal in preparation for Passover. Within hours, Temple police seized Jesus. It is recorded—Judas, the disciple, betrayed him.

Early the next morning, chief priests took Jesus to Pontius Pilate, the Roman governor of Judea. Jesus also appeared before Herod Antipas, as he, too, was in Jerusalem. Pilate felt Jesus, a Galilean, came under the jurisdiction of Antipas. Regardless, Antipas sent Jesus back to Pilate who turned him over to a crowd demanding his death. Calvary, or Golgotha (the skull), is presumed to be the site of the crucifixion (Matthew 21, 26, 27) (Mark 11, 14, 15) (Luke 22, 23) (John 13, 18, 19).

The next day, Saturday, the Jewish Sabbath, those close to Jesus remained together in grief and confusion. The Sabbath prevented them from attending to Jesus' body. Also, fear of Romans and facing the same outcome as Jesus, made them cautious. Early on Sunday, Mary Magdalene hurried ahead of other women as they made their way to the tomb where the body of Jesus had quickly been placed after the events of Friday. Stunned, Mary noticed the rock sealing the tomb had been moved. Jesus then appeared, in the flesh, telling Mary to go and share the news that he had risen from the dead.

Later, on that same Sunday, Jesus entered a locked room where the disciples had gathered. Afterwards, there were a few more reports of Jesus seen among the living. Then, fifty days after Passover, Jesus' followers gathered in Jerusalem for the Feast of Pentecost, a celebration of the wheat harvest. Suddenly, Jesus appeared—his final physical presence on earth. He instructed his disciples to go into the world and preach his message. After that, Jesus rose into heaven (Matthew 28) (Mark 16) (Luke 24) (John 20).

John the Baptist

John the Baptist, cousin of Jesus and of the lineage of David, appears to have been born a few months before Jesus. John's parents, Zechariah and Elizabeth, advanced in years, had long awaited the birth of a child. An angel appeared to Zechariah with news that a son was to be born to them and they were to name him John. Little is known of John's early years. The Gospels speak of John in the wilderness along the Jordan River and baptizing for forgiveness of sins, shortly before Jesus' baptism. John had been sent by God to pave the way for *one more powerful than I.*

At that time, Antipas, son of Herod the Great and ruler of Perea, became alarmed by John's words. John spoke against Antipas because of his marriage to his half-brother's wife, Herodias. Offended by John the Baptist, Antipas had him arrested and jailed. Herodias, also angered by John's words, involved her daughter Salome in a plot to rid them of John's condemnation. After winning Antipas' attention, Salome asked for John's head— which Antipas ordered (Matthew 3, 4, 14) (Mark 1, 6) (Luke 1, 13) (John 1, 3).

Jesus' Disciples

The Gospels vary in naming the disciples, those who became the closest of Jesus' followers. Evidence points to more than the twelve. The Gospel of Mark (3:13-15) tells: . . . *Jesus appointed twelve, whom he also called apostles, to be with him, and to be sent out to proclaim the message, and to have authority to cast out demons.* Jesus opened the disciples' minds for understanding his messages of God and gave them the ability to perform miracles. After Jesus' death, as Apostles, the disciples continued his ministry. Descriptions of the disciples, generally regarded as the twelve nearest to Jesus, follow.

Simon Peter and his brother Andrew had a fishing business on the Sea of Galilee. At their first meeting, Jesus named Simon, *Peter,* meaning *rock.* Both brothers had been disciples of John the Baptist. Peter, generally the first one named in lists of disciples, became their leader. Nevertheless, after Jesus' arrest, Peter denied him three times. Peter went on to become instrumental in the early Christian movement. Acts 2 tells of Peter, fifty days later, on Pentecost, converting a large crowd to the new faith. Peter's

travels ended in Rome where he was crucified, head down—on
his request—during the reign of Nero (54-68) (Matthew 26:69-
75) (Mark 1:16, 3:16, 14: 66-72) (Luke 22:56-62) (John 1:35-42).

Andrew and his brother Simon [Peter] worked together as
fishermen. Andrew learned of Jesus while a disciple of John the
Baptist. After the first meeting, Andrew knew Jesus to be the
messiah and took his brother, Simon, to meet Jesus (John 1:35-
42). Little is known of Andrew's ministry; one account places
him preaching in an area which became Russia and later his
crucifixion in Greece.

Brothers **James** and **John**, sons of Zebedee, fished on the Sea
of Galilee like Peter and Andrew. It is recorded both had a fierce
temper. The expectation that Jesus would be named a worldly
king led one of the brothers asking to sit at his right hand, the
other asked for the left hand. Jesus taught both brothers, as well
as the other disciples, that his kingdom was about meekness
and humility. In the Gospels, James, older than John, is usually
mentioned first when speaking of both. King of Judea, Agrippa
I, grandson of Herod the Great, had James beheaded during a
persecution of Christians. John worked with Peter in spreading
the teachings of Jesus. He held a position of respect and leadership
in the early Church (Matthew 4:18-22) (Mark 1:16-20, 3:16,
10:35-43) (Acts 1:13, 12:2).

John 13:23, in a list of disciples, notes: *the one Jesus loved*.
Ehrman identifies John as the beloved disciple. It is not clear that
the reference is in regards to John, son of Zebedee.

Philip is mentioned briefly in the Gospels. The only reliable
information comes from The Gospel of John. In Chapter 1 verses
43-44, Jesus sought out Philip, from the same town as Simon
Peter and Andrew, the day after those two joined with him. Philip
then rushed to his friend, Nathanael, telling him he had found the
messiah. Philip, in John 14, asks Jesus to show them [the disciples]

the Father [God]. In reply, Jesus explained that anyone seeing him [Jesus] saw God. Philip preached in Samaria and cities of Philistia.

Bartholomew is thought by many scholars to be the same person as **Nathanael**. The name *Bartholomew* is most often shown; however, the Gospel of John (1:44-51) uses the name Nathanael and speaks of Philip telling Nathanael he has found the one spoken of in the Law and the Prophets. Nathanael replied: *Can anything good come out of Nazareth?* When Jesus saw Nathanael, he recognized a sincere man, totally dedicated to God. That reference to unseen attributes proved to Nathanael that Jesus was the messiah. Bartholomew (Nathanael) journeyed with Philip and Thomas in spreading the message of Jesus.

Thomas is mentioned as a disciple; however, the only additional information is found in the Gospel of John. Thomas is also referred to as *Didymus*, the Greek equivalent to the Hebrew and Aramaic name for *twin*. When disciples could not change Jesus' mind about returning to Jerusalem, which lead to his death, Thomas felt they all should go and die with him (John 11:16). In John 14:5-6 Jesus tells Thomas *I am the way, the truth, and the life.* Thomas missed seeing Jesus, in the flesh, the Sunday after the crucifixion and doubted the other disciples when told of their meeting. Jesus, at another physical presence, showed Thomas the wounds in his hands (John 20:24-29). Scholars think Thomas spread the Gospel in Parthia and Persia, and later was martyred in India.

Matthew, noted as *Levi* Luke 5:27, held the position of a tax-collector when called by Jesus. The dislike of tax-collectors made Matthew an outcast to his fellow Jews.

James, son of Alphaeus is listed as a disciple in three Gospels. The name also appears in Acts 1:13 with disciples shortly after the death of Jesus. There is little else said about him (Matthew 10:3) (Mark 3:18) (Luke 6:15).

Thaddeus is a name of some confusion. In Mark 3:18, the name Thaddeus is shown as a disciple. Matthew 10:3 states: Thaddaeus is also called Lebbaeus. Luke 6:16 uses the term Judas, son of James, which is repeated in Acts 1:13. John 14:22 refers to Judas (not Iscariot), speaking to Jesus. Jude is an English form of Judas. If there was a disciple named Jude, scholars today feel it is not the same person who wrote the letter *Jude.*

Simon the Canaanite is mentioned as being a disciple; however, there is evidence that he belonged to the group known as Zealots. Zealots, a radical Jewish faction, opposed Roman rule in Judea. It is supposed that Simon gave up his life as a Zealot and became filled with justice and charity, values in keeping with the ministry of Jesus (Luke 6:15).

Judas, the only Judean among the disciples as the others came from Galilee, looked after the finances while Jesus and the disciples traveled from place to place. He is mentioned as a disciple in Matthew 10:2-4, Mark 3:16-19, Luke 6:14-16. In John 6:71, Judas is referred to as the son of Simon Iscariot. Why Jesus chose Judas is questioned. The Gospels clearly state that Judas betrayed Jesus and then took his own life in remorse (Matthew 26:14-16, 27:3-10) (Mark 14:10-11) (Luke 22:3-6, 22:47) (John 13:21-30).

Matthias, selected by casting lots, replaced Judas (Acts 1:23).

On Pentecost, the disciples came together and were filled with the Holy Spirit. After that, they continued the ministry of Jesus, as Apostles (Acts 2).

The Marys

Mary, mother of Jesus, is mentioned in Matthew 1:18:24 and Luke 2:7, 2:19 with the birth of Jesus. In Luke 2:34-35 a prophecy is told regarding Jesus and the effect it will have on Mary. The trip with Mary and Joseph to the Temple, when Jesus was a young boy, is also covered in Luke (2:41-52). Mary was present at Jesus' first miracle, turning water into wine, as reported in John 2:1-12. Also, she was one of the women at the foot of the cross at Jesus' crucifixion, at which time Jesus gave her over to *the beloved disciple John* (John 19:25-27).

Mary Magdalene, from the city of Magdala in Galilee, became a follower of Jesus after he freed her of seven demons (Luke 8:2-3). She was present at most of the events during the crucifixion; after his resurrection, Jesus appeared first to Mary Magdalene. She and other women went to the tomb and found it empty. At that time, Jesus sent Mary to tell the others he *was ascending to the Father* (John 19: 25) (John 20:11-18).

Mary, mother of James and John, helped in providing for the disciples, and witnessed Jesus' death and resurrection (Luke 2:31) (Matthew 27:55-61).

Mary of Bethany, sister of Martha and Lazarus, listened to Jesus' words while Martha worked in the kitchen. Mary anointed Jesus' feet with oil which he called *an unselfish act and a memorial to her* (Luke 10:38-42) (John 12:3).

Paul (Saul)

The primary source covering the life of Paul is his seven letters and the accounts found in Acts. Scholars date his birth within the first decade of the current era and his crucifixion to the mid-60s, in Rome. Starting with the Jewish name Saul from Tarsus (near the Mediterranean Sea in present day Turkey), he became an Apostle of Jesus. Under the Greek name Paul, he is credited with the broad and rapid spread of Christianity across the Roman world.

Saul, a Jew, inherited his father's Roman citizenship and like his father, became a Pharisee. As a youth advanced in knowledge,

Saul studied the traditions of The Law in Jerusalem. Later, he fiercely opposed the ideas of Jesus and the spread of Christianity. After witnessing the stoning of Stephen, Saul joined in the persecution of Christians in Jerusalem.

Acts 6 tells of Stephen, *a man full of faith and the Holy Spirit*, being chosen by the twelve to work with them in proclaiming the Good News. In a short time, some from the synagogues argued with Stephen and he was brought before the high priest on charges of blasphemy. Stephen's words so angered his accusers they dragged him out of the city and stoned him. Saul was a part of the killing, as recorded in Acts 7:54-60.

Saul's persecution of Christians intensified. He asked permission to go to Damascus [Syria] and bring back, to Jerusalem, any *who belonged to the Way*. Approaching the city, Saul fell to the ground when confronted by a bright light. He heard a voice asking, *why do you persecute me?* Saul wanted to know who was speaking. Jesus revealed it was he and directed Saul to continue into the city where others would tell him what to do. Travelers with Saul heard the voice but saw no one. Blinded by the light, his friends helped Saul reach the city where he was healed by a disciple. The events lead to Saul's belief that he had been called to be an Apostle. He was baptized and carried the story of Jesus to the Gentiles (Acts 9: 1-22).

When he began preaching Jesus' message, Saul left Damascus and moved southward to avoid Jews who plotted his death. After a few years, Saul returned to Jerusalem. Apostles there questioned his loyalty and qualifications for inclusion within their group. The unrest around him caused Saul to return to his home in Tarsus. There, Barnabas, one of the new Apostles, convinced Saul to join him in spreading the word of Jesus. The two journeyed to Antioch where more converts accepted the faith and the word *Christians* was first used. A short time later, Saul became known as Paul (Acts 11:25-26, 13:9).

Through the 40s, Paul continued his travels and preaching, gaining more and more Gentiles as Christians. Even with additional attempts on his life, Paul established many Christian Churches. Starting in the 50s and continuing until his death, Paul continually wrote letters of encouragement to the Churches.

CHAPTER 7

A Church Survives

Reflections   Controversy

It was after my retirement I returned to regular church attendance. When my children were mostly grown, for some reason I didn't make time for church. While a teacher, with additional university classes, lesson plans, grading papers, and extended family, I slipped away from routine church attendance. Always, I kept up with those friends of earlier years and one invited me to attend her church. She had changed from the Baptist Church we had served for many years. Her New Thought Church *re-awakened my interest in formalized religion.*

And what a fresh breath I encountered there! All people are welcome; there is no controversy over which church has the correct teachings. Never did I hear words of sin and guilt. Happy people come together for learning and growing in spirituality. I imagine it is like the early Christian communities known for their joy and love. Messages of God and Jesus are centered on ways to live in todays' troublesome times. They are uplifting. They speak of peace. They provide comfort.

Coming from that broad perspective of spirituality, it saddened me when my readings brought me to conflicting times surrounding the early centuries of Christians condemning other Christians. As a young person I was aware of terms like blasphemy and heresy; I was unaware of the many early groups called Christian *who found they had no place in the ongoing Christian community. Yet, I draw a sense of well-being from the many new experiences I've discovered about life, primarily—Good overcomes Evil.*

Related Vocabulary

Looking at the development of the Christian Church, a distinct vocabulary is listed below as a quick reference. The Glossary is an additional resource.

Aeon: Divine being, emanating from God
arcane: secret, mysterious, known only to the initiate

blasphemy: a contemptuous, disgraceful or profane act, concerning God - also, the act of claiming for oneself the attributes and rights of God

catholic: (small c) universal,

Catholic: (capital C) Catholic Christian Church

codex: book written on papyrus bound with leather

codices-plural

content: topics contained in written work

context: meaning of words or concepts contained within specific writings

Coptic: Afro-Asiatic language descended from ancient Egypt (translation of Greek [Gnostic]texts into an Egyptian dialect)

demiurge: creator of the physical universe, so named by Platonists, plus other philosophical and religious movement in Antiquity

Docetism: belief that Jesus only seemed to have a human body and to suffer on the cross

dogma: doctrines authoritatively considered absolute truth

doctrine: something taught, principles presented for acceptance or belief (religious-political-scientific-philosophic)

dualism: The concept of dualism may be older than recorded history, though the term was first used in 1700 CE to describe religious systems believing in God and the devil. There are varying levels of dualism in most all faiths past and present. Generally, it centers around two opposing principles of good and evil. One form of dualism views the forces of good and evil as equal; another places *good* as the primary principle with *evil* as a secondary. These principles are extended to concepts like: body and soul, light and dark, material and spiritual, God and Satan.

esoteric: teachings for only a few who have special knowledge or interest, secret, private

exegesis: interpretation of a passage of Scripture through careful and rigorous textual and theological analysis

Gnostics: from Greek *gnosis* meaning knowledge - individuals seeking spiritual and intellectual knowledge based on intuition and perception   Gnostic groups are noted in the second century, current era. However, they existed before and continue to present time.

heretic: from Greek meaning *to choose for one's self* The dictionary defines *heretic* as a person holding controversial opinions, especially one who publicly dissents from the official accepted dogma of the Roman Catholic Church.

heresy: an opinion or doctrine at variance with established religious beliefs, especially dissension from or denial of Roman Catholic dogma by a professed believer or baptized church member

logos: Greek meaning *speech, word, reason* - Divine wisdom manifested in the creation of the world; plus, the word of God in creative power and manifested as Jesus in the world

martyr: individual choosing death rather than renouncing religious principles

martyrdom: suffering death for one's religious faith

metaphysical: immaterial, supernatural, excessively subtle, over and above the physical world

Neoplatonism: modification of Platonism (Plato) in Antiquity, to coincide with eastern concepts of the world as formed from an indivisible being with whom the soul is capable of being reunited in trance or ecstasy

orthodox (small *o*): prefix *ortho* from Greek *orthos,* straight, correct, right, identifies acceptance of traditional and established faith or religion

Orthodox (capital O): specific religious establishments – Catholic Churches adhering to doctrine of the early Roman bishops of Rome, Alexandria, Constantinople, or Antioch (Syria), present Eastern Orthodox Church and Orthodox Judaism

papyrus: paper made from papyrus reeds, used in Antiquity

sect: group adhering to a distinctive doctrine or a leader

secular: worldly, not belonging to a religious order

Early Centuries CE

Times leading up to the crucifixion of Jesus saw growing conflicts between Jews and Romans in Judea, the birthplace of Christianity. There was little peace among the various factions of Jews and growing clashes with Rome created a volatile situation. The Romans continued to be a force both Christians and Jews faced. More religious groups appeared based on the teachings of Jesus. Some were rejected. Before long, a shift occurred between Jews and Christians. All these issues blend together in providing a broader picture of the ongoing influence of biblical times. The following breakdown of early Christianity covers the people and places through that time, including the eventual decisions on which Christian writings qualified as Scripture. Some references have previously been mentioned; additional information on others is included in upcoming chapters.

First Century 0-99

Scholars generally agree that Jesus' death occurred about the year 30. As covered in the Acts of the Apostles, instructions for the disciples came at the Pentecostal Feast, fifty days after the crucifixion. The disciple Peter became spokesman for the twelve; Matthias took Judas' place. At that time, disciples became Apostles. Many Jews, like Peter, still spoke the Aramaic language; Peter's words drew other Jews to the new faith. Later, Greek speaking Paul became an Apostle and was instrumental in converting Gentiles to the ways of Jesus. In time, *Christ* was added to the name *Jesus* and his believers became *Christians*. Christ communities led to Christian Churches. Acts 4:32-35 describes the communities as believers united in heart and soul. No individual held possessions; everything was shared with the group. Provisions were given to any in need.

In the early years of Christianity, growth was slow; yet, a steady increase took place. Individuals told friends and family about the peace and joy they found in knowing of Jesus and his deeds. Scholars feel that by the year 60, there were about 2,000 people living in Christian communities, equally divided between Judea and the rest of the Roman Empire.

The increase of Christians, in Rome, led to their persecution. Roman historian **Suetonius** (75-130) wrote of Emperor **Claudius** (41-54) banning Christians from Rome. Suetonius indicates that Jews caused disturbances with Christians. It is thought that the communities consisted of many Jewish Christians, Jews wanting to integrate the teachings of Jesus with their traditional beliefs. They were expelled with the Christians. Still, Christian communities continued. Suetonius also wrote of Emperor **Nero's** torture of Christians which increased after Rome's devastating fire in 64. Nero blamed Christians for that fire. Jews, also felt the wrath of Nero.

A few years after the fire, Jewish Zealots set out to eliminate Roman rule (detailed in Chapter 5). First, they overthrew the priestly aristocracy in Jerusalem, those who sought to maintain peace with the Romans. Then the Zealots instigated a rebellion against Rome. **Titus**, son of Emperor **Vespasian**, in 70 completely destroyed Jerusalem and the Second Temple; Jews were expelled from Jerusalem. It is not known how long that restriction lasted. The final Jewish stronghold at Masada fell to Rome three years later. Rome made Judea a providence with a Roman official as ruler. Christians, too, were affected by Rome's actions. James, leader of the Jerusalem Church; Peter, spokesman for the Jews; and Paul, a voice for Gentiles; had been put to death. Many Christians wanted to separate themselves from the Jews.

The growth of Christianity saw various factions; all claiming they alone were based on the *truth* of Jesus. No formal organization of a church existed. Regardless of the diversity, the belief of God and Jesus was the predominate focus. A few of the communities are identified as follows. The Jerusalem Church of Jewish Christians wanted the Hebrew Scriptures honored with the addition of Jesus' teachings. Gentile churches reflected the vision of Jesus portrayed by the Apostle Paul. A group called *Gnostics* believed the knowledge of God and Jesus came through inner transformation. Across the Roman Empire, the wide range of Christian communities began denouncing one another as frauds. In addition to conflicts over beliefs, communities loosely using the name *church*, became divided over the role of leadership.

Clement of Rome (ca 90-100) became spokesman for the Christian Church in Rome. A letter attributed to him declares God as ruler of all things on earth. Clement went on to delegate authority of the church to bishops, priests, and deacons, with the warning that whoever disobeyed the Divinely ordained guidance was subjected to death as heretics.

Through that first century, Paul's letters, along with other letters, and the Gospels: Matthew, Mark, John, were written. The writings, bound together, became a *codex*. Scrolls were no longer used. Christians, in their worship, turned to those writings along with the Greek version of the Hebrew Bible. Also, during that time, the Hebrew Kethuvim (Writings) had been declared Scripture, completing the Hebrew Bible.

By the end the first century, Christianity had increased dramatically, with communities in Judea, Samaria, Galilee, Greece, Italy, and it probably had spread to Syria, Turkey, Spain, Egypt, and Northern Africa.

Second Century 100-199

Through the second century, Christian communities continued to grow. There was no formal church organization so the diversity seen in the first century remained. In many cases local leaders governed the churches; however, the position of a bishop as the authoritative voice gained acceptance. By 120, the documents named Luke and Acts along with other letters, later classified as Scripture, were among the writings shaping the churches. The second letter of Peter appeared a short time later.

At that time, Judaism was a tolerated religion in the Roman Empire; Christianity was not. During most of the second century, Rome continued its persecution of Christians. Some emperors were more lenient than others. **Pliny the Younger** (ca 112), governor of a Roman province in Turkey and a noted author, collected and published some of Paul's letters. Nevertheless, he executed Christians refusing to worship Roman gods in the same manner as the Christian God. Emperor **Trajan** (98-117) approved the action.

A generation after Clement of Rome, Bishop **Ignatius** in Syria, upheld Clement's mandate of one bishop as leader of a church which the congregation must honor as if he were taking the place of God. Ignatius extended the hierarchy of the church with priests under the bishop and deacons under priests. Ignatius added: *only through the Church could humanity access God.*

Under Trajan's reign, Roman officials condemned Ignatius to death on the evidence that his statements regarding God were treasonous against Rome. In a letter to the Christians of Rome, Ignatius asked them to not interfere on his behalf as he was willing to die for God.

Before long, other Christians adopted martyrdom to proclaim their faith in God as revealed by Jesus. During the first century, Jews and Christians viewed the Greek definition of *martyr* as *witness*, one willing to *speak up* for their beliefs. In the second century, Christians adopted the name *martyr* to identify those willing to die for their beliefs. In the Roman world, affirming allegiance to other than Rome was considered treason with the penalty of death. Individuals speaking against the penalty could also face the same consequences. Christians looked up to those willing to *speak up as witnesses*; however, the term *martyr* identified only ones who actually endured death. Not all Christians believed in martyrdom; some felt it went against God's will. On the other hand, many Christians saw martyrdom as an assurance of salvation. Also, seeing the deep faith of those facing death, other individuals joined the Christian movement.

Returning to Judaism, following the destruction of the Second Temple, the number of Jews living outside of Judea greatly increased. Their dedication to the Jews remaining in their homeland often clashed with Roman authorities. Between 115 and 117 Rome crushed Jewish revolts in major centers outside of Judea. Synagogues were destroyed along with several Jewish towns in Judea. The violence led to one more Jewish Revolt against Rome.

Simon Bar Kokhba believed his rebellion (132-135) would eliminate all Romans from Judea (detailed in Chapter 5). That proved fatal for the Jews. After Roman Emperor **Hadrian's** victory, he demolished Jerusalem and built a new city on the ruins which he named *Aelia Capitolina*; Judea became *Palestinae*. Once again, Jews were exiled from Jerusalem and all of Judea. Emperor **Pius** (138-161) reinstated the practice of the Jewish religion; they could return to Judea but not Jerusalem.

Meanwhile, more Christians became martyrs and diversity of churches continued. About 140, **Marcion**, a successful shipowner in Turkey, moved to Rome in hopes of spreading his beliefs regarding God and Jesus. Marcion took with him a version of the Gospel of Luke plus ten of Paul's letters. From his understanding of the Apostle Paul, Marcion created a large following of Christians. Marcion sought to make a complete break between Christianity and Judaism based on his belief of two Gods: God of the Hebrew Scriptures and God of Jesus. The Church of Rome condemned and excommunicated Marcion as a heretic; his church continued into the next century.

Close in time, **Justin** (ca 100-165), a Samarian philosopher, converted to Christianity after witnessing martyrdom. He wrote to Emperors Pius and Aurelius (father and son) protesting the treatment of Christians. Later (ca 150-155), Justin was tried and condemned by the Romans then killed along with many of his students.

Around the time of Justin's death, Bishop **Polycarp** in Turkey, was arrested and burned alive in a public arena. **Ireanaeus** (ca 130-202), a student of Polycarp and Bishop of Lyons (France), went on to influence the organization of the Christian Church.

A differing view of Christianity came from **Clement of Alexandria** (Egypt), a teacher at the first major Christian school of higher learning. He preserved many fragments of otherwise unknown gospels. He knew Gnostics, was familiar with their documents, and accepted many of their beliefs. About 180, Clement wrote that some elements of the Gnostics could be adapted to the ever-growing Christian Church. Like the Gnostics, Clement saw both the masculine and feminine in God. He insisted men and women *share equally in perfection* and both should participate in the church. Clement's views, formed in the cosmopolitan atmosphere of Alexandria, found little agreement elsewhere. Instead, Tertullian's vision of total male church leadership prevailed.

Tertullian (ca 190) of Carthage (Northern Africa), noted as a brilliant theologian and writer, defined the Church's position as *Jesus resurrected in the flesh.* He did not mention immortality of the soul as he thought most following the faith of Jesus accepted that philosophy. Tertullian declared anyone denying the resurrection *of the flesh* was a heretic, not a Christian. He denounced the Gnostics who had differing views of the resurrection.

Tertullian, like Irenaeus, felt martyrdom led to complete forgiveness of sins and ensured salvation. Though, both thought the fear of persecution caused some people to look for other ways to be Christian. Both men shared the same belief of bodily resurrection and Tertullian agreed with Irenaeus' decision as to which Christian documents could be considered Scripture. Tertullian gave the writings the name *New Testament*. However, total agreement and authorization of the writings came years later.

Nearing the end of the second century, the variety of churches claiming to follow the true ways of Jesus created confusion and conflicts. Irenaeus, and those like him who endorsed the positions of bishops, priests, and deacons, insisted there could be only one church. A church based on the belief of the bodily resurrection of Jesus. Those outside the church would not be saved. Members of the one church must be orthodox (straight-thinkers) and be in agreement with the framework set up by Irenaeus and his friends. In addition, the church had to be *catholic* (universal). All other forms of teachings about Jesus were denounced as heresy. Irenaeus, about 180, wrote five volumes denouncing any and all beliefs not considered orthodox.

At the end of his life, Tertullian broke with the orthodox community and joined the Montanist movement called *new prophecy,* inspired by the Holy Spirit. Irenaeus remained faithful to the Christian Church he was instrumental in organizing.

Third Century 200-299

By the third century, Christians generally accepted the Gospels, Acts, most of Paul's letters, and some general letters as Scripture. During the third century the debate over other documents continued.

After their defeat at the hands of the Romans, in 135, Jews, settled into a non-threating self-government based on their religious laws. By 200, they had developed successful enterprises and Rome realized the empire would benefit from Jewish achievements. Rome loosely granted the Jews religious freedom, allowed them some control over their businesses and excused them from military service.

Jews became Roman citizens in 212 when Emperor **Caracalla** gave that distinction to all non-slave subjects of the empire. Jewish prosperity increased with the change. Jews traveled freely, increased their trade across the land and new educational opportunities brought greater professional advancement. Rome failed to extend its favors to Christians.

Within Christian communities, disagreements between orthodox Christians and others calling themselves Christians endured, despite the danger of heresy. **Plotinus** (205-270), a Neoplatonic philosopher, had an interest in different religions of the Roman Empire including the orthodox Catholic Church and Gnostic Christians. However, Plotinus began attacking Gnostics when many of his students turned to Gnosticism. He felt the foundation of *seeking God within* lacked instruction for gaining inner knowledge.

Hippolytus (170-236), a student of Irenaeus, became a teacher in Rome. He matched Irenaeus and Tertullian's admiration for martyrs and opposition to heresy. In his early teaching, Hippolytus believed that bishops of the orthodox Christian Church were the only ones shown the *truth* and in 230 he condemned all in opposition to the voice of the bishops. However, a short time later, Hippolytus objected to the election of a bishop in his own church. The bishop was respected as a teacher and witness to

Christianity, as he had faced imprisonment and torture by the Romans. Hippolytus publicly attacked the bishop's integrity, citing dishonest conduct. The majority of orthodox Christians did not believe Hippolytus, who then turned away from the church and denounced the official hierarchy. In 235, Hippolytus was arrested on orders of the emperor and was deported to an island region of Italy where he died.

Origen (ca 185-254), some thought the most brilliant theologian of the third century, interpreted passages in the Hebrew Bible in a way that turned the action into personal messages. For instance, Origen, like most of the other early church writers, spoke against all warfare. He explained killings of enemies (Joshua 15:3) as eliminating individual vices. Origen came under suspicion of heresy in his declaration that God offered salvation to all; he went on to say church teachings must be simple and offered to the common people. In addition, Origen spoke about numerous Christians holding differences of opinion on important matters.

While diversity among Christians continued, Rome was battling external threats. With its empire of vast roads, expansive cities, advanced water systems, and more—a triumph of civilization—Rome faced uncertain times. Armed rebels and mass numbers of barbarians were crossing into the Roman Empire. Trying to maintain their long-held realm, Romans returned to their ancient gods. In so doing, individuals and groups exhibiting anti-Roman behavior came under threat of treason. Emperor **Decius** (249-251) escalated the persecution of Christians.

In 260, **Gallienus** became emperor of an ever-diminishing realm. As the influence of outside forces increased, Gallienus led a revival of Roman arts, poetry, philosophy and literature to unite the Romans and preserve the Roman Civilization. A year later, he issued the first Decree of Toleration, making Christianity an officially recognized religion which then had tremendous growth for about twenty years.

In an effort to control invaders, Rome reorganized its empire. In 284, Emperor **Diocletian** realized that additional rulers were necessary to control the empire and he set up a system of shared power. Two emperors, each with a subordinate, ruled over two different sections of the empire. Italy's city of Milan, where Latin was the dominate language, became headquarters for the western region. The eastern region, largely influenced by Hellenistic culture, had Greek headquarters a few miles from the city of Byzantium. As senior emperor, Diocletian renewed the persecution of Christians. Churches were destroyed, Christian worship was forbidden, many church leaders lost their lives; numerous Christians left Palestine. Diocletian gave the empire a reprieve; survival of Christianity was questionable.

As the third century ended, Christianity saw little unity amid Roman hostility. Rome struggled with outside enemies and a reduced empire. Jews maintained their traditional ways, throughout many lands. The fourth century saw a major shift.

Fourth Century 300-399

Developments of the third century left the Roman Empire divided between the eastern and western regions while confusion over unofficial and official Christian writings continued. A bishop in Palestine, **Eusebius**, the first church historian wrote of those times. Born around 260, his writings cover the first Christian communities and extend through the time of Constantine. Eusebius died before 341.

By 305, Emperor Diocletian knew his continual persecution of Christians would not abolish that faith. He stepped down from office; his joint senior emperor did likewise. Junior emperors became senior emperors, leaving space for additional subordinates. Wars broke out as contenders fought for the positions.

A young man named **Constantine** joined his father in battle; the father died in 306 and his army declared Constantine emperor. Battles continued. In 312, Constantine had a vision of a bright cross in the sky. The next day, Constantine's troops defeated the opposing forces. Constantine believed the Christian God gave him the victory. The following year, Emperor Constantine issued the Edict of Milan, reaffirming the Decree of Toleration given by Gallienus in 261. In addition, Constantine legalized Christianity. Christians moved back to Palestine and property previously claimed by Rome was returned. In 324, Constantine defeated his one remaining contender and became the sole emperor of both the east and west regions of the Roman Empire.

In Alexandria (Egypt), the question of Jesus' relationship to God created a division among Christians. Theologian **Arius** spoke of Jesus as the son of God but *not the same substance* as God. Bishop **Athanasius** believed Jesus was the son of God *and the same substance.* To settle the matter, in 325 Constantine called close to 300 bishops to meet in Nicaea (Turkey) and come to some agreement. Athanasius' view was accepted. The wording of the Nicaea Creed remains: *We believe in one God the Father. . . and in Jesus Christ, one in being with the Father.* Arius with two bishops refused to accept the Creed and were exiled by Constantine. Also, a decree warned anyone possessing a book by Arius would face the penalty of death. Eusebius took the side of Arius.

Though condemned as a heretic, Arius continued his preaching and converted many followers to Christianity. Seeing that public opinion favored Arius, Constantine reversed his position and condemned Athanasius. However, Constantine again changed his mind and supported Athanasius, denouncing Arius once more. Arius started his own church with the backing of fellow

Alexandrians who convinced Constantine into yet another reversal. Athanasius was sent into exile, leaving Christians in Alexandria confused over who and what to believe. Arius died a short time later.

In exile, Athanasius continued to influence Christianity. By 367 he compiled a listing of Christian documents essential to the Christian faith and believed to be Scripture. Athanasius' twenty-seven books replaced those compiled by Eusebius earlier in the century. Athanasius then condemned all other Christian documents as heresy. Many scholars today feel it was at that time the Gnostics of Egypt hid their writings which were discovered in 1945.

Even before Constantine's time, the city of Rome ceased to be a practical capital, as the empire extended far to the east. When Constantine became emperor, he wanted a new capital to give the weakened Roman Empire a fresh beginning. He chose Byzantium, a simple Greek colony half way between Rome's eastern and western frontiers. Byzantium, with water on three sides, was suitable for trade between the Mediterranean and the Black Sea; plus, its seven hills reminded Constantine of the city of Rome. The project took six years, completed and dedicated to God in 330. Constantine named his new city, *Nova Rome,* which soon took the name Constantinople, a tribute to the builder. Byzantium became the capital for Christianity and the new Byzantine Empire.

Seven years later, Constantine returned to his dream of enlarging his domain; he gathered troops and set out to conquer Persia. However, his dream was short lived. At Helenopolis, a city named for his mother, Constantine became ill. He realized he would not recover and asked Bishop Eusebius to baptize him into the Christian faith. After his death, the demise of the old Roman Empire became obvious; the Greek Christian culture in the east was advancing. Before long, the Roman Empire became known as the Byzantine Empire.

Despite Constantine's ability to maintain political and religious peace, at times his actions were less than honorable. He became jealous of his oldest son who was extremely popular with the citizens. Constantine ordered the son's execution on suspicion he seduced his stepmother. Constantine then killed the stepmother.

Still, few rulers impacted history to the degree of Constantine. He became emperor when both the Roman Empire and Christianity were floundering. Constantine's acceptance of the Christian faith permanently altered the culture and social life of the empire. Byzantium became a center of advanced learning, offering civilization a new way of being.

Constantine's mother, **Helena**, was a Christian and brought about change in her own way. She was the first to make a pilgrimage to the Holy Land (Palestine). She started hostels and hospitals along the way that remained for future generations. Helena built the Church of the Nativity in Bethlehem and the Church of the Holy Sepulcher in Jerusalem. She is credited with finding the cross used in Jesus' crucifixion.

Following Constantine's death, the empire was divided between his three living sons, all with a variation of the name *Constantine*. Each received the title of *emperor*. Fighting between the brothers resulted in a civil war. After his brothers were killed in battle, **Constantius II**, as the only remaining emperor, needed help to maintain the empire. Dealing with barbarian intrusions and Persia's aggressiveness required greater force than one person could handle. Constantius II called on his only remaining relative, **Julian** to help.

Julian had declared himself a Christian and spent his youth studying Greek and Roman classics. Later he traveled abroad seeking out philosophers in hopes of learning about the disappearing Roman world. In time, Julian secretly replaced Christianity with Neoplatonism. Julian was not trained in warfare and gave no thought to becoming an emperor; however, he could not ignore his uncle's request. Surprisingly, Julian became a brilliant general and as his success continued, he publicly stated his intentions to restore paganism in the empire. In 361, after naming Julian his successor Constantius II died. Julian's rejection of Christianity and his return to paganism gave him the name *Julian the Apostate.*

Upheaval caused by wars of Constantine's three sons left a decaying empire for Julian. He believed Christianity was at the heart of the downfall and proceeded to return paganism to the realm. In so doing, he lifted the ban on paganism, placed by Constantine years before, and allowed Jews to return to Jerusalem. Nevertheless, Julian soon realized that paganism had lost its hold. Thinking victory against Persia would destroy Christianity, Julian traveled to Antioch (Syria) to plan his strategy. While in Antioch, he continued his efforts to restore paganism there and again was unsuccessful.

In 363 Julian's army entered Persia. Retreating from an unsuccessful attempt at claiming the capital, the enemy made a surprise attack in which Julian was killed. The early years of the Byzantine Empire, the time of Julian's youth, were gone. In the change, the empire, with its preservation of Roman classical works of literature, philosophy and scientific texts, became a world power.

Following Julian, a number of emperors with questionable ability tried to control the influx of barbaric invaders. Armies in the east and west were declaring their generals *emperors* at an alarming rate. Then, in 379, **Theodosius** was named emperor and given the task of restoring order to the eastern half of the empire. Relying on his strong military background, by 382, Theodosius prevented the collapse of the eastern realm, though the west saw no recovery.

Within a short time, Theodosius became ill. Wanting to enter into judgement with his sins forgiven, he asked to be baptized into the Christian faith. Theodosius' recovery left him a changed man. He had stabilized worldly issues; saved from death, he felt it his duty to do the same with spiritual concerns.

The Arian heresy still divided Christians. Some bishops endorsed the Nicaea Creed while others upheld Arius' opinion concerning the nature of Jesus. Theodosius asked a council of bishops to condemn Arians. The bishops complied and gave Theodosius sanction to persecute heresy. Arians were forced to give up their churches, scattering the congregations.

Next, Theodosius set out to eradicate paganism. Though he lacked total success, the prohibited worship ceased being a threat. In 391, Theodosius declared Christianity to be the only religion of the Roman Empire. On Theodosius's death four years later, his son Arcadius became emperor.

Late in the fourth century, the Christian theologian **Jerome** (345-420) began translating the Hebrew and Christian Scriptures into the Latin language. On completion, the two were placed together in one book with the name: Vulgate Bible, a Bible for the common people. Half of the Roman-Byzantine Empire called themselves Christians.

The growing numbers of Christians also increased the condemnation of groups, and their writings, not considered orthodox. **Epiphanius**, of the ancient city of Cyprus, about 380 wrote *Panarion* in which he summarized 80 groups and denounced each one.

The rise of Christianity impacted the Jews. Jerusalem, the home of King David and King Solomon and the Jewish capital of Judea, became the Christian Holy Land. During the reign of

Emperor Constantius II (337-361), Jews were denied the right to own slaves and Jewish men were forbidden to marry Christian women. Jewish communities were taxed heavier than Christian neighbors, leaving countless Jewish settlements in poverty. In 352, Jews, with support from Samaritans, revolted. In suppressing the revolt, many thousands of Jews and Samaritans were killed. In later years, the situation worsened to the point Jews moved away from the influence of the empire. In spite of their troubled times, in 390 the Jewish Mishnah, a written commentary of oral traditions, was completed and the Jewish calendar was formulated.

Looking Forward

The fifth century of Christianity saw fewer and fewer non-orthodox Christian movements. When condemned as heretics, they scattered or surrendered their beliefs. Orthodox Christianity was the only authorized religion of the Roman-Byzantine Empire. Yet, the Christian Church did not free itself from future struggles.

The final defeat of the Western Roman Empire came in 476. Rome remained the capital for the Christian Catholic Church in the west, with theology based on Roman law. The eastern Greek Orthodox Catholic Church had its roots in Greek philosophy. Differences between the two theologies created misunderstandings on issues related to doctrine.

After years of conflict with the Byzantine Empire, Persia, in 614, successfully took Palestine then Jerusalem. Christian buildings were destroyed and more than 65,000 Christians were killed. Survivors were exiled. Control of Jerusalem was given to the Jews, which was short lived with changes brought about with the **Islamic Muslims**. The final fall of the Byzantine Empire came in 1453 at the hands of the Ottoman Turks (Muslims).

Jews, Christians, and Muslims, overcame all obstacles; their faiths have endured into the twenty-first century.

Rejected Beliefs

With the rise of Christianity, a wide variety of groups taking the name *Christian*, emerged across the Roman Empire. Numerous groups developed beliefs and practices having little in common with the Christian Church that survived. Until recently, the long-forgotten movements received almost no attention aside from academic settings. Discoveries of hidden scrolls in the Dead Sea area of Israel (Judea) and Gnostic texts of northern Egypt have created stronger interest for the general public. Though biblical scholars have substantial knowledge of rejected beliefs, reviewing just a few provides some insight into the struggles faced in early Christianity. Following is a brief account of groups receiving current attention.

Jewish Christians

At the beginning of Christianity, Jews who followed the Law of Moses plus the teachings of Jesus were named *Jewish Christians*. They looked on Jesus as a true prophet that would lead people to a simple and nonviolent way of life. Jewish Christians emphasized Jewish Law to a greater degree than traditional Jews while applying Jesus' teachings to their own life. Some Jews of that time replaced their long held religious life with Christianity. Those individuals were not considered Jewish Christians. Paul, a Jew, rejected the Law of Moses and became a Christian. He is credited with the growth of the Gentile Christian movement.

Jewish Christians felt Jesus, a Jew, never intended to create a religion apart from Judaism. Gentile Christians did not think of themselves as Jews. This difference created divisions within the disciples and other Jews. Conflicts between the two groups are recorded in the New Testament. In Acts, Chapters 11, 15, and 21, questions dealing with the Law of Moses, specifically regarding circumcision and food, point to the early differences between Christians and Jews. Galatians 2:6-8 refers to Paul being entrusted with teaching of Jesus to Gentiles and Peter giving the message to Jews. The term *Jewish Christians* is used in those documents.

Various groups of Jewish Christians existed roughly four hundred years after the death of Jesus. Eventually, both Jews and Christians condemned Jewish Christians.

Much of the information about Jewish Christians comes from two early Christian writers, Clement of Rome (ca 90-100) and Epiphanius (380). Clement's *Recognitions of Clements* and *Clementine Homilies* are the only sizable surviving documents containing Jewish Christian writings. The writings are attributed to Clement of Rome; however, scholars generally date those writings to the third century so question Clement's authorship. The two books contain descriptions of Jewish Christianity found in Epiphanius' *Panarion*. Epiphanius describes a number of Jewish Christian groups and is considered the most knowledgeable regarding that form of Christianity. Epiphanius personally interviewed individual Jewish Christians and includes quotes from their literature. The Ebionites, mentioned more than any other, are cited as the most important of the later Jewish Christian era. Others mentioned are Ossaeans, Elchasaites, Nazoraeans, and Nasaraeans. All had similar beliefs.

Ebionites, the Hebrew term meaning *the poor,* thought of Jesus as the *True Prophet* predicted by Moses in Deuteronomy 18:15-18. Ebionites, like other Jewish Christians, believed in simple living, were pacifists, and vegetarians. They focused on Jesus' sayings and actions from sources other than those found in the New Testament. They also practiced the Jewish Law.

During the fifth century, Jewish Christianity disappeared. Islam, a religion based on messages from God to Mohammed, emerged early in the seventh century. There appears to be some similarities between Ebionite and Islamic beliefs. There is no mention of Ebionites or Jewish Christianity in early Islamic writings; however, there is evidence of Ebionite ideas in the Islamic faith. Trends of Sufism, generally considered a form of Islamic mysticism, are closely related to those of the Ebionites. Total devotion to God and living in poverty are two likenesses. The Sufis have sayings and stories of Jesus not found in Christian documents. al-Ghazali, an eleventh century Islamic mystic, wrote of Jesus in his book, *The Precious Pearl*. It might be that Jesus' teachings, and many Ebionite beliefs, were incorporated into Islam.

Gnosticism   Nag Hammadi Discovery

Twentieth century findings confirm and enlarge the knowledge of Gnostics of early Christianity. They saw themselves as seekers of greater intellectual and spiritual insight than ordinary people. The basis of Gnostic belief existed eons ago—and today—it is still witnessed.

By the middle of the second century, a growing movement calling themselves *Christians*, was given the name *gnosis*, from the Greek word meaning *knowledge obtained from insight or intuition*. There were various forms of gnosis; some held common elements while most differed. Generally, gnosis represented the belief of two Gods: the spiritual and *true* creator God and a lesser god of the physical world. According to the gnosis, in gaining spiritual knowledge, the physical world had to be overcome.

The belief of two Gods, or dualism, is based on the principal of good and evil, held by various religions past and present. Another principle of those second century gnosis dealt with Jesus' secret knowledge. The New Testament books of Matthew and Mark speak of Jesus teaching in parables to large public gatherings while he gave secret wisdom to his disciples. In turn, the disciples privately shared the wisdom with highly spiritual individuals, who again were cautioned to maintain secrecy. Often, individuals seeking or achieving inner knowledge connected to secret teachings of Jesus, joined a gnosis group. In the eighteenth century, the term was changed to *Gnostics*.

Before the discovery of texts in the twentieth century, the only knowledge regarding gnosis came from writers of early Christian centuries. In the beginning, a number of Christian groups received Gnostics rather well; later came the condemnations.

Clement of Alexandria (ca 150-215), an Egyptian Christian theologian, referred to the groups as *true gnosis*, as they were searching for understanding of the Christian life. It appears that some Gnostic groups, distancing themselves from Rome, found greater acceptance in Egypt. Other Christian writers opposing Gnosticism are: Irenaeus (second century), Tertullian (second century), Hippolytus (second century) and Epiphanius (fourth century). Plotinus (third century), a non-Christian philosopher, also, spoke against Gnosticism. The discovery in Egypt of the long-lost Gnostic texts provide direct information from the Gnostics themselves.

The ancient manuscripts were found by Muhammad 'Alī al-Sammān in 1945, near Nag Hammadi. Caves, used as grave sites more than 4000 years ago, are still visible. It was there that Muhammad 'Alī found an earthen ware jar containing thirteen papyrus books, bound in leather. The find consisted of fifty-two previously unknown texts from the early Christian centuries. The manuscripts are Coptic translations made about fifteen hundred years ago from the original Greek to an Egyptian dialect. Though the manuscripts offer only a glimpse of the complexity of the early Christian movement, they add a great deal to the present day understanding of Gnosticism. As previously mentioned, it is thought, in the fourth century when the orthodox Catholic Church condemned all writings other than their approved list, Gnostics hid their writings.

With no knowledge of the importance of the find, Muhammad 'Alī left some of the pages near the oven and his mother used them as kindling. A short time later, Muhammad 'Alī and his brother killed the man responsible for their father's death. Fearful that police would come to the house and see the remaining texts, Muhammad 'Alī took some to a priest for safe keeping. The priest gave one to a history teacher who sent it to a friend in Cairo to find its value. By then, selling of the manuscripts caught the attention of officials of the Egyptian government. They bought one book and confiscated ten and a half of the others, placing them in the Coptic Museum in Cairo. The Jung Foundation in Zürich purchased one of the books that had been smuggled out of Egypt and offered for sale in the United States.

What remained from the find are roughly fifty-two varied texts dealing with myths, instructions for mystical practices, poems, a metaphysical explanation of the universe's origin, and secret unknown gospels. Some titles are: Gospel of Thomas, Gospel of Phillip, Gospel of Truth, and Gospel to the Egyptians. Other writings attributed to Jesus' followers are: Secret Book of James, Apocalypse of Paul, Letter of Peter to Phillip, and Apocalypse of Peter. The context of the writings differs from those documents selected for the New Testament.

Scholars agree that the texts from Nag Hammadi, and others like them, circulated across the Roman Empire as Christianity was taking shape. By 180, Gnostic writings were targeted as heresy, yet, dating the original texts is unclear. Generally, between 120-150 seems a possible date. Though, the Gospel of Thomas could have been compiled about 140, as traditions included may be older than the New Testament. The papyrus, bindings, and Coptic script date the copies between 350-400.

In the translations of the Nag Hammadi texts, two Gnostic groups mentioned repeatedly are Sethians and Valentinians. Also documented are the less well-known Carpocratians, who adopted questionable ways with their practice of Gnosticism. Following is additional information regarding those three groups.

Valentinians

Valentinus (ca 100-175 CE) founder of the Valentinian school, attended schools in Alexandria, the primary center for philosophical, scientific, religious, and literary study of the ancient world. The Valentinians regarded themselves as Christians but felt they alone had the knowledge to interpret Scriptures needed in finding union with God. They were like professors of theology—educated and self-confident. Valentinians had little regard for others in the many religious movements of that time. Major Valentinian texts from Nag Hammadi are:

The Gospel of Truth
The Gospel of Philip
The Treatise on the Resurrection
The Exegesis on the Soul
A Valentinian Exposition

Sethians

The Sethians, named for the third son of Adam, incorporated aspects of other religions in combining and refining their knowledge. Of all Gnostic groups, the Sethians had the clearest sense of what constituted true knowledge. Deeper insight into their beliefs is found in their Sethian texts from Nag Hammadi, listed below. Translator, James M. Robinson provides a brief description of the titles.

Allogenes {stranger}
The Apocalypse of Adam {end of times}
The Apocryphon of John {unauthorized/secret writing}
Eugnostos the Blessed {person's name}
The Gospel of the Egyptians {mystical prayers}
The Hypostasis of the Archons {foundation/reality of Greek rulers}
Hypsiphrone {high minded person}
Marsanes {name of Gnostic prophet known from two other sources}
Melchizedek {person's name}
On the Origin of the World {unlike the Hebrew Bible}
The Thought of Norea {person's name}
The Three Steles of Seth {hymnic prayers}
The Thunder: Perfect Mind {revelation discourse by a woman}
The Trimorphic Protennoia {three forms of (name)}
Zostrianos {person's name linked to Persian Zoroaster}

Carpocratians and the Secret Gospel of Mark

Early Christian writers, Epiphanius and Irenaeus, spoke against the Carpocratians who believed every part of life must be experienced before they could transcend the material world. They understood good and evil as conditions labeled by humans, not God. The fragmented, Secret Gospel of Mark, with a letter written by Clement of Alexandria contain some controversial practices of the Carpocratians. The two sources provide documentation of the Carpocratians which held leanings of a Gnostic nature. The letter was discovered by Morton Smith, in 1958, at the Judean desert Monastery of Mar Saba.

The handwritten copy of Clement's letter condemns Carpocratians' practices. The letter was sent to a person named Theodore, unknown by historians. In the letter, reference is made to an edition of the Gospel of Mark written as *a spiritual gospel to be used by those people seeking perfection*, known today as the Secret Gospel of Mark. Also, Clement pointed out that Mark wrote one Gospel for *beginners in the faith,* plus the other more spiritual Gospel *for those being perfected in the faith*. Clement went on to say that *Mark knew of additional, arcane traditions—which he did not write down—which lead initiates into the "innermost sanctuary" of the truth*. The Secret Gospel of Mark alludes to this knowledge.

****

Gnostic groups of the early centuries of Christianity were silenced before the fifth century, yet, their voices are still heard. Today, all seekers of knowledge have documents available for guidance in deeper understanding of the physical and spiritual world. Though manuscripts were buried, ideals contained in those writings could not be hidden.

With the help of the Internet, information on groups and

events with a Gnostic foundation is just a click away. Various churches offer services structured around a distinct Gnostic calling. Ritual practices, study groups, and informal fellowship gatherings provide occasions for enlightenment. Some opportunities for learning are found apart from a specific religious content. Groups meet in homes or spaces provided for routine gatherings.

The Institute of Noetic Science is a worldwide nonprofit organization dedicated to the connection between observable facts and inner knowledge. The organization was founded by former astronaut Edgar Mitchell in 1973 after observing the World on his return from outer space. Mitchell saw the Divine presence in the creation of the universe and realized science alone did not hold answers to the complexity of reality.

Research by the institution includes meditation, consciousness, spirituality, psychic abilities and life after death. The word *noetic* comes from the Greek word *nous*, referring to inner knowing— direct and immediate access to knowledge beyond what is available to normal senses and power of reason. Around the world, small groups meet to discuss current research findings while workshops and conventions draw large audiences. More information is available at noetic.org.

In concluding this topic of Gnosticism, a look at two Gospels not found in the New Testament, is presented.

Mary Magdala   The Gospel

Close to fifty years before the discovery in Nag Hammadi, a Coptic copy of the Gospel of Mary surfaced. That Gospel, found in 1896 at an antique shop in Akhmin (Egypt), went to the National Museum of Berlin for safe keeping, where it remains. The copy was made in the early fifth century from a third century Greek fragmented copy of the Gospel. Pages 1 to 6 and 11 to 14, of the Coptic translation are missing. In studying this work, some errors and faulty translation were noted. The first translation of Coptic to French, came in 1955, by Jean-Yves Leloup. Joseph Rowe translated the French version into English, with a copyright of 2002.

The Gospel, not included in the Nag Hammadi find, and the Gospel of Thomas, uncovered at Nag Hammadi, are often compared. Thomas deals with the sayings of Jesus; Mary centers on the teachings she received from Jesus. The two Gospels are generally listed as Gnostic texts; each was written in the same Coptic dialect. However, the structure of the Universe, a characteristic of Gnosticism, is missing in both.

Of interest from the Gospel of Thomas is the indication that Thomas was Jesus' *twin brother*. The deeper meaning of the passage is that when Thomas discovered his spiritual *other self*, he was the same as Jesus, or identical to Jesus. Like Thomas, those finding their spiritual self through inner knowledge become like Jesus. Similar to the Gospel of Thomas, Mary's Gospel deals with a deep inner knowledge gained from Jesus' personal teachings.

A definite time and place of the original Gospel of Mary is unknown, though scholars feel it was written around the time of the Gospels of Matthew and Mark. However, Mary's Gospel, telling of her friendship with Jesus, did not received recognition like the others. One reason might have been its focus on a woman: Miriam of Magdala, known today as Mary Magdalene. Another consideration for the lack of acknowledgement could be its depth of metaphysical messages.

In addition to the Gospel, two books were titled after Mary. The *Questions of Mary* and the *Birth of Mary* are quoted by Epiphanus in his book *Panarion,* written in the fourth century. The original *Questions of Mary* was lost and is only known by Epiphanus' book. An edited version of *Panarion* was renamed

Pistis Sophis in the eighteenth century. It remains in the British Library.

Epiphanus' quotes, plus Gospels other than those found in the New Testament, present a previously unseen view of Mary. An example, from the Gospel of Mary, states: *Peter said to Mary: Sister, we know that the Teacher loved you differently from other women. Tell us whatever you remember of any words he told you which we have not yet heard.*

Mary's name is often mentioned in early Christian writings—some honored her—others disgraced her. The Gospels of Matthew, Mark, Luke and John refer to Mary Magdala by name. Through the years, some scholars have thought other women mentioned in the Gospels were Mary Magdala. One example is Mary of Bethany, Lazarus' sister. Another is found in Luke 7:36-50, identifying a woman as a *sinner* who anoints Jesus with precious oils. The Greek word for *sinner* is *harmartolos,* with different meanings: a person who violated Jewish Law or one who did not pay the required tax. The Greek word for *harlot* is *porin* which Luke uses elsewhere in his Gospel, but he does not relate the term to Mary. The Gospels never refer to Mary as a prostitute.

Pope Gregory I, in 591, stated Mary was the unnamed woman in Luke 7. The Pope went on to say Luke's unnamed woman [Mary] had previously used oils on her flesh in *forbidden acts* and had seven devils, or all the vices, removed from her. In 1969, the Catholic Church officially repealed the Pope's naming Mary a whore. Still, many believe the incorrect labeling.

Mary Magdala is noted as having been freed of seven demons, leading many to look at her as a *sinner.* Going back to Ancient Times, spiritualists understood the seven energy centers located throughout the body. Knowledge of these centers, common in India, Babylonia, Assyria, and Egypt, seems to be a part of Hebrew tradition. *Seven* is a number of deep spiritual significance.

There are many references to the sevenfold structure of spiritual worlds in the Hebrew Bible. The Hebrew menorah contains six candles reaching up to the seventh, the central light of the spirit. Jesus does relieve Mary of seven demons but modern thinking points to this wording as the clearing of her seven energy centers.

The Gospels John, Mark, and Matthew speak of Mary Magdala taking oils to anoint the body of Jesus on the third morning after the crucifixion. John (20:17) goes on to include Jesus' words: *Do not touch me*, as Mary reached out to Jesus. Some have misinterpreted the saying as Mary still carrying the stigma of a soiled woman. From Greek, the translation was: *Don't cling to me*, continuing on with, *for I am not yet ascended to the Father*. These words indicate Jesus was speaking of another world where life exists and Mary, perhaps because of her purified state, received the message and instructions to go and tell the others. Thus, Mary became the *Apostle of Apostles* as recognized in the Gospels of Matthew, Mark, Luke and John, and also, the Nag Hammadi Gnostic Gospels.

There is a strong belief that Mary Magdala journeyed to southern France after the crucifixion of Jesus. She lived in caves and developed the ability of clairvoyance, or clear seeing. Many say Mary spent the last of her years in the hidden part of the earth.

In recent years there has been speculation about the relationship between Mary Magdala and Jesus. Perhaps this began with The Gospel of Philip (63:36-38, 64:1-4)) found in the Gnostic Gospels of Nag Hammadi, which states:

> The Lord loved Mary more than all the disciples, and often used to kiss her on the mouth. When the others saw how he loved Mary, they said "Why do you love her more than you love us?" The Savior answered them in

this way: "How can it be that I do not love you as much as I love her?"

Research, concerning the possibility of marriage between Mary and Jesus, points to the Jewish tradition requiring men to be married in order to teach in synagogues. There are various opinions on a marriage between the two, or their relationship. Regardless, Mary Magdala remains an interest. Following is another small portion from The Gospel of Mary. The entire Gospel is little more than ten pages. [Mary is questioning Jesus]

> "What is matter? Will it last forever?" The Teacher answered: "All that is born, all that is created, all the elements of nature are interwoven and united with each other. All that is composed shall be decomposed; everything returns to its roots; matter returns to the origins of matter. Those who have ears, let them hear."

John, one of the close twelve disciples of Jesus, considered Mary the founder of Christianity as she first saw the resurrected Jesus (John 20). Other disciples acknowledged this witness.

Judas   The Gospel

From Middle Egypt, in the 1970s, a Gospel of Judas came to light. The Gospel was part of a fragmented codex, a Coptic translation of four separate Greek writings all classified as Gnostic Gospels. Then, the codex seems to have been on the black market until early 1980s. Supposedly, in 1982, antiquities dealer Frieda Tchacos viewed the writings. Thereafter, her name identified the codex. Apparently, the Swiss acquired the material in 1999.

The sixty-six-page Codex Tchacos contained a version of the

Letter of Peter to Philip and a text titled James (a version of the First Revelation of James). Both known from Nag Hammadi. Also, included was an unfamiliar copy of the Book of Allogenes (or, the Stranger, an epithet of Seth, son of Adam and Eve). The inclusion of a copy, mostly intact, of the Gospel of Judas stunned biblical scholars. The extremely poor condition of the codex prolonged translation into languages of today.

A number of antiquity collectors became interested in the codex, especially the Gospel of Judas. After a great deal of negotiation with a number of different individuals, the National Geographic Society entered into the picture in 2004. They photographed the Gospel's fragmented pages and with translations available at that time, a documentary film was produced, followed by a magazine article. The early publications contained pictures of the Gospel with commentaries by biblical scholars. By 2006, the Society published the English translation of the Gospel of Judas, a collaborative endeavor including Rodolphe Kasser.

Looking back, the first Christian writer to mention a Gospel of Judas was Irenaeus of Lyon, who, around 180, referred to a Gospel of Judas in *Against Heresies*. A strong assumption is that the Gospel was written between 130 and 170 by a Gnostic group called Cainites. Like other manuscripts of early Christianity, scholars are unable to determine exact dates and authorship. In the fourth century, Epiphanius documented the Gospel. Both, Irenaeus and Epiphanius wrote against heresies and condemned the writing, which was then suppressed.

Marvin Meyer, in his Introduction to *The Gospel of Judas*, states that the wisdom Judas gained from Jesus, dealing with the nature of God, is more advanced than can be truly comprehended by most Christians today. That deep understanding of the Infinite Deity falls under the Gnostic definition of knowing the Divine Light within. The Gospel of Judas reflects the Sethian Gnostic thought. Seth, the third son of Adam and Eve, is mentioned in the Gospel. It is implied that Seth represents a new beginning for humanity and that people with self-knowledge of God within, belong to the generation of Seth.

Judas Iscariot historically considered the one who took money for betraying Jesus—then took his own life—is one of the most well-known of Jesus' disciples. From *Judah*, the Hebrew name meaning *praised*, came the Greek spelling *Judas*. Judah is a popular name in Judaism; some think the term *Jew* resulted from the name. Judah, from time of the Patriarchs, is son of Jacob, great-grandson of Abraham and namesake of the Tribe of Judah. When the Kingdom of Israel divided (928 BCE), the southern kingdom took the name *Judah*. The Gospel of Luke (6:16) lists twelve disciples; two have the name Judas. There is no clear explanation for *Iscariot.*

The New Testament speaks of Jesus' betrayal. At the Last Supper, Jesus told Judas, the treasurer of the group, to do what he had to do. Some scholars now think the death of Jesus was a Divine plan, with Judas doing his part. Those studying the Gnostic Gospel of Judas support the theory that Judas, over his own well-being, fulfilled Jesus' request. With Judas' betrayal, Jesus was freed from the flesh so he could return to his heavenly home. His inner, Divine self was released from his body.

One point made in the Gospel is Judas, knowingly and as requested, *handed over** Jesus to the authorities. According to the Gospel, Jesus said to Judas, *You will exceed all of them. For you will sacrifice the man that clothes me.* This is closely in line with the Gospel of John 6:64 and 13:27-28 plus the Gospel of Matthew 26:25 suggesting Jesus knew of his approaching death and allowed Judas to carry out God's plan.

*Scholars question some biblical translations. An example is referring to Judas as *betraying* Jesus or as a *traitor* whereas the translation from Greek is: *give over, hand over,* or *turn in.*

Other key views presented in the Gospel of Judas are: the creator of this world is not the one true God, this world is an evil place and must be escaped, Jesus is not the son of the one who created this evil world and salvation comes through the revelation of secret knowledge that Jesus provided. These views conflict with those found in the New Testament.

Though many find the Gospel of Judas perplexing, the discovery is seen as a major find and intrigues people the world over. Early in 2006 an Italian newspaper reported that Judas would receive a favorable re-evaluation, based on the find. A day later, from London, an article indicated the Vatican (Rome) was clearing Judas' name. The Vatican replied: *words of exonerating Judas are baseless.*

CHAPTER 8

The New Testament

Reflections New Testament Revisited
Source—New Testament
   Gospels, Letters/Epistles, Documents
New Testament—A Review
   Books of the New Testament

Judith Marie Judy

Reflections   New Testament Revisited

Looking back on my years attending Christian Churches, I don't remember specific teachings about when and who wrote the New Testament. Maybe it all went over my head. I think I just assumed the Gospels were written by those names mentioned in the titles: Matthew, Mark, Luke and John. Over the past years I realized scholars today know so much more about biblical writings, like authors and dates. Information from older publications is no longer accurate. In thinking about it, many church goers probably are more interested in the messages, than how they came to be. I guess that was me. Yet, I found knowing the history behind the writings led to a deeper understanding of the people and the times. Too, for me, it is helpful to see many references of the Hebrew Bible carried forward into the New Testament. My goodness, in my youth no one mentioned that Jesus and his disciples were Jews. Attitudes were different back then.

Source—New Testament

Compilation of the Hebrew Bible, with numerous different sources, began after 458 BCE and was not completed until around 70 CE. The writings that became the New Testament relied on various sources also, one being the Hebrew Bible. The writings, in Greek, occurred between 50-130 CE, though it took until the fourth century CE before the selection of those considered Scripture, were designated as a New Testament.

Details regarding sources utilized in the writings are listed here. A description of the events covered in the writings is given in *New Testament—A Review*. As with previous dates, indecision remains with today's scholars. Also, the term *document* (few pages), often replaces *book* (lengthy reading) in reference to the writings.

Although there is no authenticated account of Jesus written during his life, works of later Roman writers support his existence. One being the Jewish Historian, Flavius Josephus, in his *Antiquities of the Jews*, he mentions: *there was about this time Jesus, a wise man who was a doer of wondrous works and drew over to him many of the Jews and many of the Gentiles. When Pilate, at the suggestion of the principal men amongst us, had condemned him to the cross, those that loved him did not cease to be attached to him.*

Jesus and his disciples, like Jews of that period, remained devoted to the Hebrew Scriptures. Christians, many were Jews, relied on the Torah, Prophets, and Writings for guidance and comfort while incorporating sayings and stories of Jesus into their lives.

It took decades before accounts of Jesus became written words. Messages pertaining to Jesus traveled slowly, passing by word of mouth across many countries. During that time, the Apostle Paul began writing letters dealing with the meaning and significance of Jesus. The letters were sent to an occasional individual but generally to Christian communities. Seven of those letters, and some written by other Christians at a later date, are part of the New Testament. Gospels, narrating Jesus' life, were written after Paul's letters. Those authors relied on each other for information, plus additional sources. Of the two remaining New Testament documents, one is based on Paul and the Apostles' work with early churches. The second looks into the future, drawing on more letters.

Gospels

Gospels, narrations of Jesus' life, are placed in the beginning of the New Testament; however, Paul's letters were written before the Gospels. Scholars feel that after decades of Jesus' messages being circulated by word of mouth, learned individuals wrote down the words. A combination of written and oral accounts was most likely consulted in creating the Gospels. It is understandable that the stories recorded had seen changes in the process of Oral Tradition.

Authors of the Gospel are unknown; they were neither disciples of Jesus nor were they eye witnesses to his ministry. The language of Jesus and his disciples was Aramaic. The Gospels were written in the Greek language. Furthermore, in the time of Jesus, most of the people close to him could neither read nor write. It is thought Jesus might have been able to read, as he was a rabbi, but it is unlikely he could write.

The first three Gospels, Matthew, Mark, and Luke are similar to one another in their messages about Jesus; they are called *Synoptic Gospels*. All three appear to have relied on stories passed down through Oral Tradition. However, as each one has material not covered in the other two, it is considered that sources no longer in existence, possibly written, were used.

Matthew, dating in the 80s, contains almost the same wording of stories found in Mark, though another source was used as Matthew contains material not found in Mark.

Mark, dating in the 70s, is generally acknowledged as the first Gospel written. It is known that a Greek-speaking Christian wrote the Gospel.

Luke, with a questionable dating around 110, also used Mark as a source. However, like Matthew, there is material in Luke not found in Mark. The same author of Luke wrote The Acts of the Apostles. At one time it was thought that Luke, Paul's companion, wrote both documents; modern scholars disagree with that assumption.

John, dated around 95, seems to have been compiled by an author who used a variety of non-surviving sources. Apparently, there was a *signs source*; a writing of the signs (miracles) that would convince others that Jesus was the messiah. The Gospel of John contains seven signs; seemingly all from the same source. The lengthy speeches of Jesus indicate another source. Chapters 18-20 (Jesus' death and resurrection) appear to come from yet an additional source, written or oral. The beginning and ending of the Gospel look to have been taken from early Christian hymns.

Letter/Epistles

Letters, from the Greek word epistles, are the earliest written and the majority of documents found in the New Testament.

Paul's Letters, beginning in the 50s, provided encouragement and guidance to specific groups of early Christians. Scholars believe, almost without a doubt, that Paul was the author of seven letters, one of which was sent to an individual. The authorship of another six is questionable.

General Letters, written by eight various individuals from the 80s to the 120s, deal with experiences that could apply to any early Christian community.

Documents

The Acts of the Apostles dates with Luke in the early second century, as they were written by the same author as a two-volume document. Acts centers on speeches given by Paul and other Apostles. Some scholars feel historical writers often made up speeches for presenting information on individuals they were writing about. In addition to speeches, more accounts might have been taken from the author Josephus in his writings dating throughout the 90s.

Revelation, dating in the 90s or early in the second century, is signed by *John*; however, he was not the disciple, not the author of three General Letters, and not the author of the Gospel of John. Letters sent to seven Christian communities, dealing with the final years before the second coming of Jesus, are the basis of Revelation.

New Testament—A Review

By the second century, groups of Christians acknowledged some documents as Scripture. However, into the fourth century, discussions continued regarding more material suitable for inclusion. It took until 367 before the twenty-seven books selected as officially meeting the standard of Scripture were canonized. Bishop Athanasius of Alexandria compiled the final listing. With a proclamation of the accepted documents, those not included were labeled as heretical.

The following review looks at each of the New Testament books.

The **Gospels**, from the Greek words *good news* became written documents beginning in the 70s and into the early 110s. The Gospel writers, in their biographies of Jesus, did not know him personally. They learned of him through stories spreading across the lands of ancient Judea after his death. The stories found in the Gospels, some the same, others different, present the character of the one from whom a new faith immerged.

Early Christians treasured the **Gospel of Matthew**. Perhaps that is the reason the Gospels start with Matthew. Matthew begins by stating Jesus as the messiah, and then traces his genealogy as *son of David* and back to Abraham. Next, Jesus' birth is related to fulfilling prophecies in the Hebrew Bible. Throughout the Gospel, the author points out ways Jesus' life is based on Jewish Law. It is stated that Jewish authorities rejected Jesus, resulting in his death. The Gospel ends with the risen Jesus directing his disciples to make disciples of all nations. . . and that he [Jesus] would *be with them always, to the end of the age.* The Gospel covers the Sermon on the Mount which includes the Beatitudes, the Golden Rule and the Lord's Prayer, some of the better-known biblical messages of Jesus.

The **Gospel of Mark**, like Matthew, deals with Jesus as the messiah sent from God to fulfill the Jewish Scriptures. Starting with a proclamation of Jesus carrying out an ancient prophecy, the Gospel then moves into the baptism of Jesus by John the Baptist. Throughout the Gospel, Jesus is referred to as the Son of God or the messiah, however, the author's writing does not indicate that Jesus used the words to describe himself. In fact, the belief that Jesus was the Son of God and messiah was kept secret during his life. A major point in Mark is the usage of the word *way, the way of the Lord,* and *the way of Jesus.* Another theme found in the Gospel is that those coming into contact with Jesus did not understand his underling messages and purpose in life. As in Matthew, Jewish religious leaders opposed Jesus. Mark ends with the women finding the empty tomb and fleeing because they were frightened.

In the **Gospel of Luke**, Jesus is shown as a prophet, similar to those of the Hebrew Bible. Too, Luke covers the movement of Jesus and his message reaching the Gentiles. The Gospel is dedicated to one named *Theophilus,* a common Greek name meaning *beloved of God,* perhaps a reference to Christians. Luke begins with the birth of John the Baptist followed by the birth of Jesus, differing from Matthew and Mark. In moving to Jesus' ministry, the episode of his sermon given in his home town is longer and more detailed than the other Gospels. Those present questioned Jesus when he implied he was *the spirit of God*; Jesus replies with two familiar stories from the Hebrew Bible where God sent prophets to Gentiles. The part about prophets to Gentiles is not included in Matthew and Mark. When the angry worshipers try to throw Jesus off a cliff, he disappears and then takes his message to other towns. In this way, Luke shows the fulfillment of the prophecy: *the prophet of God is opposed by his own people.* Other usage of *the spirit of God* is shown at Jesus' baptism, his last words on the cross, and with the promise *the Spirit of God* will descend on Jesus' followers.

The **Gospel of John** differs from the other Gospels. A number of stories not included in the first three are found in the Gospel of John. The Gospel shows Jesus in a more spiritual manner than the others. The wording of this Gospel provides a deeper understanding of Jesus as *the word of God* and the importance of Jesus' work in bringing the light of God to individuals. Like Mark, the Gospel of John begins with Jesus as an adult. Few of the recordings of Jesus' words and miracles in John are found in the other Gospels, likewise, the other Gospels do not contain the same stories that appear in John. However, the account of Jesus' death is similar to the first three Gospels.

Acts (of the Apostles), was written as a second volume to the Gospel of Luke. Acts, like the Gospel of Luke, is dedicated to *Theophilus*. Jesus' words and deeds appear in Luke; the spreading of Jesus' messages is covered in Acts. Beginning with Jesus' appearances after his resurrection, Acts continues with Jesus telling the disciples to stay in Jerusalem until they are given the power of the Holy Spirit [God]. Once received, they are to take the message of Jesus to Jews and Gentiles outside of Jerusalem where Jesus faced rejection. Over half of Acts contains the story of the Apostle Paul and his work in starting Christian communities.

Paul's Letters, beginning in the 50s, say very little about Jesus' life. For the most part, the letters were intended to assist specific Christian communities with their new faith. Ranging from tenderness and affection to conflict and anger, the letters were read to congregations; most of whom were illiterate. The following letters are the seven generally identified as being written by Paul.

1. In the letter to the **Romans**, the only community previously unvisited, Paul wrote to introduce himself, as he planned to extend his ministry to them. He spoke of his understanding of Jesus' teachings and how they pertained to the meaning of God and the transformation of a life centered on Christ.

2. Identified as **1 Corinthians**, though he had written to the community earlier, Paul's letter addresses divisions and conflicts that had surfaced over spiritual issues.

3. Scholars see in **2 Corinthians** a collection of letters reflecting Paul's steadfast dedication to that community. Some letters deal with struggles regarding the early decades of Christianity. Others focus on the strife among followers of Jesus as they interpreted their new way of life. The beginning chapters are thought to be among the most reflective of Spirit and transformation into the likeness of Christ, that is found in Paul's letters.

4. **Galatians** addresses the churches of Galatia, not a specific congregation. In this letter, Paul reacts to being accused of untruths in speaking of Jesus' mission. The communities were divided on which Jewish Laws had to be included in the new faith.

5. In **Philippians**, a letter from prison, Paul writes of his thanks for all the progress shown in the community. Words: *joy, rejoice, content, thankful, love,* are given as continued encouragement for Christ-followers.

6. **1 Thessalonians** speaks of the Christian community being a family of brothers and sisters where all members share and support each other. The letter also deals with the second coming of Jesus, which Paul expects to happen very soon.

7. **Philemon**, the only letter addressed to an individual, was another one Paul wrote from prison. Paul encouraged Philemon to take back, as a beloved brother, a runaway slave.

Six other letters, attributed to Paul, have been dated from the 80s to the 110s. Reportedly, Paul was arrested in Jerusalem in the late 50s and taken to Rome where he lived under house arrest for the rest of his life. He was executed around 64 during the reign of Nero.

Scholars feel some of the later letters signed as Paul, might have been written by members of the communities he founded. It was not uncommon for writers of that time to use a fictitious name. The following three letters, listed with Paul's, seem to have been written by one or more author(s) who were greatly influenced by Paul's work.

1. **Ephesians** differs from Paul's letters in style and subject matter. It does not seem to be addressed to a specific community. The letter stresses unity of Christian Jews and Christian Gentiles with inclusion of instructions pertaining to the *Church*.

2. **Colossians** contains an introduction, a prayer of thanksgiving, and ends with a blessing, using the same words as Paul. However, a probable date for Colossians is in the 80s. Originally, the sentences of this letter were longer than Paul's; they have been shortened in some biblical editions. Also, ideals opposite of Paul's are found in Colossians. In portraying Jesus, the author begins at the creation with Jesus being the *image of the invisible God*.

3. **2 Thessalonians** is a letter most scholars feel was purposely written in the same manner as 1 Thessalonians so it would be accepted as a genuine letter by Paul. Issues around the delay of Jesus' second coming and those joining Christian communities only to receive the sharing of food are mentioned in this letter. However, those concerns were not present in Paul's time.

The following three letters, again, listed with Paul's, were sent to Timothy and Titus, both referred to as *Pastoral,* as they offer advice on ways to fulfill that role. Most scholars today think the author, wanting the communities to accept the letters in the same faith of Paul's, signed his [Paul's] name. One reason for disputing the authorship of Paul is the term *Pastoral,* which was not used during Paul's time.

1. In **1 Timothy**, a major change from Paul's letters is the role assigned to women. Paul was open to women in leadership positions; in 1 Timothy they are forbidden to teach. Overall, the letter instructs Christians on acceptable behavior, both individually and within the community.
2. **2 Timothy**, a personal letter to Timothy, cites Paul in prison, realizing the end of his life is near. The letter commissions Timothy to continue Paul's work.
3. The letter to **Titus** instructs him, like Timothy, to carry on Paul's work. Qualification for selecting leaders is addressed as is the teaching of Church rules.

General Letters, a group of eight, date from the 80s to the 120s. They differ from those of Paul as they deal with universal problems faced by all Christians at the time they were written. Following are the details of those letters.

1. **Hebrews** is not written in a letter format and was not intended for Jews. The author, signed as *known only to God*, repeatedly used in the Hebrew Bible, addresses ways of relating Judaism to Christian beliefs.

2. **James** (not brother of Jesus), stresses the importance of doing and acting. The author, *a servant of God and of Lord Jesus Christ*, likely knew the teachings of Jesus from the Oral Tradition or from a written account other than Matthew or Luke.

3. **1 Peter** (not the disciple), gives affirmations of Jesus and God with encouragement and moral teachings. The author, *Peter an apostle of Jesus Christ*, was an elder thought to be writing from Rome.

4. **2 Peter** (neither the disciple nor author of 1 Peter), speaks to the importance of refraining from worldly ways and warns against false prophets. The author, *Peter a servant and apostle of Jesus Christ,* cites love as the true Christian virtue.

The three letters of John were not written by the disciple nor the author of the Gospel of John.

5. **1 John** could have been written by someone using that name. There are similarities and differences between this letter and the Gospel of John. Not written in letter format and with no indication as to the specific community, the letter stresses love and affirms Jesus as a human and the incarnation of God's love.

6. **2 John**, a short letter sent by *the elder* to *the elect lady and her children,* who is thought to have been a leader of an early Christian community, stresses love.

7. **3 John**, another short letter signed *elder,* was written by the same individual as 2 John and probably sent to the

same community. This letter praises the community for welcoming Christians and also faults an individual for unchristian behavior.

8. **Jude**, as signed by the author, refers to himself as *a servant of Jesus Christ and brother of James*. Scholars strongly state that the James mentioned is not the brother of Jesus. The location of the writing and the community to whom it was intended is unknown; however, Jude is faulting the community for its lack of upholding their dedication to God. The short letter refers to Jewish documents not found in the Hebrew Bible.

Scholars indicate that John, the author of **Revelation**, is neither the disciple nor the author of the John letters. The author, a religious ecstatic, wrote of his visions. He traveled through Judea as an itinerant teacher and prophet after the destruction of Jerusalem in 70. More than half of the document implies a deep understanding of the Hebrew Bible. Revelation was written in Greek, showing an Aramaic use of language.

The book of Revelation is sometimes referred to as the Apocalypse, an unveiling of the future, a common topic of Judaism in the centuries before and after Jesus. Symbolic language, often the case with apocalyptic literature, is seen in Revelation. Numbers, especially *the number 7*; animals, such as a *lamb*; women *clothed with the sun,* are symbolic examples. Contrasts, such as *good* and *evil*, are also found in Revelation. Though the wording of Revelation is often confusing, it carries forth the basic yearning of a world filled with the presence of God and the absence of suffering.

In 367 Christians gave the name *New Testament* to the twenty-seven writings approved as Scripture. They then considered the Hebrew Bible the *Old Testament*. Both Testaments still hold a place of honor in the Christian religion. Following is a listing of New Testament contents taken from: The New Oxford Annotated Bible New Revised Standard Version With The Apocrypha. Variations in titles of some books occur within differing publications.

Books of the New Testament

The Gospels: Matthew, Mark, Luke, John
The Acts of the Apostles
Letters/Epistles in the New Testament:
Romans, 1 Corinthians, 2 Corinthians, Galatians, Ephesians, Philippians, Colossians,
1 Thessalonians, 2 Thessalonians
The Pastoral Epistles:
1 Timothy, 2 Timothy, Titus, Philemon, Hebrews, James, 1 Peter, 2 Peter, 1 John, 2 John, 3 John, Jude
Revelation

PART TWO

BEYOND THE BIBLE

SECTION FOUR

MOVING ONWARD

CHAPTER 9

Biblical Translations

Reflections Bibles for All
Words Become a Bible
Jewish Translations
Christian Translations

Reflections   Bibles for All

There is a long history detailing the persecution of Jews and Christians because of their beliefs. It is strange to me that individuals wanting a Bible translated into a language of their own, would also be oppressed. Translations of the Hebrew Bible to Aramaic, Aramaic to Greek, then, Greek to Latin seems to have been well received. Even later, as the Jewish Bible, it appears there was little interference with translations to other languages. That was not the same for Christian Bibles.

The early organization of the Christian Catholic Church was based on bishops, priests, and deacons having the authority of God and the sole privilege of passing Jesus' message on to the common people. Even in the beginning of Christianity, many questioned that practice. A question I have is: Why did the Church, as the years went on, want to restrict the words and works of Jesus? In his life, Jesus spoke to the common people of a loving God. He taught acceptance and forgiveness of others. Were those who faced death, because of their work on English translations in the Modern Age, willing to forgive those who fought against them? It makes me sad even to think about such things. Always, some questions have no answers. I must remember—a few remained firm in their efforts to provide Bibles for everyone. I am indebted to those refusing to surrender their dreams of GOOD—for humankind.

Words Become a Bible

As shown previously, The Bible is a work of many authors covering numerous time periods. The terms *Bible, Scripture, Testament* and *the word of God* have slightly different meanings, though all are used in much the same way. The word *Bible* is plural, taken from the Greek word *ta biblia*, indicating a collection of material. *Bible* has come to mean *sacred religious Scriptures or, the very word of God. Canon,* from the Greek *reed* (straight stick used for measuring) is the term given to the material judged as being critical in defining a specific group of people. The word was first used by Greek writers who came after the Torah became written Hebrew Scripture. When *canon* was used for the selection of books in the Bible, all other books were excluded. The list became closed.

The canon of the Hebrew Bible came in stages. The first five books, or Torah, was designated Scripture sometime after Ezra's work in restoring the Jewish faith in Judah (458 BCE). Before 300 BCE, the books of the Prophets (Nevi'im) were designated as Scripture. It took until 70 CE before the Writings (Kethuvim) were added to the list. Between 100 BCE and 100 CE, the Apocryphal was compiled. Jews did not accept those books as Scripture; all or some were eventually accepted by various Christian denominations. By the end of the fourth century CE, the canon of the New Testament was in place. The first four centuries of Christianity were filled with disputes over which writings met the criteria of *Scripture.* Though the number of books in the Bible did not change, some wording was adjusted to the translations as languages progressed.

Additional changes, along with languages, occurred in early biblical times. They too, affected the way of life. Early in the second century CE, writings were placed on individual pages and bound together as a codex (book).The invention, by the third century BCE, of parchment, a writing surface using animal skins in place of papyrus reeds, made printing easier. Into the fifteenth century, the printing press transformed the process of reproducing written words. By that time, the Bible had seen a number of translations. In the sixteenth century, common people could purchase Bibles as a printed book.

Jewish Translations

For Jews, respect of the original Hebrew wording of their Bible is maintained to this day. A translated Bible does not replace that first Bible, rather it is a supplement to the Hebrew Bible. A modern name for the Hebrew Bible is *Tanakh (Tanak)*, taken from the Bible's three parts: *Torah, Nevi'im, Ketuvim.* The first letter of each part is separated by *a*, then often ends with *h*, the final letter of *Torah*. The title *Jewish Bible* is seen in current writings. Looking at translations, the original authors did not divide their work into chapters and verses. It took until the ninth century CE for Jewish scholars to complete their work separating the writing into verses. Chapters were the addition of Christian editors in the thirteenth century. Accounts of some of the major translations of the Hebrew Bible follow.

Though many Jews, starting about the middle of the third century BCE, adopted Greek as their primary language, they maintained their Hebrew language. At that time and extending to the present, Jews preserve some familiarity with the Hebrew text of their Bible. Chanting portions of their original biblical text is practiced in almost all contemporary synagogues of the twenty-first century CE.

Around 250 BCE, in Alexandria, beginning with the Torah, the Hebrew Bible was translated into the **Greek language**. The translation was named *Septuagint*, or *LXX*, in reference to the seventy-plus Jewish elders and the days need for the translation of the Hebrew into Greek.

Oral *Torah*, interpretations of the Hebrew text, were presented in the **Aramaic language** when it began replacing the Hebrew language. In the first century CE, the Hebrew Bible was translated into Aramaic. Scholars working with the Dead Sea Scrolls discovered some Aramaic writings and used the name

Targum to distinguish those passages. The Targum translations incorporated the community's understanding of how the Bible related to their needs.

There is no indication that Jews translated their Bible into Latin. At the end of the fourth century CE, **Jerome** studied Hebrew and consulted Jewish teachers in his Latin translation (**Vulgate**) of the Hebrew Bible, the New Testament, and the Apocrypha.

With the rise of Islam in the mid-seventh century, Jews living in the East and North Africa adopted the Arabic language. Early in the tenth century, **Saadia ben Joseph** produced an **Arabic translation** of the Hebrew Bible, written with Hebrew characters. All Jews did not accept the translation.

As Jews settled in Europe, it was some time before they were interested in translating their Hebrew Bible. Partly, it was their opposition to the Roman Catholic Church and its adoption of the Vulgate Bible. In time, however, translations occurred.

1200s **German** speaking Jews had translated portions of their Bible for use in homes and schools.

1430-1442 **Spanish** versions of the Hebrew Bible, the **Ferrara Bible** and **Alba Bible**, were produced.

1611 The **English** publication of the **King James Bible** became the most influential translation for English speaking Jews. The vocabulary and structure strongly resembled the original Hebrew language. The Bible served England's growing Jewish community as well as the Christians.

1655 The First Jewish settlement in **New York** borrowed the **Torah** scroll from the Jewish Center of Amsterdam. Later settlers brought a Torah scroll with them or borrowed one from other

Jewish communities. Jewish communal life was impossible without their Bible. The Torah scroll defined their worship service as authentic as it contains the sacred teachings of Jewish religious life.

In about 1780, **Mendelssohn** (1729-1786), a **German philosopher**, translated the Jewish Bible into the German language using Hebrew characters. He felt only a Jew could produce a proper version for fellow Jews. His version was an advanced form of German, taking the Bible from Antiquity to Modern Times.

1814 **Jonas Horwitz** produced an edition of the Hebrew Bible, the first of its kind in the **United States**.

1840-1850 **Isaac Leeser**, in Philadelphia, translated the Torah, then the entire Hebrew Bible, into the **English language**, freeing Jews from their reliance on Christian translations. The influence of his translation resulted in new editions and republications over the next seventy years.

The **Jewish Publication Society of America** (JPS), founded in Philadelphia, was committed to advance knowledge of the Hebrew Bible among Jews. The Society became an important part of formal Jewish education in the United States.

1917 Russian born, **Max Margolis**, became chief editor of a JPS committee responsible for a new English language version of a Hebrew Bible for Jews. Margolis, like others on the committee, received part of their formal Jewish education in the United States. Their Bible, *The Holy Scriptures,* gave fellow Jews pride in a production similar to Catholic and Protestant Bibles. The Holy Scriptures provided *non-Jews an understanding of Jewish tradition in the interpretation of the Word of God.* The Holy Scriptures replaced the dependence on Leeser's Bible.

1925-1961 In Berlin, two Germans, **Martin Buber** (1878-1965) and **Franz Rosenzweig** (1886-1929) collaborated on a new translation of the Hebrew Bible into the **German language**. They wanted to restore the Hebrew influence for Jews who had adopted much of the German culture. Rosenzweig died in 1929; Buber left Germany in 1938 and completed the translation in Palestine. When the translation was complete, there were no Jews left in Germany.

Most early Jews migrating to the United States possessed printed Hebrew copies of all twenty-four books of the Jewish Bible. Some Jews relied on editions of the Christian Bible; however, they studied only the books that formed part of the Jewish Bible. Most of those first immigrants preferred the Jewish Bible over the Talmud. They found the Bible easier to read. Through the nineteenth century, the Bible bound Jews together.

During the late nineteenth century and into the twentieth, over two million east European Jews migrated to the United States. They knew and respected their Jewish Bible. From Oral Tradition to written words of many languages, the Hebrew Bible remains a guiding influence for Jews.

Christian Translations

The Christian Bible, like the Hebrew Bible, has been translated into many languages. Over the years, Christians have referred to their collection of Scripture, plus the addition of the Hebrew Bible, as *The Bible*. Christians gave the name *Old Testament* to the Hebrew Bible when they titled their accepted twenty-seven books *The New Testament*, which had been written in the Greek language. As Christians combined the books, they changed the placement of some of the Hebrew books. There are no books of the New Testament in Jewish Bibles. The following listing of translations deal with the Christian Bible, sometimes called the English Bible. The many translations resulted in some differences of books included by the various forms of Christianity.

Christians looked to Jesus and his ways, plus their knowledge of the Hebrew Scriptures, for their understanding of God. At the beginning of Christianity, the Hebrew Scriptures had been translated into the Greek language. Before long, Latin replaced Greek.

Like the Jews of Alexandria, early Christians, many speaking languages other than Greek, wanted Bibles printed in their own language. There were some translations of various portions of the Bible during the second and third centuries, continuing into the fourth. As Latin became a common language, Pope Damascus (ca 383) commissioned **Jerome** to translate the entire Bible into Latin. The Bible, given the name *Vulgate,* was intended for use by common people. Following are records of some of the often-referenced translations of the Christian Bible.

1380-1397 **John Wycliffe** and his associates translated, from the Vulgate, the first English version of the Bible. After Wycliffe's death, his secretary, John Purvey was responsible for a second translation. The translations were manuscript copies only.

1408 The Archbishop of England prohibited English translations of the Bible.

1455 The Vulgate Bible, printed in Germany on the Gutenberg press, became known as the **Gutenberg Bible**.

1466 The **first German translation** of the Vulgate was based on a hand written German translation from the fourteenth century.

By 1521 twenty-four translations existed; however, only the rich could afford the Bibles. Other factors prevented common people from having a Bible they could read. The many German dialects plus opposition by the bishops limited translations.

1522-1534 **Martin Luther** translated the entire Bible into the German language. He relied on the Greek and Latin translations; for the Old Testament he used the Hebrew Bible as a back-up. At the time of Luther's death in 1546, there were 350 editions of his **Luther Bible**.

1526 **William Tyndale's** work provided Bibles for the common people of England. His English Bible, translated directly from Hebrew and Greek editions, was printed as separate books. By 1535 revised editions of the New Testament were available. A year later, his enemies strangled and burned Tyndale at the stake. Yet, his work remained. The structure reflected in his Bibles influenced future translations.

1535 The entire Bible, in English, appeared as one book. In his work, **Coverdale** translated from two Latin versions, plus Tyndale's Bibles and German translations from Luther and his reformers.

1537 **John Rogers**, under the name *Thomas Matthew*, published the **Matthew's Bible**. Roger utilized his friend, Tyndale's work, plus additions from Coverdale's version.

1538 In Paris, **Coverdale**, commissioned by Sir Thomas Cromwell, Secretary to King Henry VIII (reigned 1509-1547), began a revision of the Matthew's Bible. A year later, as the **Great Bible**, it was published in London and became the first authorized English Bible. On order of the king, it was placed in every church.

In 1568 Anglican bishops revised the Great Bible under the name **Bishops' Bible**. That, too, was revised in 1572 which became the bases of the **King James Version**.

1539 Layman and lawyer, **Richard Taverner**, published a **revision** of **Matthew's Bible**. One edition was available in sections so those unable to purchase the complete Bible could buy according to their means.

1553 **Mary**, King Henry's daughter, became **Queen of England**. Mary was a Roman Catholic and printing of the English Bible ceased and its use in churches was forbidden. Many English protestants left England, moving to less restrictive countries.

1560 A revision of the English Bible appeared in Switzerland (Geneva), an undertaking by a group who fled England. The unauthorized **Geneva Bible** became the house-hold Bible of English-speaking countries for close to a century. It was the first English version with numbered verses and paragraphs. Shakespeare and the Puritans looked to the Geneva Bible for their inspiration.

1582 Another group fleeing England settled in France (Rheims). **Gregory Martin**, trained at Oxford University in England, led other Roman Catholic scholars in the translation of the New Testament from Latin to English.

1590 The Vulgate Bible became the Bible of the Roman Catholic Church.

1609 Much like the situation in 1582, the Old Testament was translated in Douay, France.

1611 The **King James Bible** was published. Seven years earlier, King James I of England requested a translation of the entire Bible, reflecting the original Hebrew and Greek. Once completed, the King James Bible became the only version used for Divine services in all churches of England. The Bible was the work of fifty-four translators. One third of the wording of the New Testament came from Tyndale's work; the rest of the Bible followed his general pattern. The King James Bible remained the authorized version for English speaking people for two and a half centuries.

1870 The **Convocation of the Province of Canterbury** (England) appointed a committee for the **revision of the King James Bible**. Completions were: New Testament, 1881; Old Testament, 1885; Apocrypha, 1895.

1901 **American scholars** who worked on the King James Revision, wanting some changes, published the **American Standard Version** (of King James).

1928 **The International Council of Religious Education** acquired the copyright of the American Standard Version which then passed on to the ownership of the churches of the United States and Canada associated with the Council. The Council appointed a committee of Protestant scholars to have charge of any future revision. Completion of the **Revised American Standard Versions** was: New Testament 1946, Old Testament 1952, Apocrypha 1957. In keeping with the King James Bible tradition, Tyndale's basic structure is found in all revisions.

1952-1990 Many translations and revisions of English Language Bibles took place.

1966 The **American Bible Society** published **Good News for Modern Man** with simplified vocabulary.

1970 The **U.S. Bishops' Conference** published the **New American Bible**, a translation by the Catholic Biblical Association of America. Revisions followed within fifteen years.

A **New Revised American Standard Version** was published in 1990.

At the beginning of the twenty-first century, current area, The Christian Bible is found in numerous languages and a multitude of revisions.

CHAPTER 10

Expanded Christianity

Reflections Discord
Continued Heresy
    Manichaens, Massalians, Paulicians, Bogomils, Cathars
Crossroads
    East—West Schism, Crusades, Knights Templars,
Inquisition, Martin Luther, Protestant Reformation,
Reform in England, Council of Trent

Reflections   Discord

In my study of biblical times I encountered topics that had interested me for some years. I knew a little about the various topics; however, I was unable to place them in close proximity to related historical periods.

Looking deeper into those subjects helped in extending the history of Christianity into a more current period. Books I read mentioned Knights Templar, Inquisition, and Crusades. Now I am aware of their significance. Heresy, what an awful word! Not only did it cause suffering for those with differing ideas, but the fact heresy fell in the framework of religion adds to the grief. Looking back on those difficult times, I see little gain for humanity today. People are still dying for their beliefs. Does it weaken my faith? NO! Knowledge broadens the mind; ignorance restricts growth.

The number of Christian religions surfacing after the death of Jesus equals the multitude of denominations today. Times change, but hearts and minds of humankind remain on a steady course of hope. I have lived through the era of the Jewish Holocaust, the dropping of an atomic bomb, genocides too many to name, and I shudder. Still, I praise God for the wonders of life: the seen and the unseen.

Continued Heresy

Condemnations of heresy surfaced in broad areas outside of Palestine and the surrounding early Christian communities. Before and after the organization of the Catholic Church and with the development of a New Testament, groups in distant countries formed religious practices that were condemned by the Church. Covering many centuries, people joining together for religious worship differing from the Church faced threats of death. Following is a brief account of some of the major condemned groups.

Manichaens

Decades before Constantine's Nicaea Council of 325, the Persian Prophet Mani (216-275) formed a religion known as Manichaeism. As a youth, Mani lived in Babylon with a Jewish Christian sect known as *katharoi,* meaning *pure ones.* Mani, his father and two others, began teachings called *Religion of Light,* which proved to be radically dualistic. Manichaeism enjoyed widespread popularity for some time but through the fifth and sixth centuries the Church of Rome eliminated all Mani's followers. The Eastern Roman Empire, known then as the Byzantine (Greek) Empire, took similar action. Manichaeism was extinguished from Europe; however, new dualist heresies arose.

Massalians

By 447, a group with the name Massalians, meaning *the praying people,* became a heretical threat in Armenia, a kingdom of Turkey. The group, also known as Enthusiasts, are thought to have originated in north-east Mesopotamia, possibly in the late fourth century. Their basic belief centered on a demon living within every person. With prayer and renouncing the comforts of society, the demon could be banished and further sinning would be impossible. The person could return to the same life as before. Armenia, like other Christian countries, put down this threat.

Paulicians

In the sixth century a group calling themselves Paulicians surfaced. They were named for Saint Paul [of the New Testament]. Again, this new heresy appeared in Armenia. It appears Paulicians did not become dualists until sometime after their formation.

Unlike some heretical groups, Paulicians were fighters with a military force. In 717, the Armenia Church condemned Paulicians as *sons of Satan* and *fuel for the fire eternal*. Though denounced, Paulicians apparently survived into the seventeenth century.

Bogomils

The establishment of the first Bulgarian Empire (681-1118) appears to be influential in the establishment of the heretical Bogomils. Bulgaria, bordering on the Black Sea, was a pagan country. Constantinople, the Christian capital of the Eastern Roman Empire, or Byzantine Empire by modern historians, also bordered the Black Sea. The Church at Constantinople feared the pagans of Bulgaria; to reinforce Christianity, Greek Christians were re-settled along the land between Bulgaria and Constantinople. This action brought more trouble of heresy to the Christian Church because many of those relocated were Paulicians who, history says, influenced Bogomilism.

Bogomilism, supposedly a mixture of Manichaeism and Paulicians, was first recorded in the reign of Bulgarian Tsar, Peter (927-969). It is assumed Bogomilism was formed by a priest named Bogomil. The meaning of the name, Bogomil, is not certain; however, the general connotation connects it to *love and worthiness of God's mercy*. The Bogomils are defined as rejecting both the Old Testament and the Christian Church. They were moderate dualists with missionaries spreading the word of their faith. When first noted, they had become a distinct group with their own teachings. By 928, Byzantine's oppression toward the Bogomils probably drove some of them west. France reported this heresy around 1003. As the eleventh century progressed, persecution of heretics increased. It isn't known if this centered on Bogomils; at that time, the Church used the term *Manichaean* in reference to all heresies. By 1050, heresy seemed to diminish; most of the condemned groups could not survive their severe punishment. Although, there are reports of Bogomils into the eighteenth century.

Cathars

Scholars note a religious group with the name Cathars, in Cologne, Germany as early as 1143. Those Cathars, widely known as the *heresy* of the Middle Ages, had no connection with a group also named Cathars who were condemned as heretics during the Council of Nicaea. That earlier group had taken the name *Cathars*, from the Greek *Katharoi,* meaning *pure ones.* They did not believe in dualism; however, they did speak against the Catholic Church. The first Cathars died out in the fifth century. [Note the use of *Katharoi* in Manichaeism.]

The German Cathars challenged the Catholic Church which they called *the church of Satan.* The Cathars became highly organized in their opposition to Rome and were persecuted by the Church as heretics. Within a few years, Cathars had settled in the area of southern France called the Languedoc.

Cathars claimed their beginning came from early Christianity; their central belief was of morality—only the pure of heart would be saved. They lived an austere life. Unlike the earlier Cathars, they saw the world as divided by forces of heaven and hell, good and evil. Another principle of Cathars, revealed only to a select few, portrayed Jesus as an apparition, not a flesh and blood human. This concept, *Docetism,* was declared heresy by the Church.

The quickly spreading Cathars called themselves the *Good Christians.* Members came from ordinary men and women with normal jobs living in towns or villages. They did not live in seclusion; they gathered in homes, barns, or fields. Cathars only prayed the Lord's Prayer and did not honor the cross, a symbol of torture. Equality among women and men existed. Cathars lived "*in* the world—but not *of* the world."

Persecution followed the expansion of Cathars. In 1208, the Catholic Church called for a Crusade against the Cathars. A year later, nine thousand Cathars lost their lives at the start of the Albigensian Crusade, centered in southern France. Cathars' fortresses continued to fall. By 1231 (1233?), the Inquisition reached the Cathars. Killings continued. Catharism nearly came to an end in 1244 with the fall of the fortress of Montségur in the Pyrenees, the mountain range along the French-Spanish border. A few Cathars survived until 1389, when the remaining members were arrested and put to death.

Cathars and their faith were extinguished; stories of the Holy Grail and Cathars remain. The Grail myth is not just the imagination of current writers; it has long been part of the Cathar story. The first written account of the Grail was around 1180 when Knights of King Arthur searched for the Grail. There are different interpretations of what the Grail actually represents. It has been thought of as a chalice, texts of ancient wisdom, and also, as the blood line of Jesus and Mary Magdalene. One of the Cathars' inner teachings, passed on only to those of the highest rank, was that the two were married.

Some reports of the Grail say it was smuggled out of Montségur shortly before its fall and hidden in a nearby cave or given to the Knights Templars. Cathars, the Knights Templars, and the Troubadours, shared the Languedoc during the thirteenth century. Troubadours, wandering poets, wrote of love, bravery and honor. Many love songs spoke about an unattainable woman. Some poems and songs were allegories, in which symbols are used to tell of moral or religious principles. Often, inferences included the Virgin Mary.

Knights Templars, the most powerful military religious order of that time, were major landowners in the Languedoc. History shows some connection between the Templars and the Cathars, though it is not clearly detailed. The Templars refused to participate in the Albigensian Crusade. Later, they, like the Cathars, faced charges of heresy.

During a time of profound change in Europe, Cathars appeared. It is noted—heresy played a large part in shaping the concept of witchcraft and the persecution of innocent thousands during the Witch Craze of the sixteenth and seventeenth centuries.

Crossroads

Early Christianity saw the formation of the Roman Catholic Church. As in all times, changes and conflicts continued. Following is a brief mention of some of the noteworthy issues faced as the growth of Christianity became interwoven into the fabric of life across many nations.

East—West Schism 1054-1204

With the establishment of the Catholic Church, differences surfaced regarding Church organization. Questions regarding the nature of God and religious truths became major concerns. For some time, the Church in Rome and the one in Constantinople tried to settle their differences over those issues. With little success, formal separation of the two began in 1054, though it took until 1204 before the irrevocable split. The Church of Constantinople, the Eastern (Greek) branch became known as the Eastern Orthodox Church while the Western (Latin) Church became the Roman Catholic Church. That division, called the *Great Schism*, permanently altered the Church.

Crusades 1099-1291

Crusades, a series of Holy Wars between European Christians and Islamic Muslims, lasted close to two centuries. Starting in 622, from Mecca in Arabia, Mohammed began uniting the Arab tribes under his belief of one God. The religion of Mohammed is Islam and the followers are Muslims. Mohammed's proclamation that Muslims had permission to fight against their enemies turned the tribes into fierce warriors. In 638, Jerusalem, Holy City to Jews and Christians, fell to the Muslims. Jerusalem became a Muslim holy place and Palestine was organized into military districts. Conflicts between Christians and Muslims led to the Crusades.

In the First Crusade (1099), Jerusalem was reclaimed by European Christians. After that victory, Christian soldiers sewed red crosses on their uniforms to indicate they were following Jesus' words from Matthew 16:24: *If any man wishes to come after me, let him deny himself, and take up his cross, and follow me.* Crusades continued across Muslim held lands. Jerusalem once more fell to Muslims. Christians recaptured their Holy City two more times between 1229 and 1244 when again the city reverted to Muslims. Muslim control lasted until World War I when Jerusalem was captured by the British.

Accounts dating the ending of the Crusades differ. Some place it at 1244, others 1291. Too, the number of Crusades differ as there were some less intense than others.

Knights Templars 1120-1312

Forming of the Knights Templars came after the First Crusade when Christians reclaimed Jerusalem. Christians, once again, set out on pilgrimages to the Holy City; they required safe passage through the surrounding battle fields. The Knights provided that service.

Research suggests the Knights were probably first associated with an Augustinian Order who provided lodging for the Knights until 1120 when the Order of Knights Templars was officially recognized. The original name for the Order was the *Poor Fellow-Soldiers of Christ*, as the Knights were poor monks and dressed in donated clothing. Later, they had uniforms of white with a red cross. The king of Jerusalem granted the Knights a place to live in a temple surrounded by other holy structures. After their temple headquartering, the Order was known as *Knights Templars*; in time, they became wealthy and powerful.

Donations given by wealthy land owners began in 1127 and continued. From France, England and Scotland, came gold, silver, housing, and more. All given for the defense of the Holy Land and for the donors' salvation. Before long, the Templars were asked to assist in warfare against enemies of Christians. They became a determining force of the Crusades.

Pope Innocent II, in 1139, established the Templars as an independent and permanent Order within the Catholic Church; the Pope had sole jurisdiction over the Templars. The Templars became one of the most powerful financial and military organization in the Medieval World. However, this came to an end in less than two hundred years.

In 1291, the Templars were dealt a major defeat in Acre of Syria. Continued losses left no Christians in the land of Syria. The Templars, as a military knighthood, were to preserve the

Holy Land; at this, they failed. In 1292 Jacques de Molay, became the Templars Grand Master with renewed hope of recovering the Holy Land.

Pope Clement V and King Philip IV of France, in 1307, began plans for a new Crusade. With the help of the Templars, they planned to gain back the Holy Land. However, conflicts between the pope and Philip halted the mission. Jacques de Molay traveled to Paris seeking the king's favor, unknowing that the French king planted spies among the Templars and had reported suspected heresy among them. After a seemingly warm welcome, on Friday, October 13th, the king, on charges of heresy, had Jacques de Molay arrested along with all the Templars across France. King Philip's reason for the arrests was his wish to confiscate the wealth of the Templars.

The Templars were severely tortured until confessing to the charges brought against them. In less than two weeks, the honor of the Templars was lost. A year later, Pope Clement absolved Jacques de Molay and other Templars of any wrong doing.

After years of infighting between the pope and the king, in 1312, under pressure, the pope abolished the Order and forfeited his power over the fate of the Templars. Penalties placed on the majority of Templars, still in the hands of the French court, varied from lengthy imprisonment to life in a monastery. The leaders were held until 1314 before a final sentencing. After seven years in the king's prison, Jacques de Molay and Geoffrey of Charney, the Master of Normandy, loudly protesting their innocence, were burned at the stake.

Other accounts claim a number of Templars hid their wealth and fled to Scotland before the arrest in France. Merriam-Webster's definition of Knights Templars includes the term Freemasonry. *Haag does not address the outcome of Templars in other parts of the Christian world.*

Inquisition 1231 (1233?)-late Eighteenth Century

The Inquisition, a force of the Roman Catholic Church, combated heresy with severe questioning and punishment. The first official Inquisition targeted Cathars of France. Those accused had no way of defending themselves. During times of the Protestant Reformation (1517-1648) and the Catholic Counter-Reformation (1545-1563), the Inquisition expanded to other European countries. Colonies of Spain and Portugal were included in the effort to maintain strict adherence to the Catholic doctrine. With expansion, the focus of persecution included Witch Hunts of the sixteenth and seventeenth centuries.

Martin Luther 1483-1546

Luther, after being a monk, was ordained as a priest in 1507. Five years later, with a doctorate degree, he began teaching theology at the university at Wittenberg, Germany. During that time, Luther began writing essays on the doctrine of the Catholic Church. By 1514 he was appointed minister of the town's church. There, the congregation enjoyed his telling of biblical stories spoken in simple words. As Luther gained responsibility within the Church, he began questioning its doctrine.

Not only did Martin challenge the rituals, he rejected the priests' role in interpreting the Bible in the way they saw fit for the common people. Priests told the people what was right and wrong. In so doing, emphasis was placed on following the rituals and asking for forgiveness of sins. Priests had the only authority to forgive sins. If one did not receive forgiveness of sins and repent, salvation and ever-lasting life could not be attained. Luther's belief was based on *justification by faith alone.* He spoke of a direct relationship with God; priests were not necessary for individuals to reach God. Salvation came from faith, not from following rules set by the Church.

Another custom of the priests Luther addressed was the selling of religious positions and *indulgences.* Indulgences provided forgiveness of sins at a cost. Depending on the amount of money paid for an indulgence, the sinner could reduce or eliminate the number of years in purgatory. Priests saw this practice of buying forgiveness as an individual's act of repentance. Selling both indulgences and religious positions became a major source of fundraising for many Churches.

In 1517, Luther wrote his complaints regarding indulgences in *Ninety-Five Theses* which he attached to the door of the Church, then sent a copy to his bishop and the archbishop. Rome retaliated by formally alleging *suspicion of disseminating heresy,* against Luther. In addition, Luther was ordered to Rome and to face the Inquisition. In 1521, Luther was excommunicated.

Luther continued his work. He and his followers took the name *Lutherans.* Luther had begun translating the New Testament into a German dialect in 1517; it was completed and ready for sale in five years. Between 1523 and 1530, the translation of the Old Testament was on the market and three years later, every German household had a Luther Bible. A full Luther Bible, with both Testaments, was released in 1534. Luther was the most published writer in the world; his translations left a lasting impact on the German language. In England, William Tyndale drew from Luther's work as he translated the Bible into the English language. In later years, Luther's position on the Peasants' War in 1524-1525 and his anti-Semitic writings left lasting criticism.

Protestant Reformation 1517-1648

In the sixteenth century, opposition within Christianity came from a number of different individuals. John Wycliffe, Jan Hus, Martin Luther, and John Calvin were among those labeled as *reformers.* They protested doctrines, rituals, leadership and structure of the Roman Catholic Church. Their efforts led to the formation of Protestantism, taken from the word *protest.* The Reformation sought to end the questionable practices of the Catholic Church and place the Bible as the authority of spiritual guidance. The invention of the printing press in 1452 strengthened the efforts of the reformers.

The Protestant Reformation is commonly noted as beginning in 1517 with Martin Luther's publication of *The Ninety-Five Theses.* The 1555 Peace of Augsburg gave both Catholics and Lutherans the right to practice their own religion in Germany. In 1648 the Peace of Westphalia ended the Thirty Years' War bringing an end to the Reformation at which time Lutheranism was the state religion in Germany.

Reform in England 1534-1559

King Henry VIII (1509-1547) began England's reformation movement in 1534 when Pope Clement VII refused to grant him an annulment from his wife, Catherine of Aragon. The queen had not provided a male heir and the king wanted to remarry. Following the Pope's decision, Henry declared he alone had authority over churches in England and formed the Church of England. He abolished monasteries and confiscated their holdings. Another change came with Bibles being made available for the common people as they were placed in the newly formed churches.

On Henry's death, a large number of England's population upheld the new Church of England through the reign of King Edward VI. Henry's daughter, Queen Mary I, followed Edward. Mary, daughter of Catherine returned Catholicism to England. When Henry's other daughter Elizabeth, daughter of his second wife, became queen in 1559, the Church of England continued; however, individuals were not held to a specific religion.

Council of Trent 1545-1563

First meeting in 1545, the Council of Trent, a Catholic Counter-Reformation action, is noted as one of the Catholic Church's most important Councils. Conducting meetings for close to twenty years, critical issues regarding the Protestant Reformation and the continued influence of the reformers were studied. The Council resolved to stress additional literacy and education in an effort to promote strict religious practices throughout their lands. To combat Protestant heresies, the Inquisition in Spain and Rome were reorganized. Additionally, the Council declared the Apocrypha books equal to other approved Scripture.

CHAPTER 11

Biblical Lands Past-Present

Reflections Changes
The Promised Land
  Israel/Palestine, Galilee
Regional Ties
  Jordan, Syria, Egypt, Turkey, Lebanon, Yemen, Iraq, Iran

Reflections   Changes

Like the rest of the world, the region called the Promised Land sees unending changes. Land surfaces and climate phases accompany empire shifts. Names and terminology are altered with differing rulers. The rise and fall of civilizations divided the land that once was Canaan and the countries that were instrumental to that history. Fighting and wars seem to dominate biblical times in the same way they tear apart countries today. It appears humanity continues on in destructive ways. Conflicts that have been—and continue—into the current century, are too numerous to cover in this writing.

Currently, strife and unrest in and around the Promised Land draws worldwide attention with shared concerns of safety and peace. Starting with Canaan, some countries had close ties; others, separated by distance, were a vital part in the balance of ongoing life. So it is, today.

New generations and new names will determine the future of the Middle East.

The Promised Land

Presently, as in the past, other nations impact the region referred to as *the Promised Land*. Following, a review of previously documented times offers a historical perspective in looking at current circumstances. Of interest is the designation of *Near East* and *Middle East* seen and heard often in the twenty-first century. There are various definitions, a common one is: **Near East**, the ancient Holy Land of Israel, Lebanon, Syria, and Jordan, while the **Middle East** includes Iraq, Iran, Afghanistan, Kuwait, United Arab Emirates, Turkey, Qatar, and Bahrain. Some accounts include Egypt in the Middle East, as well as other regional countries.

The land of Israel today has known many names. After Noah's Flood, lands were divided between his sons and their sons. A grandson settled in the area bordering the eastern Mediterranean Sea which then carried his name, Canaan. In early times Egyptians defeated a group of sea people they called Philistines who seemed to have moved into the area of Canaan. Assyrians knew this group as *Pilisti* or *Palastu,* the bases for the word *Palestine.* Biblical accounts name Canaan as the Promised Land God gave to Abraham (Abram) and his descendants. Abraham was a Hebrew. During the life of Jacob (Israel), grandson of Abraham, the large Hebrew family left Canaan because of a famine in that land. They journeyed to Egypt where they multiplied and eventually became slaves, remaining for four hundred years. Moses led his people, the Hebrews, out of Egypt with the intent of returning to their Promised Land. After forty years at the foot of Mount Sinai, Joshua, a descendant of Jacob, led his people into Canaan. Historians have placed the return in the year 1240 BCE.

It took hundreds of years before the Hebrews were able to regain their Promised Land. The Hebrew tribes were successful and Canaan became the **United Kingdom of Israel** and then, Hebrews called themselves Israelites. After more years, the kingdom divided into the **Kingdom of Israel** in the north and the **Kingdom of Judah** in the south. Judah was another descendant of Jacob. In time, the Kingdom of Israel fell to the Assyrian Empire and its inhabitants were lost to history. When Judah fell to the Babylonian Empire, the Israelites were taken into bondage. In 539 BCE, Cyrus of Persia defeated the Babylonians and gave the Israelites an option of returning to their home land. On their return, they called themselves *Jews* with the religion of Judaism. Under Greek rule, the spelling of their land was changed to **Judea**. Following years under Egyptian and Syrian control, Jews again ruled over their own independent country of Judea.

Changes came in 63 BCE with the Romans. In 135 CE, Rome defeated a second major Jewish revolt, expelled surviving Jews and named Abraham's Promised Land **Palestine**. Jerusalem was named Aelia Capitolina, denoting the Roman Emperor and a Roman god.

With the rise of Christianity, Palestine became the Christians' Holy Land. However, in 638, Muslims conquered Palestine. A few times during the Crusades, Christians managed to regain their Holy Land. Yet, the Muslim Ottoman Empire held the land of Palestine from 1517 until World War I.

Israel/Palestine

Before World War I, Jews began a migration to Muslim controlled Palestine. A Zionist movement sought a Jewish state with freedom to govern themselves. They saw their settling in Palestine as a return to their Promised Land. At the beginning of the war, about 100,000 Jews, 550,000 Muslims, and 70,000 Christians lived in Palestine. Muslim rule ended with the War. Palestine, with other surrounding countries, came under the control of Britain.

In 1917, led by an influential Zionist, the Belfour Declaration was sent to Britain. The document requested Palestine be declared a national home for the Jewish people. The British government supported the action; however, no plan was proposed for carrying out the declaration. Nevertheless, Jewish population in Palestine greatly increased with settlements spreading across Palestine, including the city of Jerusalem.

The influx of Jews changed the lives of the Palestinian Muslims. Jews purchased farmlands from Muslim landlords, forcing long time Muslim tenant farmers to relocate. In 1919, most Palestinian Christians and Muslims worked to form a

United Arab State. Their action was overruled four years later by a British mandate formally incorporating a Jewish national home in Palestine. Again, no official allocation of territories was included in the plan. Situations worsened for non-Jewish communities who lacked strong leadership plus the means to provide health care and education for their people. Around that time, Palestinian Muslims became known as *Palestinian Arabs,* or simply *Palestinians,* as a way to separate them from the Jewish sector.

Conditions deteriorated further for Palestinians in **1947** when Britain turned Palestine over to the **United Nations** (UN) and a **political partition of Palestine** was approved. Sixty percent of Palestine became a *Jewish State* even though Jewish settlers were only one-third of the population. The Palestinians received Galilee, Gaza (a narrow strip at the southern end bordering the Mediterranean Sea), and the West Bank (a larger area west of the Jordan River). Former Judea and Samaria fell in the West Bank. The city of Jerusalem, in the West Bank, remained under the jurisdiction of the United Nations.

As conflicts escalated, surrounding Arab countries became involved. Early in 1948 an Arab Liberation Army was formed in part by Syria, Egypt, Jordan, Lebanon, and Iraq. The joint forces were insufficient in facing the Jewish organization and their advanced military. More Palestinians fled Palestine. On **May 14, 1948**, the prime minister of the Jewish partition proclaimed their allocated land as the **State of Israel**. The name *Israel* replaced the name *Palestine.*

The **Israel-Arab War of 1948-1949**, Arab countries against Israel, began the next day. With Israel's victory, new boundaries gave Israel 70% of the land, Palestinians retained most of the West Bank (controlled by Jordan) and the Gaza Strip (administered by Egypt). Israel claimed Galilee, a portion of the West Bank, and a few other smaller areas. The city of Jerusalem was divided. The

Old City (east), a religious site for Jews, Christians, and Muslims, went to Jordan. Eventually the Old City became *East Jerusalem*. Israel received the western part of the city, where Jews had settled earlier.

Following their loss, an additional 700,000 Palestinian refugees left what had become the State of Israel. Regardless of the divisions of land, some Palestinian communities remain in the Israel sections; likewise, Jewish communities exist in areas allocated to the Palestinians.

In 1955, Egypt obtained Soviet funds for arms and to build a dam. Seeking to repay the Soviets, Egypt seized the Anglo-French Suez Canal Company and the entrance to the Gulf of Aqaba, located on Israel's southern tip. In turn, Israel attacked across the Sinai Peninsula and closed the Gulf. Known as the **1956 Suez War**, the UN halted further action. They demanded Israel's withdrawal and left an Emergency Force on the Egyptian side to ensure safety. The Gulf of Aqaba was left open.

An Arab Summit Council, in **1964**, established the **Palestine Liberation Organization (PLO)** for providing Palestinians a larger role in protecting their allotted territory. As the only representative for Palestinians, the PLO denied Jordan any claim to the West Bank. Regardless, Jordan's status was unchanged. Ongoing PLO's guerrilla attacks on Israel from Syria and Jordan increased Israel's military action against Palestinians.

The **War of 1967 (Six Day War)** began when the Egyptian president ordered the UN forces, in place since 1956, to leave and moved his troops into Sinai, closing the entrance to the Gulf of Aqaba. Jordan and Syria joined with Egypt over the issue; Israel retaliated with full force. Within a few hours, Egyptian forces were defeated. By the end of the war, Israel had taken the West Bank and the Old (east) City of Jerusalem from Jordan, plus Golan, a strip of northern Syria. Israel settled more people into its increased areas. Later that year, under the UN Security Council Resolution for Peace, Israel was to withdraw from the newly claimed territories. Israel did not comply.

In **1973**, Egypt dismissed Soviet military units and other personnel. Then with Syria, opened war on Israel, targeting Israeli occupation in the two Arab countries. Again, the combined Arab forces were no match against Israel's superior defense. Israel contained an entire Egyptian army and Syria retreated. In the end, both sides realized their wars were ineffective. The following years, the United States (US) became involved in a lengthy disengagement agreement.

A peace settlement in **1979**, between Egypt and Israel, stipulated that Israel withdraw troops from the Suez Canal and the Sinai oil fields they had claimed ten years earlier. Egypt allowed Israel non-military use of the Suez Canal. Egypt restored diplomatic relations with the US; a few years later, Arab nations broke diplomatic relationship with Egypt. (Egypt returned to the Arab League in 1989.) The disengagement agreement did return to Syria a narrow portion of their Golan. Through it all, peace was not achieved and conflicts continued.

The **1987 Arab protest** of Israeli occupation in the West Bank and Gaza drew attention to the plight of the Palestinians against Israel. The Western World voiced its outrage toward the violence directed on Palestinians by Israel. Little changed but a short time later Jordan withdrew any claim to the West Bank. The UN Security Council declared, in **1988, Palestine's Independence**; many countries do not acknowledge the decision.

An agreement in the early **1990s**, stipulated Israel's withdrawal of Jewish settlements in Palestinian allocated partitions. Israel did remove some of its settlements. However, additional Arab violence halted Israel's efforts to abide by the agreement. In **1994**, the **PLO** took control of Gaza. Jewish settlements remain in Gaza, the West Bank, Eastern Jerusalem and the narrow strip in Syria. Also, that year a **Jordan-Israel peace treaty** was signed.

An **Arab uprising in 2011**, given the name *Arab Spring*, brought uncertainty to much of the Middle East while creating greater awareness to other nations of the growing turmoil in the region. As in other countries, protesters in Jordan, Egypt, and Syria, demanded change. Lasting effects of the movement are uncertain.

Another change for Israel came in May of **2018** when the United States President, Donald Trump, moved the **US Embassy** from Tel Aviv to Jerusalem, thus recognizing the Holy City as the capital of Israel. Palestinians continue to claim East Jerusalem and look to the day it will be the capital of a Palestinian state. They oppose President Trump's actions. Jerusalem remains the capital city of Israel, yet few nations recognize this directive. Israel is governed from Tel Aviv where other foreign embassies remain.

The World Today Series 2017-2018, The Middle East and South Asia, by Seth Cantey, details numerous agreements and treaties related to the Israel-Arab situation, from the time of the first Jewish immigration and into the present. Discord continues. Through the years of changes in leadership and governments of Israel and Palestinians, policies and agreements are altered. Also, both parties contain a number of varying factions; each wanting their own concerns addressed. Other countries have helped in negotiating peace, that too lacked the desired outcome. Wars have come and gone, even before the time of the Hebrews. The World asks: "Will there ever be a time of peace?".

Galilee Past-Present

Jesus spent his childhood in Galilee and later, most of his ministry occurred in that area. Centuries before, King Solomon gifted twenty cities in Galilee to a neighboring king in payment for cedar and other materials. After Solomon's death, northern kings ruled over Galilee. When Assyria conquered the region, they resettled the inhabitants farther north. Galilee became a region of foreigners, as neighboring kingdoms often moved their conquered people to that area. During the Hasmonean period (164-63 BCE), Galilee was included in the Jewish realm. Under Roman rule, Herod the Great (37BCE-4CE) was given the country of Galilee.

In the political partition of Palestine in 1947, Galilee fell into the Arab Palestinian portion of land. Although, after the 1948-1949 Israel War of Independence, Israel claimed Galilee.

Regional Ties

Middle East borders, separating territories into individual countries, in many instances, appeared in Modern Times. Yet, even without borders, nomadic tribes had a keen sense for the land that was theirs. Territories, then and now, have been defended, growing or shrinking with the rise and fall of civilizations. For the sake of history, the changing of names and lines are updated on maps and globes, holding visions of intrigue, adventure, and heartbreak. Accounts of the following countries hold all three.

Jordan

In Biblical times, the Jordan River, as it makes its way down to the Dead Sea, formed the eastern boundary of Judea. The Gospels of the New Testament tell of John the Baptist speaking of repentance and a return to the ways of God, along the banks of the Jordan. He baptized Jesus in the River. Both Romans and Byzantines farmed the plateaus east of the River, as it continues its descent into desert, where only *Bedouin* nomads survived. Until the nineteenth century, Bedouins dominated the area. Eventually, settlements appeared along with Ottoman control.

During World War I, Bedouins fought with Arabs and Britain against the Ottomans. After Britain's victory, their *League of Nations* included the Jordan Valley as part of the *Palestine Mandate*. At that time, the name *Jordan* referred only to the river and its banks. On the west bank, established cities, some including Zionists, existed and prosperous farms dotted the fertile valley. A far different condition lay on the east bank of few towns, warring Bedouins, meager farms, and scant government. Britain gave the name *Emirate of Transjordan* to the lands east and west of the Jordan and appointed **Abdullah** as ruler. Previously, he had ruled the area and was loyal to Britain. Abdullah formed a military, the *Arab Legion*, who then brought some law and order to the east bank.

Abdullah's Legion joined Britain again as allies during World War II. A treaty in 1946 gave independence to Transjordan and Abdullah claimed the title of *King*. A year later, the United Nations (UN) partitioned Palestine between Jews and Arab Palestinians. Transjordan, consisting of both the west and east banks of the Jordan River was included in an area designated for the Arab Palestinians. Jerusalem, centered in the west bank, remained undivided as an International City, under British control.

The Arab Legion fought against Israel in the Israeli-Arab War of 1948-1949, capturing the Jewish section of Jerusalem's Old City (east). Within the year, a Palestinian congress named Abdullah king of all Palestine territories. In 1949, Abdullah formally annexed the portion of Israel controlled by his troops.

Israel claimed the newer city of Jerusalem (west) and a portion of the West Bank. Remaining as a Palestinian holding, Gaza came under Egyptian administration. The reduced West Bank fell under the control of Jordan. Abdullah named his realm the *Kingdom of Jordan,* with Amman as capital. In 1951 Abdullah was assassinated; a grandson, **Hussein**, began his rule two years later.

Hussein, in 1967, formed an unwanted treaty with Egypt resulting in the Jordan-Egypt War against Israel. Partially, Jordan joined in the war over issues of water rights. Israel, shortly after statehood, through the use of canals and pipelines, directed irrigation water from the Jordan River. In four days of fighting, Jordanian units west of the Jordan River fell to Israel who then seized the richest portions of that kingdom. After the 1987 Arab Dispute, Jordan gave up its West Bank. Conflicts with Israel continued until 1994 with the signing of a peace treaty between Jordan and Israel. Jordan regained water rights, a small amount of Israel held land, plus, US waived nearly one billion dollars on loans. Hussein died of cancer in 1999 leaving the throne to his son Abdullah.

Jordan's rough times continue with issues related to ISIS (Islamic State in Iraq and Syria)* and Syria. Plus, their sluggish economy, water shortages, and countless refugees add to Jordan's uncertainty while dealing with the chaos of their neighbors. Nevertheless, Jordanians today see the brutality in Syria and find a degree of security and stability in their own royal government.

*Islam: Muslim's religion ISIS: militant Islamic group

Syria

Saul of Tarsus, on his way to confront Christians in Damascus (Syria), encountered a vision that changed his life. Under the name Paul, he joined other Apostles in spreading the word of

Jesus. Syria was one of the places early Christians gathered, as it was somewhat removed from the threat of Rome. In today's world, few would travel to Syria for safety.

Syria flourished during the seventh and eighth centuries; however, as various Muslim Empires weakened, Syria's geographic location led to ongoing invasions. In the late 1800s, Damascus was an important Ottoman province. The present international borders did not exist at that time.

Preceding World War I, different factions in Syria worked at establishing an Arab independence. After the war, the Arab army administered Syria though French troops occupied a small portion in the west. In 1920, Damascus, the capital, declared independence for Syria; however, it was short-lived as France invaded and imposed their rule over Syria. They divided Syria into small regions for various ethnic minorities plus the region of Lebanon.

Syrians protested the French government. In time, some who opposed the French took control of the government. Nevertheless, other groups vied for leadership. Discord between the groups led to corruption which did little to unite the government. At the end of World War II, France withdrew from Syria; its independence came in 1946. Historians feel problems remaining today stem from the separations made by France.

After World War II, Syria joined Egypt and Jordan in the 1948-1949 War against Israel. The joint Arab forces were defeated; at that time, Syria did not suffer loss of territory. Regardless, Syria was left in a weakened state. The military, headed by **Husni al-Za'im**, overthrew the government. He arranged a cease-fire with Israel and a verbal alliance with Iraq. Five months later, al-Za'im was executed, resulting in more military coups and continued instability.

In the mid-1950s, Syria received Soviet military equipment

and in 1958, with Egypt, formed the short-lived *United Arab Republic.* Both countries faced their own economic problems and were unable to support the joint effort.

Clashes with Israel continued. In 1967 Syria, Egypt, and Jordan attacked Israel. The Arab nations could not match Israel's strength. At the end of six days, Syria had lost Golan, a small stretch of land bordering Israel.

General **Hafiz al-Assad** seized power in 1970 and was elected president a year later. He was instrumental in establishing a new constitution that included an elected legislature. Regardless, the legislature had little power as decisions were made by the president, his close circle of family, and military officers.

The fifty years of Hafiz al-Assad's presidency saw no change in policies and unrest remained. One highly vocal group of opposition, the illegal *Muslim Brotherhood* wanted an Islamic State and an end to military rule. Eventually they revolted with violence and killings.

Syria, in 1973, joined Egypt in an attempt to rid themselves of Israel's occupation. At the end of the conflict, a portion of Golan was returned to Syria. Meanwhile, wanting to strengthening its military, Syria sought high-tech weapons from the Soviet Union. The request was refused as Syria lacked funds for payment. Al-Assad was against the Camp David Accords and ended its country's friendship with Egypt, the United States, and Palestinian Arabs. Conflicts between Iran and Iraq occurred through the 1980's; Syria backed Iran, then condemned the United States invasion of Iraq in 2003.

Hafiz al-Assad died in 2000 and his son **Bashar al-Assad**, became president. Reform issues Bashar spoke of saw little change. During the Arab Spring of 2011, al-Assad and his ruling circle rejected changes proposed by a new cabinet. Demonstrations were crushed, killing many participants. Efforts to end the repression and fighting were ineffective. The United Nations' attempts to offer aid were blocked by Russia.

A number of groups opposing al-Assad's regime failed to unite and by 2012 a Civil War erupted. The brutality and use of chemical weapons that followed alarmed the World. Retaliation from the United States brought condemnation from Iran and Russia.

Another try to unite opposing rebels for establishing a government of moderation was unsuccessful. The *Islamic State (IS)** was extremely aggressive in seeking territory, for that reason, other rebel groups did ban together in fighting the *IS*. Additional joint forces, the United States and Iraq being two, helped in curtailing *IS*. Reports in 2017 indicate *IS* had lost close to fifty percent of land held in Syria. It seems likely *IS* will be unable to regain its former status. Also, in 2017, the support of Russia and Iran firmly secured the current regime. Unrest in Syria is likely to last many more years.

*_IS_: often referred to as ISIS, the name that identified the *Islamic State of Iraq and Syria*

Egypt

Egypt, an ancient civilization of pharaohs and pyramids, still holds mysteries. The heritage of all humanity lies along the country's Nile River basin. In biblical times, Egypt offered refuge to the family of Abraham. Much later, Joseph with Mary and the infant Jesus, found safety in Egypt when they fled the threat of Herod the Great. Today, sitting at the crossroads between Africa and Asia, Egypt's population of Arabs far exceeds the other Arab nations. It is considered the center of Arab culture.

During the seventh century CE, under the Byzantine Empire,

Egyptian Coptics, descendants of ancient Egyptians, were the predominate inhabitants. Muslim armies, with little opposition from the Coptics, conquered the land. Egyptians adopted the Arabic language and the Islamic faith. With time, Muslims lost their control over Egypt and local governments took over, lasting until 1517 when the Ottoman Empire claimed Egypt.

Egypt fell to Napoleon of France in 1798. Three years later, **Muhammad Ali** of the Ottoman army arrived with the task of removing the French occupants. However, on his success, Ali claimed power for himself. In maintaining Egypt as part of the Ottoman Empire, in 1806, Ali was assigned to head the government and Egypt became a self-governed region of the Ottoman Empire. Ali's reorganization of Egypt brought it to a modern state. Through all the changes, Cairo remained the capital.

Following Ali, his son, in 1856 commissioned the French construction of the Suez Canal from the Mediterranean Sea to the Red Sea. Under another administration, Egypt sold its share of the Canal to Britain. In 1882 Britain sent troops to Egypt in an attempt to overthrow the Ottomans. Britain was able to place its own Consul General in power, though Egypt remained part of the Ottoman Empire until Britain's victory in World War I. In 1923, persistent disagreements between Egypt and Britain led to Britain granting Egypt's Independence, with conditions. A succession of monarchs followed with little gain for Egypt. Hostility left the country in disarray and friction mounted after Egypt's loss to Israel in 1949. At that time, the political Islamicist group, *Muslim Brotherhood*, increased their influence in the government. The *Brotherhood*, a long-standing political Islamist group, promotes Islamic Law.

The military, by 1952, seized control of the government, initiating programs to provide the country with an honest government, a reduction in poverty, and increased educational opportunities. The leader of the movement, **Abdul Nasser** became president two years later. Arms were purchased from Communist Czechoslovakia, increasing Soviet influence in the Middle East. In bringing about change, a policy of *Arab Socialism* was adopted; citizens saw only small benefits.

In 1970, Nasser died unexpectedly and **Anwar Sadat** became president. Three years later he dismissed many of the Soviets and then, with Syria, made a final attack on Israel. On his defeat, Sadat realized the penalties Egypt suffered were not worth more fighting. He accepted a truce with Israel, although, attempts at peace settlements were ongoing. Sadat was assassinated in 1981 and **Husni Mubarak** became president.

During Mubarak's presidency, a new phase of Islamic values appeared. Some groups were peaceful, while others were extremists and violent. Demonstrations and protests, some involving arson and murder, increased. The government made little gain in attempting to end Islamist opposition. Muslim-Christian relationships suffered. Coptic Christians were targets of repeated assaults. Amid protests in 2011 (Arab Spring) Mubarak resigned; charges against him led to his imprisonment. The military gained leadership.

After a complicated election battle **Mohammed Morsi**, a Muslim Brotherhood candidate, was elected president. By June of 2013, the military intervened and Morsi and other leading members of the *Brotherhood* were arrested.

A step toward democracy came in 2014 with the election of **Abdul Fattah al-Sisi** who imposes harsh sentences to combat terrorism. Morsi was sentenced to death for his part in the Arab Spring and charges of spying. With the new regime, many *Brotherhood* members and supporters have been killed. In 2017, Mubarak was released from jail and Morsi's conviction awaited an appeal.

While preparing this book for publication, The Denver Post printed an article, from the Associated Press in Cairo, stating the death of Morsi, which occurred at his trail. During the sessions, he was held in a glass cage. After addressing the court and revealing he had *many secrets*, Morsi collapsed; he did not regain consciousness.

Nations watching Egypt from abroad, hope for the best. Kings, presidents, military rulers, have come and gone—mysteries of the pyramids last.

Turkey

Roman Emperor Constantine, in 325, called for 300 bishops to attend a meeting in Nicaea, Turkey, to decide on a statement of belief that all Catholic Christian Churches would uphold. The Nicaea Creed is still repeated in many Christian Churches today. Also, Constantine chose the Greek city of Byzantium for the site of his new capital. Given the name Constantinople, it became the center of the Byzantine Empire, where Hellenistic influence flourished. In 1435 the empire fell to the Ottomans who changed the name to Istanbul and it became the culture and economic center of Turkey.

Turkey, the heart of the Ottoman Empire, experienced the shuffling that occurred after World War I. The Arab portions of the country fell to Britain and France. Turkish speaking provinces were partitioned among Italy, Greece, Armenia, and Turkey. The Ottoman Empire ended; however, some Ottomans remained in the new breakdown of Turkey. In 1920, an Ottoman army official, **Mustafa Kemal** sent a delegate of citizens to Ankara, in an effort to save the nation. Kemal was elected president and established an independent Turkey. French troops were forced out, Italy and Britain withdrew, and the new Turkey claimed Armenia. After a bitter war, Greece and Turkey made peace. Turkey's borders today are much as they were under the Ottomans.

Kemal took the name **Atatürk** (*Father of the Turks*), proclaimed Turkey a republic in 1923 and major changes took place. The Caliph (spiritual head of Islam) and religious laws were abolished. The new constitution declared a democratic government and Kemal made Ankara, near the center of Turkey, the capital. Regardless of words on a paper, Atatürk was a dictator. Viciously, he put down opposition, especially the Kurds. Arabic script was replaced with the Latin alphabet. Religious schools were closed and harsh treatment forced most Christian Armenians and Greeks to leave the country. Atatürk wanted to remove all aspects of the Ottoman culture and move forward into a modern European society. Atatürk died in 1938; many in the country thought him a hero.

The following decades brought tremendous changes in governments, mostly violent in nature. The Kurds, overlooked in the World War I divisions, still seek recognition. Parliamentary elections in 2015 left uncertainty for the future. However, after the long years of conflict, Turkey is now seen as a major regional economic and political power.

Lebanon

The Hebrew Bible (1 Kings 5:8-10) tells of King Solomon using cedars from Lebanon for his building projects. Cedars of Lebanon are mentioned elsewhere in the Bible. In early history, Lebanon was conquered by Egypt, Babylonia, Rome, and the Ottoman Empire in 1516. In the late eighteenth century, international borders did not exist and the area of Lebanon reported to Damascus, an ancient city in the Syria region.

At the close of World War I, the territory of Lebanon/Syria was assigned to France. In 1918 French troops landed in Beirut (capital of Lebanon) and two years later invaded the rest of Lebanon. France proclaimed the area as the Republic of Lebanon in 1926, a country evenly divided between Christians and Muslims.

The British and French invasion of Syria and Lebanon in 1941 was followed by the separation of Syria and Lebanon into individual countries, with past declarations of independence negated. Lebanese Christian and Muslim politicians united and with pressure from Britain and the United States, France was forced, in 1943, to grant independence to Lebanon. Syria's independence came in 1946.

The agreement that led to Lebanon's independence provided for a government split between specific groups of Christians and Muslims; smaller religious groups were kept from participating in the highest offices. In 1958, corruption forced the first president out of office and dissatisfaction with the second president caused a disturbance referred to as a *restrained civil war*. In resolving the conflict addressing Christian versus Muslim control, the country's basic interests were not addressed. By the late 1960s, disapproval of the government reached throughout Lebanon; the gap between the rich and poor had grown. A government of individuals vying for power offered no solutions to the growing unrest.

Adding to the problems, in 1967, Palestinian Arabs who migrated to Lebanon launched guerrilla raids into Israel. Israel retaliated with attacks directed at Lebanese civilians, whose government could not control the Palestinians. By 1975, assassinations and small-scale violence between rival groups were signs that the Lebanese government and society were collapsing. Christians, wanting to regain control and restore order, tried to force Palestinian fighters out of Lebanon. Palestinians fought back and civil war between Christians and Muslims took hold.

The war created involvement with Syria, who invaded in 1976 to limit the Palestinians' influence and to aid the Christians. Israel invaded in 1978. United Nations forces nor the Arab League were able to bring peace, although a short period of less violence followed.

In 1982, Israel invaded to destroy Palestinians' military. The Lebanese government struggled to find a solution to the growing war. Finally, the United States (US) and European troops stepped in to end the fighting. They maintained order as Israel units withdrew. However, in trying to reorganize the army, they became part of the ongoing conflict. After US Marines were killed in the bombing of their barracks, American forces withdrew and the war continued.

Most of Lebanon fell under the control of local militias or foreign troops. A new president, in 1988, was determined to unite Lebanon and drive out the troops. Syria retaliated with attacks on civilians. No nation came to the aid of Lebanon until 1989 when Saudi Arabia assisted members of the Lebanese parliament to form a new constitutional arrangement. A change of presidents took place and the temporary occupation by Syria was established.

Under the new president, with support of Christian factions, fighting in parts of the country was eliminated. The Lebanese army secured the south in 1991. Although, the terrorist group, *Hizballah*, continued attacking Israeli troops. Finally, in 2000, the troops withdrew from Lebanon. The twenty-year civil war ended. It appears, the Lebanese war against Israel was the only Arab victory through a century long struggle.

Protest and political opinion against Syria caused their withdrawal in 2005. Even with the removal of foreign troops, turmoil among the various factions in Lebanon remain. With a new Lebanese president in 2016, the country has a chance of stability.

My heart skipped a beat when I read about the bombing of the United States Marine's barracks in 1982. My son, a Marine, was on a US carrier off the shore of Lebanon waiting to disembark. He stood looking at those waters, knowing he was next in line to face battle.

A moment of lasting questioning for him, before word came to turn back. Interesting—a crucial episode in a person's life is minimized to a sentence in a history book.

Yemen

Not really a part of the Promised Land, an episode in 1 Kings 10:1-13 deals with this country far to the south of present-day Israel. In biblical times, it was known as *Sheba,* an ancient and civilized kingdom. The Queen of Sheba and King Solomon became friends. They seemed to be drawn together by their great wisdom and wit. The Queen traveled to the Kingdom of Israel for discussions with the king on issues pertaining to trade routes and commerce. Costly gifts were exchanged.

Little is known of that queen, but there remains curiosity regarding the relationship between the two. Was there more than an intellectual connection? Into present time, *Queen of Sheba* is often heard in reference to a young lady expecting special attention—like that given the queen. The question: *"Who do you think you are, Queen of Sheba?"* is asked from time to time.

In its early days, Yemen, in the southwestern corner of the Arabian Peninsula, was occupied by indigenous people with feuding tribal chieftains fighting for power. Ottomans claimed Yemen in the sixteenth century CE. However, because of Yemen's remote location, the Ottomans withdrew in the seventeenth century. Then, Britain established a trading station there. Ottomans tried to regain the coast after 1849, but had little success. In 1914 Yemen leaders agreed to Britain handling their foreign affairs in return for protection. After 1918, the Ottomans were no longer in the picture and local tribes began fighting for leadership and expansion. Yemen's capital city is Sana.

Yemen's history is filled with internal and external conflicts.

It is an Arab country with an Islamic religion representing two different factions of Muslims. The future is unsure for the fragmented country of Yemen.

Iraq

In ancient times, Assyrians and Babylonians occupied Mesopotamia, between the Tigris and Euphrates rivers, the area of modern-day Iraq. Ur, by the Euphrates River before it connects with the Tigris, is thought to be the home of Abraham. He later sent his servant to Mesopotamia to find a bride for Isaac (Geneses 24:10).

In time, the region served as capital to a vast Islamic Empire, followed by years of mass invasions. In 1258, Baghdad, the capital, was destroyed and most of the population were killed or forced into exile. The Ottoman Empire ruled the area from 1554-1918. During that time, the border between Iran and Iraq was negotiated. Governors controlled the main towns and tried to maintain some order among the various individual tribes. The country saw little development; schools and hospitals appeared in the late nineteenth century.

At the end of World War I, Britain established a new nation out of the Mesopotamia region, with the name *Iraq*. In 1932, it received its formal independence and became a member of the League of Nations. Regardless, the British remained. Iraqis revolted in 1958 and the new Republic became neutral in international affairs and renounced all treaties with Britain. Revolts and wars followed with little change into present day.

After years as a strong influential leader, in 1979 **Saddam Hussein** gained additional power as president. In 1998, the United States (US) began seeking a regime change in Iraq. After the leveling of New York's Twin Towers in 2001, the United

States (US) President Bush took military action to eliminate dictator Hussein. By 2003, US and Iraq were at war over the threat of Iraq's *supposed* Weapons of Mass Destruction. The end of Hussein's rule came quickly; he was executed in 2006. After more years of violence, US troops withdrew in June, 2009.

Iraq has yet to find peace. The *Islamic State of Iraq and Syria (ISIS)*, starting in 2013, terrified the world with its violence in seeking power and territory. *ISIS'* savage attacks shook Iraq with devastating loss of life and property. With the help of other nations, reports show that *ISIS* is slipping from power. Iraq's long history of internal and external conflicts has created a questionable future.

Iran

Within the Kethuvim (Writings) of the Hebrew Bible, the book of Esther recounts her life as a Jewish queen. Her family, part of the Babylonian exile (587 BCE), remained there when that empire fell to Persia in 539 BCE. After banning his reigning queen, King Xerxes chose Esther as his new queen. Xerxes honored Esther by allowing Jews to defend themselves and to destroy their enemies. The Jews of Persia survived. There are a number of references to Persia (centuries before it became Iran) in the Hebrew Bible.

Outstanding kingdoms of ancient history are woven into Persia's countless years of civilization. In time, Arab Muslims and Turkish warriors added to the Persian culture. Presently, Tehran is the capital of a modern Iran; still, nomads from the largely un-inhabited territory cross from south to north.

Through centuries of the rise and fall of various dynasties, Persia was ill-equipped to keep pace with the advancement of other nations. Into the nineteenth century, Persia remained under the rule of a *shah*, one who held supreme power. Even then, interests from other nations seeped into the country. Both the Russian Empire and the British Empire sought portions of Persia. In 1906, the common people of Persia wanted a role in political matters and forced the *shah* to grant a constitution and form a parliament. The change offered little improvement in the government and foreign influence continued to affect the country.

In 1907, Russia and Britain agreed that Russia could maintain a presence in the north of Persia, while the south was reserved for Britain. A neutral zone crossed the middle of the designated territory. During World War I, the government of Persia collapsed. In addition to the Russians and British, Ottomans occupied part of the country. **Reza Khan**, a high-ranking military official, in 1921 created an army to replace the foreign-influenced forces; two years later he was named prime minister. After eliminating rivals, Reza Khan proclaimed himself *shah* in 1925.

Shah Reza established order across Persia. He worked for complete independence and strove to make the country much like modern Europe. He replaced Islamic laws with non-religious ones. Stability of the government provided improvements for all Persians. In 1942, to show the world his country had progressed with the times, Shah Reza changed the name *Persia* to *Iran*.

During World War II, Soviet and British troops occupied Iran to prevent the country from siding with Germany, plus they wanted to maintain oil production and transportation routes. After the war, the troops withdrew and a new *shah*, **Muhammad**, son of Reza, faced opposition from factions repressed by his father. Over the next three decades, tensions grew over political and economic issues, forcing Shah Muhammad Reza to leave the country in 1979. Voters, under **Ayatollah Khomeini**, then approved the creation of the *Islamic Republic of Iran*. Major problems followed.

Ethnic minorities threatened rebellion, the economy needed improvement, and rival groups fought for power. The United

States (US) became involved when Iran took the US embassy and held hostages. Khomeini was instrumental in the approval of a new Islamic Constitution authorizing the Supreme Leader (chief theologian) to interpret religious laws. Also, the constitution sanctioned twelve clergymen to ensure the laws conformed to Islam. Those opposing the constitution were put down with brutality and torture.

Iraq invaded Iran in 1980; after eight years, Iran accepted a ceasefire without peace. Khomeini died in 1989; the Islamic Constitution lives on. Violence continues between reformers and those wanting to maintain strict religious control.

Revolving leaders of Iran brought little change in policies, while violence and reprisals remain a major threat to the people of Iran and other nations. Though many feel Iran has supported terrorism, it viciously opposes the *Islamic State of Iraq and Syria (ISIS).*

Reports of Iran's nuclear weapons as early as 2003, led to an agreement in 2015 stating Iran would not seek, develop, or acquire nuclear weapons. The world watches to see how the nuclear deal will work out as the US President Trump, elected in 2016, seeks assurance that Iran keeps its word.

IN CONCLUSION

Completing this writing, I grieved over the extent of violence in our world, today and all the yesterdays. Then I recalled a recent televised series on civilizations which explained that early humans, for survival, needed to join together as clans. As the number of clan members increased, they required a larger territory for hunting and gathering, leading to defeating others with the same need. So, civilizations gave birth to battles. What is understood intellectually is difficult to comprehend by the heart.

When my children were small, other moms and I talked about the seemingly natural occurrence of children pretending to kill. Even without toy guns, hands and fingers became weapons. While my daughter and her friends played with Barbies, my son and his friends played with little plastic soldiers killing one another. As parents, we questioned the violence on TV and even in books geared to children. At that time, I was told the effect of violent movies is lessened when an adult watches with the child. Also, talking to the child about fear and sadness arising from violence, along with the need of getting along with others, is important. Although, recognizing that others see the world in a different perspective generally comes later in a child's life.

Looking further back in my growing up years, we didn't have TV then, but World War II had ended and I remember the boys at school playing *war*. They probably used sticks as weapons. No one wanted to be the enemy. I wondered if boys in other countries were playing and not wanting to be Americans.

That was around the time my family, with seven children, lived on a farm. We had few toys and friends lived in the city. My brothers, sisters, and I created our own fun. One game we played centered around a rather small hay stack near the barn. Corn-cobs, left from feeding the animals, were scattered around. Talk about devising toy weapons, those corn-cobs became ours as we chose up teams. Some of us got to be on those bales of hay; others were on the ground. I don't remember us calling it war, but if hit by a cob, we had to *pretend dead*. It didn't take us long to realize the team on the hay stack had the advantage, so we needed to take turns being up or down. Also, some had better coordination than others; changing team members helped keep things even. And— no hard hitting! That game taught us; we had to be fair. No one told us! Maybe, just maybe, learning to be fair is as ingrained in a civilization as the tendency to fight.

I pondered over battles, near and far, for some days before my mind rested once again on the *Good* stemming from a belief of a Divine Source, ever present, regardless of games.

END NOTES

Introduction

Barry L. Bandstra, *Reading the Old Testament Introduction to the Hebrew Bible* 4th ed. (Belmont, California: Wadsworth Cengage Learning, 2009) 31, 351, 368.

Michael Douma, curator, "The Christian Calendar." *Calendars through the Ages*, (2008, Institute for Dynamic Educational Development), 16 March 2011 <*http://webexhibits.org/calendars/calendar-christian.html*> 1, 2.

Michael Douma, curator, "The Jewish Calendar." *Calendars through the Ages*, (2008, Institute for Dynamic Educational Development), 16 March 2011 <*http://webexhibits.org/calendars/calendar-jewish.html*> 1.

Bart D. Ehrman, *A Brief Introduction to the New Testament* 3rd ed. (New York: Oxford University Press, 2013) 7.

Johnnie Godwin, Phyllis Godwin, and Karen Dockrey, *The Student Bible Dictionary: Expanded and Updated Edition* (Uhrichsville, Ohio: Barbour Books, 2014).

Jean-Pierre Isbouts, *The Biblical World: An Illustrated Atlas* (Washington D.C.: National Geographic, 2007) 22, 45.

The Jewish Study Bible. 2nd ed. Eds. Adele Berlin and Marc Zvi Brettler. Jewish Publication Society TANAKH Translation (New York: Oxford University Press, 2014) 2124-2126, 2153, 2154, 2222-2224.

Merriam-Webster's Collegiate Dictionary 11th ed., (Springfield, Massachusetts: Merriam-Webster, 2012).

Ronald R. Youngblood, F. F. Bruce, and R. K. Harrison. *Compact Bible Dictionary* (Nashville: Thomas Nelson, 2004).

Chapter 1 Background (Hebrews—Israelites)

Ancient Civilizations

Barry L. Bandstra, *Reading the Old Testament Introduction to the Hebrew Bible* 4th ed. (Belmont, California: Wadsworth Cengage Learning, 2009) 203, 241,314,475,508.

Jean-Pierre Isbouts, *The Biblical World: An Illustrated Atlas* (Washington D.C.: National Geographic, 2007) 26, 34, 35, 39, 157, 211.

The Jewish Study Bible. 2nd ed. Eds. Adele Berlin and Marc Zvi Brettler. Jewish Publication Society TANAKH Translation (New York: Oxford University Press, 2014) 2250.

Lawrence Joffe, *The History of the Jews: From the Ancients to the Middle Ages* (London: Southwater an imprint of Anness Publishing Ltd., 2014) 8.

Merriam-Webster's Collegiate Dictionary 11th ed., (Springfield, Massachusetts: Merriam-Webster, 2012).

Ronald R. Youngblood, F. F. Bruce, and R. K. Harrison. *Compact Bible Dictionary* (Nashville: Thomas Nelson, 2004).

Language Development

Bart D. Ehrman, *A Brief Introduction to the New Testament* 3rd ed. (New York: Oxford University Press, 2013) 4, 40, 41.

Johnnie Godwin, Phyllis Godwin, and Karen Dockrey, *The Student Bible Dictionary: Expanded and Updated Edition* (Uhrichsville, Ohio: Barbour Books, 2014).

Jean-Pierre Isbouts, *The Biblical World: An Illustrated Atlas* (Washington D.C.: National Geographic, 2007) 17, 27, 29, 31, 35, 39, 49, 50, 56, 62, 81, 116, 156, 157.

The Jewish Study Bible. 2nd ed. Eds. Adele Berlin and Marc Zvi Brettler. Jewish Publication Society TANAKH Translation (New York: Oxford University Press, 2014) 2117, 2135, 2144, 2148, 2222, 2254, 2255.

Merriam-Webster's Collegiate Dictionary 11th ed., (Springfield, Massachusetts: Merriam-Webster, 2012).

The New Oxford Annotated Bible: New Revised Standard Version with The Apocrypha 4th ed., (New York: Oxford University Press, 2010) 1361, 1744, 2190.

Source-Hebrew Bible

Barry L. Bandstra, *Reading the Old Testament Introduction to the Hebrew Bible* 4th ed. (Belmont, California: Wadsworth Cengage Learning, 2009) 17, 18, 19, 20, 21, 22, 24, 25, 26.

The Jewish Study Bible. 2nd ed. Eds. Adele Berlin and Marc Zvi Brettler. Jewish Publication Society TANAKH Translation (New York: Oxford University Press, 2014) 4, 5, 6, 429, 433, 1263, 1264, 2153, 2154, 2156.

Chapter 2 The Hebrew Bible

Hebrew Bible—A Review

Barry L. Bandstra, *Reading the Old Testament Introduction to the Hebrew Bible* 4th ed. (Belmont, California: Wadsworth Cengage Learning, 2009) 17-19, 187, 188, 196, 203, 213-214, 224, 235, 246-251, 256, 272, 273, 283-285, 299, 304, 306, 307, 311, 313, 318, 322, 324-326, 329-331, 335, 360, 366-369, 463-468.

John L. Esposito, *Islam: The Straight Path* 3rd ed. (New York: Oxford University Press,1998) 2, 5.

Bruce Feiler, *Abraham A Journey to the Heart of Three Faiths* (New York: HarperCollins Publishers Inc., 2002) 76.

Jean-Pierre Isbouts, *The Biblical World: An Illustrated Atlas* (Washington D.C.: National Geographic, 2007) 145, 229, 192, 197.

The Jewish Study Bible. 2nd ed. Eds. Adele Berlin and Marc Zvi Brettler. Jewish Publication Society TANAKH Translation (New

York: Oxford University Press, 2014) 429, 434-436, 763, 2153, 2223.

Lawrence Joffe, *The History of the Jews: From the Ancients to the Middle Ages* (London: Southwater an imprint of Anness Publishing Ltd., 2014) 8-9, 37, 43.

The New Oxford Annotated Bible: New Revised Standard Version with The Apocrypha 4th ed., (New York: Oxford University Press, 2010) 1361.

Books of the Hebrew Bible and Old Testament

Bart D. Ehrman, *A Brief Introduction to the New Testament* 3rd ed. (New York: Oxford University Press, 2013) 2, 7.

Early Hebrew Lineage

Barry L. Bandstra, *Reading the Old Testament Introduction to the Hebrew Bible* 4th ed. (Belmont, California: Wadsworth Cengage Learning, 2009) 30-31.

Lawrence Joffe, *The History of the Jews: From the Ancients to the Middle Ages* (London: Southwater an imprint of Anness Publishing Ltd., 2014) 8.

Samuel T. Jordan, comp. *The Time Chart of Biblical History,* (New York: Chartwell Books, 2014)

Chapter 3 Background (Spanning Old and New)

Condensed Timeline

Barry L. Bandstra, *Reading the Old Testament Introduction to the Hebrew Bible* 4th ed. (Belmont, California: Wadsworth Cengage Learning, 2009) 24, 270, 314, 351, 464, 475.

Marcus J. Borg, *Evolution of the Word: The New Testament in the Order the Books Were Written* (New York: HarperOne, 2012) 31, 32, 423, 424.

Bart D. Ehrman, *A Brief Introduction to the New Testament* 3rd ed. (New York: Oxford University Press, 2013) 42.

Jean-Pierre Isbouts, *The Biblical World: An Illustrated Atlas* (Washington D.C.: National Geographic, 2007) 245-247.

The Jewish Study Bible. 2nd ed. Eds. Adele Berlin and Marc Zvi Brettler. Jewish Publication Society TANAKH Translation (New York: Oxford University Press, 2014) 2156.

Lawrence Joffe, *The History of the Jews: From the Ancients to the Middle Ages* (London: Southwater an imprint of Anness Publishing Ltd., 2014) 37.

Michael Kerrigan, *A Dark History: The Roman Emperors: From Julius Caesar to the Fall of Rome,* (New York: Metro Books, 2008) 150-155.

The New Oxford Annotated Bible: New Revised Standard Version with The Apocrypha 4th ed., (New York: Oxford University Press, 2010) 2257.

Lands and People

Audi, Robert, gen. ed., *The Cambridge Dictionary of Philosophy* 3rd ed. (New York: Cambridge University Press, 2015).

Barry L. Bandstra, *Reading the Old Testament Introduction to the Hebrew Bible* 4th ed. (Belmont, California: Wadsworth Cengage Learning, 2009) 24, 301, 314, 449, 450, 466, 475, 480.

Jean-Pierre Isbouts, *The Biblical World: An Illustrated Atlas* (Washington D.C.: National Geographic, 2007) 216, 217, 231, 235, 244-245, 258, 260, 267, 268, 277, 318, 328, 330

Lawrence Joffe, *The History of the Jews: From the Ancients to the Middle Ages* (London: Southwater an imprint of Anness Publishing Ltd., 2014) 37, 46-49, 51-53, 61, 74, 81.

Michael Kerrigan, *A Dark History: The Roman Emperors: From Julius Caesar to the Fall of Rome,* (New York: Metro Books, 2008) 10-16, 19, 20, 26, 30, 152-155, 223, 251.

Ronald R. Youngblood, F. F. Bruce, and R. K. Harrison. *Compact Bible Dictionary* (Nashville: Thomas Nelson, 2004).

Related Writings

Barry L. Bandstra, *Reading the Old Testament Introduction to the Hebrew Bible* 4th ed. (Belmont, California: Wadsworth Cengage Learning, 2009) 8, 372, 373.

Bart D. Ehrman, *A Brief Introduction to the New Testament* 3rd ed. (New York: Oxford University Press, 2013) 36.

The Jewish Study Bible. 2nd ed. Eds. Adele Berlin and Marc Zvi Brettler. Jewish Publication Society TANAKH Translation (New York: Oxford University Press, 2014) 2229.

Lawrence Joffe, *The History of the Jews: From the Ancients to the Middle Ages* (London: Southwater an imprint of Anness Publishing Ltd., 2014) 70-73.

The New Oxford Annotated Bible: New Revised Standard Version with The Apocrypha 4th ed., (New York: Oxford University Press, 2010) 1361.

Morton Smith, *The Secret Gospel: The Discovery and Interpretation of the Secret Gospel According to Mark*, Forward: Elaine Pagels, (Middletown, California: The Dawn Horse Press, 2005) 356.

Chapter 4 Judaism

Need for Change

Barry L. Bandstra, *Reading the Old Testament Introduction to the Hebrew Bible* 4th ed. (Belmont, California: Wadsworth Cengage Learning, 2009) 368, 465, 469, 470, 475, 476, 482, 483, 487, 516, 517, 519, 520, 522.

John J. Collins, *The Dead Sea Scrolls A Biography*, (Princeton: Princeton University Press, 2013) vii-ix, 4, 5, 9, 11, 35, 37, 39, 40, 41, 63, 76, 82, 83, 84, 86, 91, 92, 94.

Bart D. Ehrman, *A Brief Introduction to the New Testament* 3rd ed. (New York: Oxford University Press, 2013) 35, 37, 38, 40, 41, 42.

Jean-Pierre Isbouts, *The Biblical World: An Illustrated Atlas* (Washington D.C.: National Geographic, 2007) 247-249, 260, 317.

The Jewish Study Bible. 2nd ed. Eds. Adele Berlin and Marc Zvi Brettler. Jewish Publication Society TANAKH Translation (New York: Oxford University Press, 2014) 141, 438, 2244, 2256.

Lawrence Joffe, *The History of the Jews: From the Ancients to the Middle Ages* (London: Southwater an imprint of Anness Publishing Ltd., 2014) 43, 44, 47, 48, 49, 50, 51, 55, 60, 61, 64, 67, 68, 74, 75.

The New Oxford Annotated Bible: New Revised Standard Version with The Apocrypha 4th ed., (New York: Oxford University Press, 2010) 2280, 2282.

Ronald R. Youngblood, F. F. Bruce, and R. K. Harrison. *Compact Bible Dictionary* (Nashville: Thomas Nelson, 2004).

Chapter 5 Roman Rule

Judea Under Rome

Jean-Pierre Isbouts, *The Biblical World: An Illustrated Atlas* (Washington D.C.: National Geographic, 2007) 257, 258, 260, 261.

Lawrence Joffe, *The History of the Jews: From the Ancients to the Middle Ages* (London: Southwater an imprint of Anness Publishing Ltd., 2014) 52, 53, 54.

Michael Kerrigan, *A Dark History: The Roman Emperors: From Julius Caesar to the Fall of Rome,* (New York: Metro Books, 2008) 12, 13, 16, 19, 223.

Heirs to Herod's Kingdom

Jean-Pierre Isbouts, *The Biblical World: An Illustrated Atlas* (Washington D.C.: National Geographic, 2007) 263, 277, 292, 294, 303, 315.

Lawrence Joffe, *The History of the Jews: From the Ancients to the Middle Ages* (London: Southwater an imprint of Anness Publishing Ltd., 2014) 55, 62, 63, 64.

Ronald R. Youngblood, F. F. Bruce, and R. K. Harrison. *Compact Bible Dictionary* (Nashville: Thomas Nelson, 2004).

Jewish Revolts Against Rome

Jean-Pierre Isbouts, *The Biblical World: An Illustrated Atlas* (Washington D.C.: National Geographic, 2007) 315, 316, 318.

Lawrence Joffe, *The History of the Jews: From the Ancients to the Middle Ages* (London: Southwater an imprint of Anness Publishing Ltd., 2014) 62, 63, 64, 65, 67, 68, 69.

Michael Kerrigan, *A Dark History: The Roman Emperors: From Julius Caesar to the Fall of Rome,* (New York: Metro Books, 2008) 119, 155.

Chapter 6 Background (Christians)

Terms Linking Faiths

Barry L. Bandstra, *Reading the Old Testament Introduction to the Hebrew Bible* 4th ed. (Belmont, California: Wadsworth Cengage Learning, 2009) 521.

Marcus J. Borg, *Evolution of the Word: The New Testament in the Order the Books Were Written* (New York: HarperOne, 2012) 1, 6, 12, 15, 17, 219.

Bart D. Ehrman, *A Brief Introduction to the New Testament* 3rd ed. (New York: Oxford University Press, 2013) 16, 51, 62, 63, 155, 161, 162, 350, 352, 353, 355.

The Jewish Study Bible. 2nd ed. Eds. Adele Berlin and Marc Zvi Brettler. Jewish Publication Society TANAKH Translation (New York: Oxford University Press, 2014) 763, 1131, 1325, 1650.

The New Oxford Annotated Bible: New Revised Standard Version with The Apocrypha 4th ed., (New York: Oxford University Press, 2010) 1641, 1774.

Huston Smith, *The World's Religions,* (New York: HarperOne, 1991) 318, 319, 336.

Roman World of Jesus

Marcus J. Borg, *Evolution of the Word: The New Testament in the Order the Books Were Written* (New York: HarperOne, 2012) 7, 9.

Bart D. Ehrman, *A Brief Introduction to the New Testament* 3rd ed. (New York: Oxford University Press, 2013) 3, 15.

Huston Smith, *The World's Religions,* (New York: HarperOne, 1991) 296, 297.

People of the New Faith

Marcus J. Borg, *Evolution of the Word: The New Testament in the Order the Books Were Written* (New York: HarperOne, 2012) 20, 21, 23, 24, 31, 401.

Bart D. Ehrman, *A Brief Introduction to the New Testament* 3rd ed. (New York: Oxford University Press, 2013) 4.

Jean-Pierre Isbouts, *The Biblical World: An Illustrated Atlas* (Washington D.C.: National Geographic, 2007) 268, 269. 273, 280, 281, 291, 307.

Ronald R. Youngblood, F. F. Bruce, and R. K. Harrison. *Compact Bible Dictionary* (Nashville: Thomas Nelson, 2004).

Chapter 7 A Church Survives

Related Vocabulary

Sean Martin, *The Cathars: The Most Successful Heresy of the Middle Ages,* (Edison, New Jersey: Chartwell Books, Inc. a division of Book Sales, Inc., 2006) 16-18.

Early Centuries CE

Keith Akers, *The Lost Religion of Jesus: Simple Living and Nonviolence in Early Christianity* (New York: Lantern Books, 2000) 10, 25, 94, 187, 188.

Marcus J. Borg, *Evolution of the Word: The New Testament in the Order the Books Were Written* (New York: HarperOne, 2012) 12, 31, 32.

Lars Brownworth, *Lost to the West: The Forgotten Byzantine Empire that Rescued Western Civilization* (New York: Three Rivers Press, 2009) xvi, 1, 15, 16, 23-38, 40, 44, 46, 301, 309.

Bart D. Ehrman, *A Brief Introduction to the New Testament* 3rd ed. (New York: Oxford University Press, 2013) 7, 47, 311-313.

Jean-Pierre Isbouts, *The Biblical World: An Illustrated Atlas* (Washington D.C.: National Geographic, 2007) 268, 269, 313-319, 321-330, 332, 334, 337-341.

The Jewish Study Bible. 2nd ed. Eds. Adele Berlin and Marc Zvi Brettler. Jewish Publication Society TANAKH Translation (New York: Oxford University Press, 2014) 2156.

Lawrence Joffe, *The History of the Jews: From the Ancients to the Middle Ages* (London: Southwater an imprint of Anness Publishing Ltd., 2014) 11, 68, 69.

Michael Kerrigan, *A Dark History: The Roman Emperors: From Julius Caesar to the Fall of Rome,* (New York: Metro Books, 2008) 150-155, 251.

The New Oxford Annotated Bible: New Revised Standard Version with The Apocrypha 4th ed., (New York: Oxford University Press, 2010) 2189-2191, 2277.

Elaine Pagels, *The Gnostic Gospel,* (New York: Vintage Books A Division of Random House, Inc., 1989) xiii, xviii, xxiii, 4, 5, 7, 23, 34-36, 67, 68, 77-80, 82, 84, 88, 89, 92, 100, 108-110, 135, 147, 149.

"Schism of 1054," (2015, Encyclopædia Britannica, Encyclopædia Britannic Online, Encyclopædia Britannic Inc.), 14 August 2015 <http://www.britannica.com/event/Schism-of-1054> 1.

Richard Valantasis, *The beliefnet Guide to Gnosticism and Other Vanished Christianities,* Preface by Marcus Borg, (New York: Doubleday, 2006) 63, 148, 149.

Rejected Beliefs

Keith Akers, *The Lost Religion of Jesus: Simple Living and Nonviolence in Early Christianity* (New York: Lantern Books, 2000) 3, 7, 8, 21-25, 29, 34, 206-215.

Ron Cameron, ed. *The Other Gospels: Non-Canonical Gospel Texts,* (Philadelphia: The Westminster Press, 1982) 67.

Rodolphe Kasser, Marvin Meyer, and Gregor Wurst, eds., *The Gospel of Judas,* Additional Commentary by Bart D. Ehrman, (Washington D.C.: National Geographic, 2006) 4-7, 11, 13, 14, 70; 75, 102, 103.

Jean-Yves Leloup, Trans. from Coptic and Commentary, Joseph Rowe, English Trans. And Notes, *The Gospel of Mary Magdalene,*

Forward, Jacob Needleman, (Rochester, Vermont: Inner Traditions, 2002) xii, xiv-xviii, xxi, xxii, xv, 4-8, 10, 25.

Elaine Pagels, *The Gnostic Gospel,* (New York: Vintage Books A Division of Random House, Inc., 1989) xiii, xvi-xix, xxxv, 14, 15, 18.

James M. Robinson, *The Secrets of Judas: The Story of the Misunderstood Disciple and His Lost Gospel,* (New York: HarperSanFrancisco, 2006) 33, 34, 39-41, 48, 53, 91, 108, 121, 159, 161-164, 178-180.

Richard Valantasis, *The beliefnet Guide to Gnosticism and Other Vanished Christianities,* Preface by Marcus Borg, (New York: Doubleday, 2006) 10-12, 16, 17, 35, 37-39, 45-50, 55, 56.

Chapter 8 The New Testament

Source—New Testament

Marcus J. Borg, *Evolution of the Word: The New Testament in the Order the Books Were Written* (New York: HarperOne, 2012) 24, 25, 31, 32, 363, 364, 423-425.

Bart D. Ehrman, *A Brief Introduction to the New Testament* 3rd ed. (New York: Oxford University Press, 2013) 5, 6, 47, 48. 57, 60, 61, 119, 120, 165, 182, 183, 297.

Jean-Pierre Isbouts, *The Biblical World: An Illustrated Atlas* (Washington D.C.: National Geographic, 2007) 268, 269.

New Testament—A Review

Marcus J. Borg, *Evolution of the Word: The New Testament in the Order the Books Were Written* (New York: HarperOne, 2012) 11, 12, 19, 24, 29, 31, 32, 36, 39, 45, 46, 57, 85, 86, 91,101, 102, 104, 119, 151, 153, 193, 194, 203, 204, 275, 277, 278, 301, 351, 352, 363-370, 401, 402, 405, 406, 415, 419, 423, 490, 547, 553, 554, 563, 575, 583, 587, 588

Bart D. Ehrman, *A Brief Introduction to the New Testament* 3rd ed. (New York: Oxford University Press, 2013) 2, 7, 49, 56, 57, 60, 75, 77-81, 89, 92, 95, 97, 98, 103, 112, 122, 166, 167, 184, 185, 276, 297, 353.

Chapter 9 Biblical Translations

Words Become a Bible

Bruce Feiler, *Abraham A Journey to the Heart of Three Faiths* (New York: HarperCollins Publishers Inc., 2002) 121.

The Jewish Study Bible. 2nd ed. Eds. Adele Berlin and Marc Zvi Brettler. Jewish Publication Society TANAKH Translation (New York: Oxford University Press, 2014) 2153, 2154.

The New Oxford Annotated Bible: New Revised Standard Version with The Apocrypha 4th ed., (New York: Oxford University Press, 2010) 2185, 2191, 2197, 2199.

Jewish Translations

The Jewish Study Bible. 2nd ed. Eds. Adele Berlin and Marc Zvi Brettler. Jewish Publication Society TANAKH Translation (New York: Oxford University Press, 2014) 1939-1941, 2081, 2082. 2084, 2091, 2092-2095, 2097, 2098.

David Rosenberg, Trans. from Hebrew. *The Book of J,* Interpreted by Harold Bloom, (New York: Vintage Books a division of Random House Inc., 1991) 4, 5.

Christian Translations

Bart D. Ehrman, *A Brief Introduction to the New Testament* 3rd ed. (New York: Oxford University Press, 2013) 1-3.

The New Oxford Annotated Bible: New Revised Standard Version with The Apocrypha 4th ed., (New York: Oxford University Press, 2010) 2196-2201.

Adam Nicolson, "The Bible of King James," (*National Geographic,* December 2011) 47.

James Reston, Jr., *Luther's Fortress: Martin Luther and His Reformation Under Siege,* (New York: Basic Books 2015) 137-139, 216, 217.

Chapter 10 Expanded Christianity

Continued Heresy

Sean Martin, *The Cathars: The Most Successful Heresy of the Middle Ages,* (Edison, New Jersey: Chartwell Books, Inc. a division of Book Sales, Inc., 2006) 24-28, 30-36, 52, 53, 154, 159, 161, 174-177, 179.

Crossroads

"Causes of the Protestant Reformation," ([n.d.], What caused the Protestant Reformation? | Reference.com), 24 May 2018 <*www. reference.com/history/caused-protestant-75b4667fde8fa6907*> 1.

Michael Haag, *The Tragedy of the Templars: The Rise and Fall of the Crusader States,* (New York: Harper, 2013) 19, 102, 103, 120, 126, 127, 132-134, 139, 140, 329-333, 340-345, 348, 349, 352, 358, 365-368.

History.com Staff, "The Reformation," (2009, A & E Networks), 24 May 2018 <*http://www.history.con/topics/reformation*> 1-4.

"The Inquisition," *Christian-Jewish Relations,* (2015, American-Israeli Cooperative Enterprise), 10 October 2015 <*www. jewishvirtuallibrary.org/jsource/History/Inquisition.html*> 1.

Sean Martin, *The Cathars: The Most Successful Heresy of the Middle Ages,* (Edison, New Jersey: Chartwell Books, Inc. a division of Book Sales, Inc., 2006) 106, 161.

The New Oxford Annotated Bible: New Revised Standard Version with The Apocrypha 4th ed., (New York: Oxford University Press, 2010) 1361.

James Reston, Jr., *Luther's Fortress: Martin Luther and His Reformation Under Siege,* (New York: Basic Books 2015) x, 1, 4, 7-11, 15, 46-47, 138, 214, 216-219, 224, 238.

"Schism of 1054," (2015, Encyclopædia Britannica, Encyclopædia Britannic Online, Encyclopædia Britannic Inc.), 14 August 2015 <*http://www.britannica.com/event/Schism-of-1054*> 1.

"Timeline for the History of Jerusalem (4500 BCE - Present)," *History of Jerusalem*, (2014, American-Israeli Cooperative Enterprise of Jerusalem), 7 April 2014 <*http://www.jewishvirtuallibrary.org/jsource/Peace/jerutime.html*> 2.

Chapter 11 Biblical Lands Past-Present

The Promised Land

Seth Cantey, *The Middle East and South Asia The World Today Series 2017-2018 51st* ed., (Lanham, MD: Rowman & Littlefield, 2017) 39, 52, 53, 97, 99-104, 106, 107, 118, 148-151, 284.

Jean-Pierre Isbouts, *The Biblical World: An Illustrated Atlas* (Washington D.C.: National Geographic, 2007) 267.

Isabel Kershner, "9 Things to Know About Jerusalem as U.S, Embassy Opens," 13 May 2018 (New York Times) 7 November 2018 <*https://www.nytimes.com*>.

Regional Ties

Samy Magdy, "Ousted president Morsi collapses, dies in court." (*The Denver Post*, [The Associated Press] June 18, 2019) Sec. A, p. 10, cols. 2-40.

Seth Cantey, *The Middle East and South Asia The World Today Series 2017-2018 51ˢᵗ* ed., (Lanham, MD: Rowman & Littlefield, 2017) 49-53, 56, 57, 59, 60, 62-72, 75, 79, 80-83, 87, 90, 91, 93, 96, 99, 100-102, 116-123, 131-135, 136, 139, 141, 150, 175-184, 187-189, 191, 197, 207, 208, 214.

MAPS OF BIBLICAL LANDS

In compiling maps from different sources, slight variations occur. Some names change through the years. A few are:

Great Sea = Mediterranean Sea
Sea of Chinnereth = Sea of Galilee
Salt Sea = Dead Sea
Arabian Gulf = Red Sea.

The Red Sea is not the location where water parted when Moses led the Hebrews out of Egypt. At that time, there was a *Sea of Reeds* near present day Suez Canal. It seems the Greek version of the Hebrew Bible (Septuagint) contained a mistake in the translation. The lasting result is reference to Moses parting the *Red Sea*. There is no longer a Sea of Reeds.

Maps shown (not drawn to scale)
Biblical Lands Ancient-Modern
United Kingdom of Israel 1200-928 BCE
Divided Kingdom 925-721 BCE
Roman Times 63 BCE-476 CE
Twenty-First Century CE

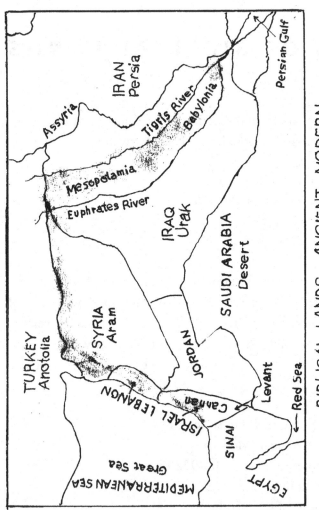

BIBLICAL LANDS   ANCIENT - MODERN

Fertile Crescent ▢
Ancient - lower case

250

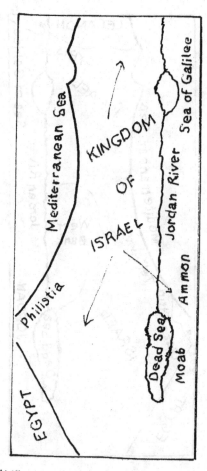

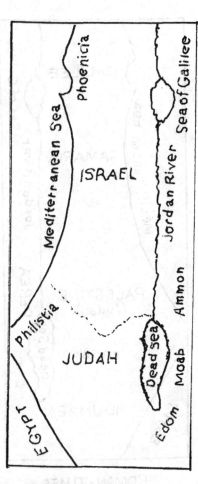

UNITED KINGDOM OF ISRAEL
1200-928 BCE

DIVIDED KINGDOM
925-721 BCE

251

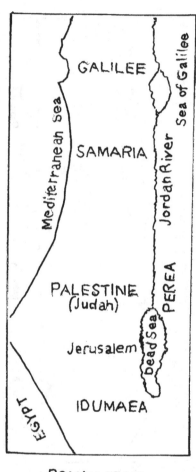

ROMAN TIMES
63 BCE-476 CE

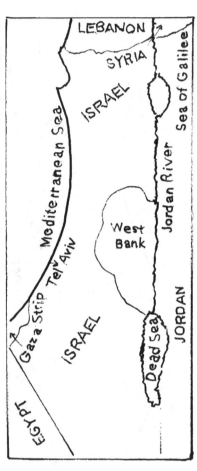

TWENTY-FIRST CENTURY
CE

252

TIMES OF INTEREST—
ANCIENT TO MODERN

In compiling notes from my collection of biblical books, it became clear that a chronological record was needed. So, I started with the Hebrew Bible, a history of the Jewish people, and then moved on through the New Testament, the beginning of Christianity. Of course, the four hundred years between the two had to be inserted. Also, I wanted to include some information on biblical translations as well as ongoing developments and discoveries. Early on I realized this was not an easy task. It helped to create the following comprehensive timeline where I could easily see the relationship of events. I returned to this list time after time as a quick reference for my writing.

Dates are the biggest obstacle in preparing a timeline of this sort. Scholars generally acknowledge that verification of early historical biblical events is nearly impossible. Nevertheless, through various means, dates that seem appropriate are given to the history of those ages. I thought scholars could determine more reliable dates because of modern advancements used in dating. This is not always the case. Different calendars cause confusion and many records have been lost. Even today, recently published books vary in recording dates of Ancient Times. Of the many resources I used in creating the following timeline, a number prefaced the word about (ca) in reference to dates. Unless noted within the text, dates I use are consistent with the following list. Items listed are contained in the text in greater detail.

Before Current Era

4004 God created the universe then Adam and Eve; Hebrews were a wandering tribes people. The fifth chapter of Genesis tells of Adam's death and the Hebrew lineage continuing with a son, Seth.

3300-3100 Egyptian *hieroglyphics*, a form of writing, were in use. Mesopotamia developed *cuneiform* writings, consisting of wedge-shaped characters on tiles then baked in ovens.

2500 Egyptians invented a writing paper from the plant *papyrus* which was used through the writing of the New Testament.

2348 Noah, descendant of Seth, built an Ark to save his family and animals from the Flood God sent to cleanse the earth. After the Flood, lands were divided among descendants of Noah. Canaan, a grandson of Noah, settled in the land that carried his name.

2247 God created the Tower of Babel; He muddled speech and Hebrews were dispersed.

2000-1700 The Age of Patriarchs dates from the birth of Abraham until Hebrews left Canaan and journeyed to Egypt because of famine.

1921 Abraham followed God's call directing him to Canaan; God promised all the land to Abraham and his descendants.

1898 God destroyed the towns of Sodom and Gomorrah. Lot, nephew of Abraham, had settled in Sodom.

1700-1300 Hebrews became slaves of Pharaoh after famine took Jacob's families from Canaan to Egypt where a son, Joseph, prospered.

1280 Moses, Hebrew born but raised as Pharaoh's son, led the Hebrews out of Egypt. They spent forty years in the shadow of Mount Sinai.

1240 Joshua, from the tribe of Ephraim, led the Hebrews into Canaan. Moses did not live to enter that land promised to Abraham and his descendants. (The name *Israelites* replaced *Hebrews*.) The conquest and division of Canaan was a long and complex process.

1200-1025 Judges ruled over the independent tribes of Israelites.

1050 Samuel became leader of Israel.

1025 Israelites asked Samuel, the last judge and a prophet, to find a king for uniting the tribes. He anointed Saul as that king. Saul proved to be unworthy so Samuel anointed David as king. Nevertheless, Saul continued serving until his death in 1005. Prophets communicated between God and people. There is a long history of prophecy in the Bible, with the role of prophets changing as times changed.

1005-965 David ruled as King of Israel.

968-928 Solomon, son of David, on his father's death became King of Israel.

950 Solomon's Temple in Jerusalem, was completed after seven years of construction.

928 Solomon's death was followed by the separation of United Israel into two kingdoms: Kingdom of Israel in the north, Kingdom of Judah in the south.

900-800 The Yahwist narrative, referred to as *J,* recorded Israel's history. Additional histories attributed to the compilation of the Hebrew Bible are: the Elohist document (800-700 BCE) from the Northern Kingdom of Israel, the Deuteronomic source (600 BCE) found in the Temple, and the Priestly document (500-400 BCE) recorded during the Babylonian exile.

850 Inscriptions on the Moabite Stone, discovered in 1868, indicate the Israelites had developed a written language.

721 The Kingdom of Israel fell to the Assyrian Empire. They dispersed the Ten Tribes of Israel farther north.

587 After previous assaults, the Kingdom of Judah fell to the Babylonian Empire. The Temple in Jerusalem was destroyed and most of the Israelites were taken as bondage to Babylon (capital of Babylonia).

539 Babylonia fell to King Cyrus of Persia; he allowed Israelites to return to Judah and the name *Israelite* became *Jew.*

515 The rebuilt Temple in Jerusalem was dedicated.

458 Ezra, born in Babylon, arrived in Judah and helped restore the Jewish faith. Ezra, in reading and reinterpreting the Hebrew writings, is considered highly instrumental in the compilation

of The Torah, the first five books of the Hebrew Bible. The Law of Moses, The Law, and Pentateuch, also are names for those books. Before long, the collection of writings Ezra and other scholars designated as key to the Hebrew faith were considered Scripture—*the very word of God.*

After the first five books of the Hebrew Bible (Torah), additional sections were added. One covered prophets (Nevi'im) and later, another with writings of treasured history and literature (Kethuvim). Both, shown on this timeline, received the designation of Scripture.

Through many decades of opening the Bible it never occurred to me that there was close to 400 years between the Hebrew Bible (I called the Old Testament) and the New Testament. Studying those years of history led me to a greater understanding of the New Testament and the relationship between Jews and Christians. The timeline continues with inclusion of outside forces and changing times for Jews.

333 Alexander the Great, of Greece, defeated Persia. Judah, with a Greek spelling of Judea, fell under Greek rule.

323 After the death of Alexander, Judea changed hands five times.

301 Judea became part of the Egyptian Ptolemaic Empire.

300 At some prior time, unknown scholars compiled Hebrew writings into the Nevi'im, or Prophets, which, like the Torah, became Scripture.

250 The Septuagint translation, Hebrew to Greek, of the Torah became available. Over time the other two sections were added to

the translation. Parchment, invented in the third century BCE, produced a writing surface from animal skins.

198 Judea became part of the Syrian Seleucid Empire.

164 A Jewish family, Maccabeans, revolted against the Seleucids. Victory led to the Hasmonean period (164-63 BCE) of Jewish rule over Judea. Two Jewish groups, Pharisees and Sadducees, fought for power during that time.

100 BCE-100 CE A segment of Jewish historical literature was compiled as the Apocryphal. That collection, not recognized as Jewish Scripture, was included as Scripture in some Christian Bibles in 1546 CE.

63 Pompey entered Jerusalem, beginning Roman control.

47 Julius Caesar made Judea a direct subject of Rome.

44 Caesar, wanting to be named King of Rome, was assassinated. Octavian, nephew and heir of Caesar, sought to replace his uncle. Fighting among Romans continued.

37-04 Herod the Great, appointed by Rome, ruled as King of Judea. Herod, a cruel ruler, part Jewish and a Roman Citizen, was disliked by Jews.

30 Roman, Mark Antony, and Egyptian, Cleopatra, committed suicide when their plot to replace Octavian failed.

27 Octavian, named the first Emperor of Rome, took the name Caesar Augustus.

04 Jesus was born, followed by the death of Herod the Great.

Current Era

First Century

30 Jesus was crucified.

33-35 After the conversion of Saul of Tarsus, as Paul, he joined disciples of Jesus in spreading the Christian message. At that time, disciples became known as Apostles.

50-60 Paul wrote letters to early Christian Churches.

64 After a devastating fire in Rome, Emperor Nero accelerated the persecution of Christians and Jews. Apostles Peter and Paul were killed.

67 Jewish Zealots overthrew the priestly aristocracy in Jerusalem, instigating a rebellion against Rome.

68 Nero ordered his own killing after the Roman Senate declared him a public enemy.

69 General Titus Flavius Vespasian became Emperor of Rome. Vespasian's son, also named Titus, was charged with bringing the Zealots, under control.

70 The Gospel, Mark, was written about the life of Jesus. Titus, the son, destroyed Jerusalem and the Temple. Approximately 100,000 Jews were killed and as many taken to Rome as slaves. Judea became a Roman province. Jews could no longer live in Jerusalem. Around that time, Jewish scholars approved additional writings pertaining to history and literature of their people, the Kethuvim, or Writings, as Scripture.

73 Masada, the last Jewish stronghold, fell to Rome.

80 The Gospel, Matthew was written about the life of Jesus.

90-100 The Gospel of John, about the life of Jesus, and the book of Revelation, about the second coming of Jesus, were written.

As the first century of Christianity ended, Bishop Clement in Rome was influential in structuring the Christian Church. A number of Christian religions surfaced through that century. Jewish Christianity, noted in the New Testament, vanished in the fifth century. Forms of Gnosticism (a heretical Christian group) were condemned; many of their manuscripts were found in Egypt in the twentieth century.

Second Century

100 Christianity experienced rapid growth. A number of Christians voiced their understanding that Christian writings, like the Hebrew Bible, met the standard of Scripture.

110 The Gospel of Luke, about Jesus' life, and the book of Acts, about the spread of Christianity, were written.

132 Under Roman Emperor Hadrian, another Jewish revolt, led by Simon Bar Kokhba, returned Judea to an independent Jewish state.

135 Rome recaptured Jerusalem, then all of Judea. It is estimated that over half a million Jews were killed, survivors fled or were sold into slavery. A thousand villages were destroyed. Rabbis (teachers) were executed and worship as set forth in the Torah

was banned. Jerusalem was renamed *Aelia Capitolina* and Judea became *Palestina.*

At the close of the second century of Christianity, there remained no union of Christian Churches and no agreement regarding Christian writings. Yet, Bishop Irenaeus and his followers had declared there was to be only one *orthodox* (straight thinking) Christian Church and it had to be *catholic*, meaning universal. The Christian Catholic Church rejected all other religions based on Jesus' teachings, labeling them heretical. Other writers influencing the times were: Clement of Alexander, Hippolytus, Ignatius, Justin, Marcion, Pliny the Younger, Polycarp, Origen, and Tertullian.

Third Century

Conflicts among Christian groups continued. Within the orthodox Church, the four Gospels, Acts, and Paul's letters were generally seen as official documents. More writings of Hippolytus, Ireanaeus, and Origen opposed groups labeled as heretics. Works of Philosopher Plotinus attacked the Gnostics. Roman hostility endured, though, in 261 Emperor Gallienus issued the first Decree of Toleration, officially recognizing the Christian Church.

Fourth Century

303 Many Christian writings were lost in Roman Emperor Diocletian's persecution of Christians.

306 Constantine, a new emperor, later converted to Christianity.

313 Constantine issued the Edict of Milan which reaffirmed Gallienus' Decree of Toleration, but added: complete freedom of worship to Christians.

325 As a result of Arius, in Alexandria, questing his deacon on the nature of Jesus Christ, Constantine called all bishops to meet at Nicaea (Turkey) for agreement of doctrinal belief to bind all Christian Catholic Churches. The adopted Creed stated Jesus as the Son of God. Those refusing to adhere to the Creed were persecuted as heretics.

330 Constantine made the colony of Byzantium his capital, changing the name to Constantinople, which replaced Rome as the capital of the Roman Empire.

At an uncertain time, early in the fourth century, Bishop Eusebius created the first accepted listing of Christian writings that eventually were included in the New Testament. At that point, additional writings were questioned.

367 Bishop Athanasius compiled the final list of Christian writings designated as the New Testament. Disputed books from Bishop Eusebius list were included. Christians gave the name *Old Testament* to the Hebrew Bible.

The compilation of the Bible covered nearly eight centuries. Work on the Torah was completed around 440 BCE; by 135 BCE other portions of the Hebrew Bible were compiled and looked on as Scripture. Again, in the first century of the current era, more Jewish writings were added to their Scriptures. The accepted books of the New Testament came in 367.

380 Christianity became the state religion of the Roman Empire, which at that time had two governing regions: Rome (Latin) in the west and Constantinople (Greek) in the east.

383 Jerome began the Latin translation of the Bible. Completed about 400, it is known as the Vulgate translation. The translation for the common people included the Apocrypha books. Later, individual churches removed some or all. They are not included in the Hebrew Bible.

Writers of the fourth century were: Airs, Athanasius, Constantine, Eusebius, Epiphanius, and Jerome. Growth of the Orthodox Catholic Christian Church forced heretical groups to the outside.

Fifth Century

476 The Western Roman Empire collapsed after invasions from a number of rivals.

Continuing

610 The Islamic faith of Muslims surfaced, based on the messages from God given to Prophet Muhammad, of Mecca, Arabia.

634-644 Muslims forced the Byzantine Empire back to Turkey, claimed Syria, Palestine, and Egypt. Muslims absorbed the Persian Empire. Muslim expansion continued.

1050 Heresy which had seen a resurgence within the Christian Church, seemed to have died out as the groups did not survive the harsh treatment placed on heretics.

1054 The East-West Schism separated the Christian Church into the Roman Catholic Church in the west and the Greek Orthodox Church in the east (Constantinople).

1055 Muslim Turks invaded southwest Asia, defeating parts of Turkey.

1099 Conflicts between Christians and Muslims led to the Crusades, a series of Holy Wars lasting almost two hundred years. The first Crusade successfully returned Jerusalem to the Christians for a short period.

1120 Knights Templars were formed to offer safety for Christians traveling to Jerusalem. Eventually labeled heretics, the organization became extinct in 1312.

1231 (1233?) The Roman Catholic Church formally instituted the Inquisition to combat the rise of Catharism. The Inquisition spread over Central and Western Europe, lasting into the eighteenth century.

1299 Ottoman Turks (Muslims), expanded into Europe and became an Empire.

1453 The Eastern Roman Empire (Byzantine) fell to the Ottoman Turks. Constantinople was renamed Istanbul.

1512-1520 Ottomans captured all of Turkey, Syria, Palestine, Egypt, and Iraq.

1517 The Protestant Reformation further divided the Roman Catholic Church with Martin Luther, and others, protesting Catholic doctrine.

1545-1563 The Council of Trent, formed by the Roman Catholic Church, declared the Apocrypha books equal to the other approved Scriptures, addressed Church doctrine, the Protestant Reformation, and the organization of the Inquisition in Spain and Rome.

1917 The end of World War I brought defeat to the Ottoman Empire. The League of Nations (1922) divided Ottoman territories between England and France. Under the mandated, Britain administered Palestine as a National Jewish State.

1947 After World War II, the United Nations Mandate partitioned Palestine into sections for Jews and sections for Palestinian Arabs.

Into the twenty-first century, conflicts remain in the biblical lands.

GLOSSARY

Some entries in this glossary are not contained in the text of this book; however, they are found in related readings.

Age of Patriarchs: 2000-1700 BCE, birth of Abraham to death of Jacob

Allegory: symbols are used to tell of moral or religious principles

Amphitheater: outside theater

Anarchy: no form of political authority

Anthropomorphism: giving human characteristics to inanimate objects

Antiquity: Ancient Times (before Middle Ages)

Apocalypse: prophetic disclosure, revelation (last book of New Testament)

Apocrypha (plural): hidden writings, Jewish history during the four hundred years between the Hebrew Bible and the New Testament

Apocryphon (singular): secret writing (Apocryphon of John)

Apostasy: abandonment of one's religious faith

Apostle: disciples and others as they took the messages of Jesus throughout the lands

Aramaic: common language of Jews following Babylonian exile

Arcane: secret, mysterious, obscure

Aretalogical: collection of miracle stories

Ascension: rising (Christ's ascension into heaven)

Ascetic: one who gives up comforts of society to live a life of austerity: (rigid economy/somber/grave)

Atonement: to make amends (from sins)

August: inspiring

Augustus: venerable, worthy of respect, honored above all others/dictator

Bar Kokhba: led revolt against Rome 132 CE, Rome recaptured Judea 135

Bigot: one rigidly devoted to own religion, intolerant of those who differ

Bishop: position in Christian Church elected to teach church doctrine, sometimes called Elder or Presbyter (hierarchy of Catholic Church: bishop, priest, deacon)

Blasphemy: contemptuous, disgraceful or profane act, utterance, or writing concerning God, also claiming attributes of God

Book of Law: first five books of Hebrew Bible: Torah, Pentateuch, Law of Moses, The Law

Caesar: dictator or autocrat, surname of early Roman emperors

Calvary: thought to be the place Jesus was crucified, called the Skull or Golgotha

Canaan: land God promised to Abraham (Promised Land)

Canon: standard of measurement used in acceptance of material judged as Scripture

Catholic: universal (Christian Church)

Christian Church: establishment developed by those who believed Jesus was the Christ (Messiah/Savior)

Christians: followers of Jesus who considered him the Christ

Christmas: Christian celebration held on December 25, as the anniversary of Jesus' birth

Church of England: church started by King Henry VIII (1509-1547 CE) after he abolished the Roman Catholic Church

Cleopatra VII: last and most famous Ptolemaic queens of Egypt

Client State: country dependent on another country

Codex: pages written on papyrus, bound into a book

Coptic: language/people descended from ancient Egypt

Cosmology: branch of philosophy dealing with structure of the universe

Council of Nicaea: called by Constantine (325 CE) for Catholic Churches to agree on doctrinal belief binding all churches

Council of Trent: Catholic Counter-Reformation action (1545-1563 CE) condemned Protestants, approved doctrinal issues

Covenant: treaty between God and His people

Crucifixion: death by hanging from a cross, used by Romans

Crusades: Holy Wars by Christians of Europe against Saracens (Muslims) (1099-1291 CE)

Cuneiform Script: from southern Mesopotamia (3300 BCE), small wedge-like shapes on clay tablets (form of writing)

Dark Ages: early Medieval Age (500-1000 CE), plagues, movement of peoples, invasions,

Day of Atonement: holiest Jewish holiday, day set aside for amending sins or faults (Yom Kippur) 10th day of Tishri (Sept.-Oct.)

Deacon: member of the Christian Church who assists the priest or bishop

Diaspora: movement or dispersion of Jewish people from their homeland

Disciples: close followers, chosen by Jesus, to learn of God's glory and continue the teaching after Jesus' death

Divine: Godlike, proceedings directly from God

Docetism: belief of Jesus as an apparition, not a flesh and blood human

Doctrine: something taught, principles presented for acceptance or belief (religious-political-scientific-philosophic)

Dogma: doctrines authoritatively considered absolute truth

Dualism: believing in God and the devil, good and evil (sprit as good, matter as evil)

East-West Schism: Catholic Church split: Eastern Orthodox Church and Roman Catholic Church (1054-1204 CE)

Easter: Christian celebration of Jesus' resurrection from the dead, held on Sunday following full moon of March 21

Ekklesia (Ecclesia): assembly or Church organized by the Apostles

Elohist (E): historian from Northern Kingdom of Israel, recorded Hebrew history using the term Elohim for God, incorporated in the Torah

Epiphany: intuitive realization, unseen presence of a Divine being, celebration of Wise Men reaching baby Jesus (January 6)

Epistemology: study of the nature and origin of knowledge

Epistle: formal letter (New Testament)

Esoteric: teachings for only a few who had special knowledge or interest, private and secret

Essenes: group removed themselves from other Jews to live a monastic desert life (around 150 BCE)

Essentialism: fundamental, inherent

Ethereal: intangible, unearthly, spiritual

Ethnarch: ruler of a province or a people (Rome)

Exegesis: critical analysis of text

Exodus: Hebrews left Egypt (1280).

Exoteric: Jesus' teachings for general public, not inner circle

Extant: still in existence (not destroyed)

Fertile Crescent: semicircle of cultivated land bordering the Mediterranean Sea, reaching through Tigris and Euphrates Rivers

Gaius Julius: given name of Julius Caesar

Galilee: from King Solomon's time, the land of Cabul, foreigners settled

Gentiles: non-Jewish people

Gnostics: groups focusing on gnosis (Greek: insight, under-standing, intuitive perceptions)

Good News: from the Greek word meaning *Gospels* (narratives of Jesus' life in the New Testament)

Handmaiden: female attendant to another female

Hannukah: Jewish celebration in December noting the reclaiming of the Temple by the Maccabean Revolt (164 BCE)

Hasmonean Dynasty: following the Maccabean Revolt (family name of Hasmonean) against Syria, a free Jewish state existed, ruled by the Hasmoneans (164-63 BCE)

Hebrew: term for Jewish people before their return from Egypt to the Promised Land (also a language)

Hegemony: predominant influence of one state over another

Hellenistic: pertaining to Greek Culture

Heresy: opinion not agreeing with established religious belief, profane speaking against God

Heretic: to choose for one's self, person holding controversial opinions, especially against Catholic dogma

Herodians: Jewish politicians in the time of Jesus, thought restoration of Kingdom of Israel should come from a **son** of Herod

Holy Spirit: reality of Divine inspiration coming from a higher realm

Homilies: sermons to educate congregation on practical matters

House of David: lineage from David

Hun: fierce barbaric race of Asiatic nomads

Inquisition: Catholic Church's effort to combat heresy (1231 [1233?]-18th century CE)

Instinct: intuition

Intrinsic: inner knowledge

Israeli: Jewish citizen living in post 1947 Israel

Islam: faith based on God's messages given to prophet Muhammad (7th century CE Arabia)

ISIS: Militant Islamic group: Islamic State in Iraq and Syria (2013 CE)

Jahwist (J):   German spelling of historian recording Hebrew history using the term for God (Southern Kingdom of Judah), incorporated in the Torah (also spelled Yahwist)

Jew/Jewish: term for Jewish people after their return to Judah from years of exile in Babylonia

Jewish Christians: Jews wanting to incorporate their traditional ways into the Christian faith

Jewish Revolt (69-70 CE):   influence of Zealots led to a revolt against Rome resulting in the destruction of the Temple and Jerusalem

Jubilee: after seven land Sabbaths (50th year), on Day of Atonement, all possessions were to be returned to previous owner (Jewish)

Judaism: faith of the Jewish people after their return from Babylonian exile

Kabbalah: ancient Jewish mysticism

Kethuvim: Sacred Writings, stories of wise men and national heroes, a section in Hebrew Bible (stories integrated in Christian Old Testament)

King: male monarch, most powerful of a particular group/place (At times, high priests were kings.)

Knights Templars: religious order to preserve the Holy Land (1120-1312 CE), became rich and powerful, associated with the Crusades

Kohen: Hebrew word for priest

Maccabees: family who started the successful Jewish rebellion against Syria (164 BCE) (see Hasmoneans)

Martyr: individual choosing death rather than renouncing religious principles

Messiah: a savior who would liberate Jews (Christians believe Jesus (4 BCE-30 CE) was the messiah.)

Metaphysical: immaterial, supernatural, excessively subtle, over and above the physical world

Middle Ages: Medieval Period (500-1500 CE), between Antiquity (Ancient Times) and Modern Period

Mishnah: written collection of Jewish Oral Law with interpretations by scribes (Second Law)

Monotheistic: belief in one God

Muslim: follower of the Islamic faith

Muslim Brotherhood: long standing political Islamic group, promotes Islamic State

Nevi'im: Prophets and/or Judges, a section in the Hebrew Bible (incorporated in the Christian Old Testament)

New Testament: twenty-seven books declared Christian Scripture (367 CE)

Nicaea Creed: partial wording. . . We believe in one God the Father. . . and in Jesus Christ, one in being with the Father. (see Council of Nicaea)

Noetic: Greek word for *nous*, inner knowledge

Oracles: proclamations of prophets

Oral Law: Law of Moses before written as the Torah

Ottoman Empire: vast European Muslim Empire (1554-1918 CE)

Pagan: worship of idols

Palestine: previously Judea, changed by Romans in 135 CE

Palestinians: Muslins living in present-day Israel

Parables: short simple stories, with deeper meanings, told by Jesus

Parchment: writing surface using animal skins in place of papyrus reeds, invented in 3rd century BCE

Passover: Jewish celebration from the time they were *passed over* by the plague of death (before their Exodus from Egypt)

Paul (Saul):   Apostle, wrote letters of encouragement to early Christian Churches

Pentateuch (Torah):   first five books of Hebrew Bible (books also in the Old Testament)

Pentecost: Jewish celebration at completion of wheat harvest (50 days after Passover)

Pharisees: rejected scribe's interpretation of the Torah, followed the Oral Law (200-100 BCE)

PLO: Palestine Liberation Organization, governing entity protecting Palestinians' territory in Israel

Polemic: argument or attack on a specified opinion or doctrine

Potentate: having power to rule over others (monarch)

Presbyters: priest, elder, of the Christian Churches

Priest (Jewish): Kohen, religious official with duties as given to Moses from God, beginning with Aaron and the Tribe of Levi

Priestly Code: used in Babylonian exile, text written from memories of priests and Levites

Printing Press: Gutenberg's invention (mid 1400s CE) using a machine to print written words

Proconsul: Roman provincial governor of consular rank (chief magistrate)

Procurator: responsible for governmental matters, authority of military and judicial concerns (Rome)

Prophets: informed Israelites of God's warnings or revelations plus His comforting words, they knew *The Law*, were teachers

Protestant Reformation: group (1517-1648 CE) protested doctrines of Roman Catholic Church, began with Martin Luther

Province: territory governed by a country or empire

Puritans: Protestant groups (16th-17th centuries CE) opposing the Church of England formed by King Henry the VIII

Qumran: area in Judea near Dead Sea (Dead Sea Scrolls)

Q (Quella): German: *source*, documents of Jesus' sayings believed in use while Gospels were written

Quran (Koran): Islamic Holy Book

Rabbi: Hebrew/Jewish teacher

Redactor: editor

Renaissance: Modern Period, Age of Discovery (14th-15th centuries CE) revival of Classical art, literature, learning

Sabbath (Christian): day of rest, changed from seventh day to the day Jesus' ascension, three days after his crucifixion (Sunday)

Sabbath (Jewish): seventh day, a day of rest (sundown on Friday to sundown on Saturday)

Sabbath (land): every seventh year, the land was to be at rest

Sacred: pertaining to religious objects, rites, or practices

Sadducees: priests who placed themselves above other priests, devoted to scribes' interpretation of the Torah (200-100 BCE)

Sanhedrin: Jewish Council or Senate recognized in 69 BCE, authority only in Judea, tried, accused, set punishment (not death)

Saracen: name used for Muslims during the Crusades

Scribes: copied, interpreted, and taught the Torah

Scripture: sacred religious writings, the word of God

Sect: group within a larger group with distinct beliefs or practices

Secular: worldly rather than spiritual

Separatists: group protested against the Church of England, left England and settled in Holland

Septuagint: Greek translation of the Hebrew Bible, also referred to as LXX, for the number of days and scholars taken for the translation (rounded off from 72)

Sophia: wisdom, Divine mind of God

Spiritual: not tangible or material, concerned with the soul, pertaining to God, sacred

State of Israel: name given to Palestine after the Jewish Allocation in 1948

Synagogue: place where ten or more adult men gatherer to study and worship the Torah (In time, women were included.)

Synoptic Gospels: Matthew, Mark, Luke (all with similar accounts of Jesus)

Tabernacle: portable sanctuary Israelites used to carry the Ark of the Covenant (Tablets of God's words given to Moses)

Talmud: text containing the collection of Jewish traditions and explanations of Scripture (Mishnah followed by Pharisees' commentaries.)

Tanakh: acronym for the three sections of the Hebrew Bible

Targum: translation, from Hebrew to Aramaic, of the Torah

Ten Commandments: original Law given to Moses by God

Ten Tribes of Israel: descendants of Jacob/Israel joined together as the Northern Kingdom of Israel (lost to history)

Testament: covenant with God

Tetrarch: government by priests or officials clamming Divine sanction

Theoretical: abstract

Theology: study of the nature of God and religious truth

Theosophy: religious philosophy based on mystical insight into the nature of God and Divine teachings

Torah (Pentateuch): The Law of Moses, first five books of the Hebrew Bible (Believed to be given to Moses from God, during the forty years at the foot of Mt. Sinai, after the Exodus.)

Transcendental: rising above common thought or ideas, mystical

Treatise: formal systematic writing

Triumvirate: government by three people

Twelve Tribes of Israel: descendants of the twelve sons of Jacob/Israel

Vassal: under foreign power but with religious freedom

Vulgate: Latin translation by Jerome (383 CE) of the Septuagint (Greek translation of the Hebrew Bible and New Testament)

Wadi: Arabic: dry water drainage that fills with heavy rainfall

Yahweh: Hebrew: God of Jews, Christians, Muslims (see Jahwist)

Zealots: Jewish patriots, fought Romans

Ziggurat: temples of towers in ancient Assyria and Babylonia (like a pyramid), earthly and Divine realms meet at the top

Zion: fortified hill within Jerusalem, often used as a name for Jerusalem

Zionist: individual, or movement, seeking the establishment of a Jewish national state in Palestine and later for the support of modern Israel

Zoroastrianism: religion surfacing around 1200-1500 BCE in Ancient Persia (Iran) with the focus of good and evil

WORKS CITED

Akers, Keith. *The Lost Religion of Jesus: Simple Living and Nonviolence in Early Christianity.* New
York: Lantern Books, 2000. Print.

"Ancient Greece," History of Ancient Greek World, Time Line and Periods, Archaic, Classical, Hellenistic. 2003-2017. University Press Inc. Web. 17 January 2017. <*www.ancientgreece.com/s/History/*>.

"The Arab-Israeli War of 1948." Milestones: 1945—1952. [n.d.]. Office of the Historian. Web. 17 August 2015. <*https://history.state.gov/milestones/1945-1952/arab-israeli-war*>.

Audi, Robert, gen. ed. *The Cambridge Dictionary of Philosophy.* 3rd ed. New York: Cambridge University Press, 2015. Print.

Baigent, Michael. *The Jesus Papers: Exposing the Greatest Cover-Up in History.* New York: HarperSanFrancisco, 2006. Print.

Bandstra, Barry L. *Reading the Old Testament: Introduction to the Hebrew Bible.* 4th ed. Belmont, California: Wadsworth Cengage Learning, 2009. Print.

Bard, Mitchell G. "Pharisees, Sadducees, and Essenes." 2012. The Jewish Virtual Library. Web. 10 May 2012. <*http://www.jewishvirtuallibrary.org/jsource/History/sadducees_pharisees_essenes.html*>.

Borg, Marcus J. *Evolution of the Word: The New Testament in the Order the Books Were Written.* New York: HarperOne, 2012. Print.

Brownworth, Lars. *Lost to the West: The Forgotten Byzantine Empire that Rescued Western Civilization.* New York: Three Rivers Press, 2009. Print.

Cameron, Ron, ed. *The Other Gospels: Non-Canonical Gospel Texts.* Philadelphia: The Westminster Press, 1982. Print.

Cantey, Seth. *The Middle East and South Asia The World Today Series 2017-2018 51ˢᵗ* ed. Lanham, MD: Rowman & Littlefield, 2017. Print.

Collins, John J. *The Dead Sea Scrolls A Biography.* Princeton: Princeton University Press, 2013. Print.

"Causes of the Protestant Reformation." [n.d.]. What caused the Protestant Reformation? Reference.com. Web. 24 May 2018. *<www.reference.com/history/caused-protestant-5b4667fde8fa6907>*.

Douma, Michael, curator. "The Christian Calendar." *Calendars through the Ages.* 2008. Institute for Dynamic Educational Development. Web. 16 March 2011. *<http://webexhibits.org/calendars/calendar-christian.html>*.

Douma, Michael, curator. "The Jewish Calendar." *Calendars through the Ages.* 2008. Institute for Dynamic Educational Development. Web. 16 March 2011. *<http://webexhibits.org/calendars/calendar-jewish.html>*.

Ehrman, Bart D. *A Brief Introduction to the New Testament.* 3ʳᵈ ed. New York: Oxford University Press, 2013. Print.

Esposito, John L. *Islam: The Straight Path.* 3ʳᵈ ed. New York: Oxford University Press, 1998. Print.

Feiler, Bruce. *Abraham: A Journey to the Heart of Three Faiths.* New York: HarperCollins Publishers Inc., 2002. Print.

Godwin, Johnnie, Phyllis Godwin, and Karen Dockrey. *The Student Bible Dictionary: Expanded and Updated Edition*. Uhrichsville, Ohio: Barbour Books, 2014. Print.

Haag, Michael. *The Tragedy of the Templars: The Rise and Fall of the Crusader States*. New York: Harper, 2013. Print.

Hirst, K. Kris. "Chalcolithic Period." 2013. Web. 10 June 2013. <*http://archaeology.about.com/od/cterms/g/chalcolithic.htm*>.

History.com Staff. "The Reformation." 2009. A & E Networks. Web. 24 May 2018. <*http://www.history.con/topics/reformation*>.

"History of IsraelBritish Mandate." [n.d.]. Stand for Israel. Web. 17 August 2015. <*http://www.ifcj.org/site/PageNavigator/sfi about history british*>.

The Holy Scriptures. According to the Masoretic Text. A New Translation. Philadelphia: The Jewish Publication Society of America, 5677—1917. Print.

"IONS Institute of Noetic Sciences." *What are the Noetic Sciences?* 2018. IONS. Web. 20 March 2018. < *https://notic.org*>.

"IONS Institute of Noetic Sciences." *IONS Overview*. 2018. IONS. Web. 21 March 2018. <*http://noetic.org/about/overview*>

"The Inquisition." *Christian-Jewish Relations*. 2015. American-Israeli Cooperative Enterprise. Web. 29 October 2015. <*www. jewishvirtuallibrary.org/jsource/History/Inquisitian.html*>.

Isbouts, Jean-Pierre. *The Biblical World: An Illustrated Atlas*. Washington D.C.: National Geographic, 2007. Print.

The Jewish Study Bible. 2nd ed. Eds. Adele Berlin and Marc Zvi Brettler. Jewish Publication Society TANAKH Translation. New York: Oxford University Press, 2014. Print.

Joffe, Lawrence. *The History of the Jews: From the Ancients to the Middle Ages*. London: Southwater an imprint of Anness Publishing Ltd., 2014. Print.

Jordan, Samuel T. comp. *The Time Chart of Biblical History*. New York: Chartwell Books, 2014. Print.

Kasser, Rodolphe, Marvin Meyer, and Gregor Wurst, eds. *The Gospel of Judas.* Additional Commentary by Bart D. Ehrman. Washington D.C.: National Geographic, 2006. Print.

Kerrigan, Michael. *A Dark History: The Roman Emperors: From Julius Caesar to the Fall of Rome.* New York: Metro Books, 2008. Print.

Kershner, Isabel. "9 Things to Know About Jerusalem as U.S, Embassy Opens." 13 May 2018. New York Times. Web. 7 November 2018. <*https://www.nytimes.com*>.

Leloup, Jean-Yves. Trans. From Coptic and Commentary. Rowe, Joseph. English Trans. and Notes. *The Gospel of Mary Magdalene.* Forward: Jacob Needleman. Rochester, Vermont: Inner Traditions, 2002. Print.

Leloup, Jean-Yves. Trans. from Coptic and Commentary. Rowe, Joseph. English Trans. and Notes. *The Gospel of Thomas: The Gnostic Wisdom of Jesus.* Forward: Jacob Needleman. Rochester, Vermont: Inner Traditions, 2005. Print.

Linder, Doug. "Bishop James Ussher Sets the Date for Creation" 2004. Web. 2 June 2011. <*http://law2.umkc.edu/faculty/projects/ftrials/scopes/ushser.html*>.

Magdy, Samy. "Ousted president Morsi collapses, dies in court." *The Denver Post,* [The Associated Press] June 18, 2019, sec. A, p, 10, cols. 2-4. Print.

Martin, Sean. *The Cathars: The Most Successful Heresy of the Middle Ages.* Edison, New Jersey: Chartwell Books, Inc. a division of Book Sales, Inc., 2006. Print.

Merriam-Webster's Collegiate Dictionary. 11th ed. Springfield, Massachusetts: Merriam-Webster, 2012. Print.

The New Oxford Annotated Bible: New Revised Standard Version with The Apocrypha. 4th ed. New York: Oxford University Press, 2010. Print.

Nicolson, Adam. "The Bible of King James." *National Geographic,* December 2011, 36-61. Print.

"1993 Oslo agreement." 2013. BBC News: Middle East. Web. 4 April 2014. <*http://news.bbc.co.uk/2/hi/middle_east/7385301. stm*>

Pagels, Elaine. *The Gnostic Gospels.* New York: Vintage Books A Division of Rand House, Inc., 1989. Print.

Reston, James Jr. *Luther's Fortress: Martin Luther and His Reformation Under Siege.* New York: Basic Books, 2015. Print.

Robinson, James M. *The Secrets of Judas: The Story of the Misunderstood Disciple and His Lost Gospel.* New York: HarperSanFrancisco, 2006. Print.

Rosenberg, David. Trans. from Hebrew. *The Book of J.* Interpreted by Harold Bloom. New York: Vintage Books a division of Random House Inc., 1991. Print.

"Schism of 1054." Encyclopædia Britannica. Encyclopædia Britannica OnLine. Encyclopædia Britannica., 2015. Web. 14 August 2015. <*http://www.britannica.com/event/ Schism-of-1054*>.

"Sinai Peninsula." 2013. Encyclopædia Britannica. Web. 4 April 2014 <.*http://www.bitannica.com/EBchecked/topic/545586/ Sinai-Peninsula*>.

Smith, Huston. *The World's Religions.* New York: HarperOne, 1991. Print.

Smith, Morton. *The Secret Gospel: The Discovery and Interpretation of the Secret Gospel According to Mark.* Forward: Elaine Pagels. Middletown, California: The Dawn Horse Press, 2005. Print.

Starbird, Margaret. *Mary Magdalene, Bride in Exile.* Rochester, Vermont: Bear & Company, 2005. Print.

Starbird, Margaret. *The Woman with the Alabaster Jar: Mary Magdalen and the Holy Grail.* Santa Fe, New Mexico: Bear & Company, 1993. Print.

Tabor, James D. *The Jesus Dynasty: The Hidden History of Jesus, His Royal Family, and the Birth of Christianity*. New York: Simon & Schuster, 2006. Print.

"Timeline for the History of Jerusalem (4500 – Present)." *History of Jerusalem*. 2014. American-Israeli Cooperative Enterprise. Web. 7 April 2014. <*http://www.jewishvirtuallibrary.org/jsource/Peace/jerutime.html*>.

"Under Persian Rule." 2009. BBC – Religions – Zoroastrian. Web. 15 November 2013. <*http://www.bbc.co.uk/religion/religions/zoroastrian/history/persia 1.shtml*>

Valantasis, Richard. *The beliefnet Guide to Gnosticism and Other Vanished Christianities*. Preface by Marcus Borg. New York: Doubleday, 2006. Print.

Youngblood, Ronald R., F. F. Bruce, and R. K. Harrison. *Compact Bible Dictionary*. Nashville: Thomas Nelson, 2004. Print.

"Zoroaster." 2009. BBC – Religions – Zoroastrian. Web. 15 November 2013. <*http://www.bbc.co.uk/religion/religions/zoroastrian/history/zoroaster 1.shtml*>.

INDEX

J

Jacob (Israel) xviii, xix, xx, xxi, 2,
5, 7, 8, 10, 11, 14, 15, 17, 19,
22, 25, 26, 27, 29, 30, 31, 32,
34, 35, 36, 39, 40, 41, 42,
46, 48, 49, 59, 60, 68, 69,
70, 95, 102, 103, 108, 140,
154, 201, 202, 203, 204,
205, 206, 207, 208, 210, 211,
212, 213, 215, 216, 219, 220,
221, 243, 249, 255, 256, 267,
270, 271, 272, 274, 276, 277,
278, 281, 282

Jeremiah 28, 29, 33, 34, 36, 38,
39, 62

Jerome 15, 61, 138, 179, 182,
263, 277

Jewish Publication Society 180,
230, 231, 232, 234, 236,
237, 239, 241, 244, 245, 281

Jewish Revolt (Rome) xviii, 11, 15,
45, 46, 47, 52, 57, 58, 59, 60,
62, 63, 74, 76, 80, 81, 83, 85,
86, 87, 88, 90, 91, 92, 93,
94, 95, 106, 107, 113, 116,
123, 124, 125, 126, 127, 128,
129, 131, 132, 133, 134, 135,
139, 141, 143, 155, 166, 168,
189, 191, 193, 198, 200, 204,
212, 218, 234, 235, 237, 238,
241, 258, 259, 260, 262, 263,
265, 268, 270, 272, 275, 282

John the Baptist 11, 80, 90, 91, 99,
103, 104, 108, 109, 111, 112,
113, 163, 209

Josephus, Flavius 45, 60, 62,
107, 159

Joshua 27, 28, 29, 30, 38, 39, 70,
132, 203, 255

Judaism 34, 35, 37, 51, 53, 63, 67,
68, 71, 73, 74, 76, 79, 94, 95,
107, 123, 127, 128, 129, 141,
154, 168, 169, 203, 236, 272

Judas Iscariot 154

Julian, Apostate xviii, 136, 137

Julius, Caesar 46, 58, 86, 234, 235,
238, 241, 258, 271, 282

K

Kemal, Mustafa 217

Khan Reza 224

Kingdom of Israel 5, 8, 17, 31, 32,
36, 46, 48, 59, 68, 154, 203,
221, 249, 256, 270, 271, 277

Kingdom of Judah 17, 31, 32, 33,
46, 59, 203, 256, 272

King James Bible 179, 185

L

League of Nations 210, 222, 265

Leeser, Isaac 180

Lost Tribes 32, 59

Luther, Martin 183, 187, 197, 199,
245, 247, 264, 275, 283

M

Maccabean Revolt 47, 53, 76,
82, 271

Magdalene, Mary 111, 116, 149,
192, 242, 282, 283, 291

Marcion 128, 129, 261

Margolis 180

Martin 181, 183, 184, 187, 197,
199, 240, 245, 246, 247, 264,
275, 282, 283

ACKNOWLEDGEMENTS

Gratitude to God and the *unseen* for help in all my undertakings, is ever present in my mind. Thanks to my children, husband, sisters and brothers, for their patience in hearing: *I'm still working on it*! I am indebted to all the authors that I drew from—their willingness to write and share their knowledge made my book possible.

Specifically, I acknowledge those who critiqued my writing from a historical and religious view, along with grammatical assistance: April Favara, a PhD candidate at the Iliff School of Theology; Scott DuPree, a recent doctoral graduate of Denver University; Bray Weaver, priest of the St. Mary Magdalene Parish of the Apostolic Johannite Tradition; and Rachel Green, editor.

Some shared in other ways. My twin, Joanne Dulmaine, gave encouragement through the long years of writing; we share the same beliefs. John Weir, my brother, insisted I look further into writers of the Gospels. Suzanne Shapiro gave me her father's Bible, *The Holy Scriptures*, printed in 1917. His hand-written name, G. M. Herzel plus his personal reflections on the Torah, became a spiritual connection to that faith. Reverend Michael James Buckley, a long-time friend, offered metaphysical enlightenment. Donna Rabbitt, my *spiritual buddy*, kept me going with her heart-felt interest in the book. William Blanning's up-dates on new (or old) materials of a philosophical nature balanced my spiritual and worldly views.

ABOUT THE AUTHOR

Thoughts of God have been with me since a very young age. As a child, I remember feeling comforted while sitting beside my father during church services. My life progressed and at the age of thirty-five, I graduated Summa Cum Laude from Metropolitan State College in Denver and became a reading teacher. Written words have long been my guide to other times and places. Studies at the University of Colorado led to advanced degrees. Following retirement from Denver Public Schools, I taught at Denver Community College and the University of New Mexico in Taos. Over the years, I developed and taught courses focusing on Southwest Culture for Adams State College, which took me to Taos in the summers. Then, while living there, I self-published an eleven generational biographical account of a local family: *Life on Torrez Road A Northern New Mexico Family History*. Later, I compiled and printed *Family Recipes Mirrored in History* for my family. Volunteer work included helping a beginning library and years as a church treasurer. Finally, I dedicated my time to write about the *Word of God*. With gratitude, I acknowledge the Divine Source and the power and love which has sustained me—always.

Judith Marie Judy

A FINAL WORD

This I Know
A Divine Source I call God
created
All that has been
All that is
All that will be

A Divine Plan exists
connecting
Visible and invisible
Yesterdays and tomorrows
Lifetimes and lifetimes

Jesus appeared as man
for teaching
Of God
Of Love
Of Peace

This I Know
I am part of ALL

Printed in the United States
by Baker & Taylor Publisher Services

Printed in the United States
by Baker & Taylor Publisher Services